D0872230

Work, Technology, and Education

Work, Technology, and Education

DISSENTING ESSAYS IN THE INTELLECTUAL
FOUNDATIONS OF AMERICAN EDUCATION

Edited by Walter Feinberg and Henry Rosemont, Jr.

University of Illinois Press   *Urbana Chicago London*

LIBRARY OF CONGRESS CATALOGING IN PUBLICATION DATA

Main entry under title:

Work, technology, and education.

  Includes bibliographical references.
  1. Education—United States—Addresses, essays, lectures. 2. Education—Philosophy. I. Feinberg, Walter,
1937– II. Rosemont, Henry, 1934–
LA212.W67   370′.973   75–4854
ISBN 0–252–00252–0

To KATHY, CONNIE, GENNY, DEBBIE, JILL, AND SAMANTHA

Acknowledgments

The editors are indebted to JoAnn M. Rosemont, whose critical reading, typing abilities, and editorial assistance helped significantly to transform a collection of papers into an integrated series of essays. We are also grateful for the assistance of Carole S. Appel of the University of Illinois Press.

Contents

Introduction

Walter Feinberg and Henry Rosemont, Jr.

SCHOOLING: THE NEW FRONTIER

In the nineteenth century the American frontier became the symbol of identity and freedom. Those who felt themselves trapped by the demands of an industrial society could dream of a place beyond the river and over the mountain where they could re-establish themselves and become free. The dream of the frontier was as important as its reality. To some it was an opportunity, a way to translate their discontent into personal action; but to others, unable to move to new lands, it was a statement that the source of their discontent was an internal weakness of will. For most, the frontier remained a dream, a fantasy that turned their hostility inward; and for some, who left and returned, it had become a nightmare, a continuous reminder of grand plans, unsettling reality, and failure. They had set out to tame the frontier and had instead been tamed by it.

As the era of the frontier was ending, the era of the public school was beginning. The frontier had become "pocked with settlements" and the settlements, connected by machines, linked as a net anchored in the East. To the machines came the people, first from Europe's shores and then from the farms that were once homesteads. It was now time for a new dream. Domination replaced escape as the primary theme of the new freedom. Opportunity was no longer a matter of moving from one territory to another, but of altering one's relationship to the machine—of dominating where one had been dominated.

The public school picked up where the frontier had left off.

Just as the frontier had been pictured as settling people of different nationalities, forming out of them a similar character and set of allegiances, now the school was to serve those functions. And just as it was believed that the frontier had provided the nation with an escape valve whereby the discontented could move out to break new ground if they had the stamina, now the school was to provide another kind of escape valve whereby the discontented could move up—if they had the talent. Like the frontier before it, the school became a symbol of upward mobility for the tired, the poor, and the huddled masses.

To insure that the new escape valve did relieve the pressure which might otherwise lead to unwanted social change, compulsory schooling and attendance laws were passed by the score, and at that time schooling became much more than a quaint sideshow of life in the United States. As the most significant instrument for socializing the young into a new and often foreign set of values, the school became the most important avenue for entrance into the mainstream of society and for staking a claim to a portion of society's wealth. The frontier wars had ended, the land had been tamed, and the Indians who could no longer resist were put away; the era of public schooling was at hand.

Seen as the modern frontier, the schools became the new focus of hope, and the optimism that marked national life throughout much of the twentieth century found its most significant expression in beliefs about the value of the public school. Different groups, however, had different reasons for their optimism; the school was an institution for all seasons supported by people of various political and economic persuasions. To the poor it was perceived as a clearly defined avenue for climbing out of poverty and squalor and for offering a better life to the next generation. To the rich it was a way to preserve law and order and to insure the stability of their place and property. To the patriot, school was a place to develop national allegiance, discipline and pride, while to the reformer it was a way to assure orderly change while adjusting people to the requirements and the rigor of the developing machine age; to everyone the school was an instrument of social control.

Public school was the great compromise, a meeting place for private conflicts and differing public visions. But the compromise did not represent all sides equally, for some groups exercised almost all of the control. The teachings of the school, for example, were carried on in the context of an economic system that functioned on the universally held belief in the necessity of onerous work even when the system could not economically afford full employment. This universal belief supported the level of competition needed to hold wages at an acceptable level—acceptable to the industrialists—and to control the inflation that often accompanies a tight labor market. As the need to rationalize the economy and to thereby avoid some of the harsher conflicts of the marketplace became more and more apparent, the schools began to teach each youngster to compete within a level of competition that was acceptable for his ascribed skills and abilities. Talent identification and vocational training increasingly became primary activities of schooling. Testing programs were devised to measure intellectual capacity and curricula were established to train each and every child for a role that was consistent with his or her assigned capacity. In this way the meritocracy was born, and the capitalist concept of fairness was insinuated on the nation: from each according to demonstrated abilities, to each in precisely the same measure. For millions of people, of course, even this dubious idea of fairness was never realized.

SCHOOLING: THE "OLD" CRITICS

The schools have never been without critics, and as public education became more significant during the first half of this century its more significant critics came from the progressive education movement. The aim of many in this movement was to reconstruct society by reconstructing the values that were transmitted in the schools, and thus they focused their writings on the interrelationship between the school and society. The progressive educators who addressed the issue of these interrelations had come to understand that the machine had initiated a fundamental change in the nation's economic and political life. Technology, as Dewey expressed it, was the new logos, the principle around which all other relations were now to be ordered. The task of the educational critic was to be accomplished by projecting developments in technology and then by readjusting the schools to meet the new requirements. To those on the fringes of the progressive movement, recognizing that technology required new modes of industrial training, such needs were defined primarily in terms of jobs. To others like John Dewey or George Counts, there was an understanding that technological change required attitudinal changes as well and that the school must not only expand its socializing function but significantly alter its goals as well.

The debates about schooling in the first half of the twentieth century were primarily concerned with the goals of education and the ends toward which children should be trained and socialized. There was little question that the schools could or should do the jobs that were desired although there were important differences about which specific set of jobs was desirable. Conservatives argued that the national welfare demanded one thing, and liberals argued that the individual and the social welfare required something else. Such arguments were not, however, totally in conflict with each other. Each side was addressing the requirements of technology at a somewhat different level. The educational conservative would guide schooling by the projected shifts in manpower needs, the liberal by projected requirements in attitude change. Both, however, agreed that the schools should be guided by the requirements of technology, and so too should everyone who passed through their doors.

Whatever the political and pedagogical persuasion of the educational critic may have been then, it was simply assumed that the primary task of educational reform could be accomplished first by determining the societal adjustments required by the movement of technology, and then by adjusting the schools to alter the social norms accordingly. The impact of the school upon the child was examined only abstractly because it was childhood rather than children which was seen to constitute the clientele of the school. The pivotal assumption was that the primary attribute of children was their malleability, and the problem was first to determine the end toward which they should be led and then to invent the techniques which would best do the leading.

Progressives frequently wrote of the need to allow the individual interests of the child to work themselves out in a social setting, but they were persistently aware that the setting was indeed a social one extending far beyond the walls of the schoolhouse. This awareness dominated many of their perceptions and with it, their criticisms of the school. Their focus concentrated heavily on the curriculum and the methods of teaching along with the social implications that these entailed. Their evaluation of the effects of the educational process was limited to the compilation of data about the relative success of one program or another in terms of standard criteria such as how well students from progressive high schools did in college. Conspicuously absent from their writings is any sensitive description of the effects of schooling upon the feelings and the dignity of the flesh-and-blood children who occupied the classroom.

SCHOOLING: THE NEW CRITICS

The style and the focus of recent educational critics has shifted from the role of the school in the social order to a description of the interaction between the school, the teacher, and the child. Beginning with John Holt's impressionistic analysis of how children fail, a series of other works has followed, each describing in its own way the psychological and spiritual effects of the learning process. In part, the recent critics have served to intensify people's sensitivity by exposing the sham that is often practiced in the schools under the most enlightened educational rhetoric. Not surprisingly, much of the recent criticism has been directed at the education of black people, an area in which the earlier progressives had been conspicuously deficient. But these works have become more than simply descriptive of the education of black youngsters. Jonathon Kozol's *Death at an Early Age* was written in the middle sixties to describe his experience in a ghetto school in Boston and the effects of this school upon the black children who populated it; it is at the same time a statement of the concerted and systematic effort that can be made to beat down the spirit of other human beings.

Much of the flurry of educational criticism that issued from this period arose at the same time that black activists and white civil rights workers were marching on places like Selma and Montgomery. Images of southern sheriffs and governors confronting black children and their parents filled the screens of television sets across the nation, as did the pictures of fire hoses, electric cattle prods, and police dogs. But the media had yet to penetrate the classroom when critics like Kozol revealed that brutality did not only come from the night stick of a southern sheriff. The physical neglect of the ghetto school—the broken windows and falling plaster—was of secondary importance when compared to the psychological and physical harassment that went on inside its crumbling walls.

Nevertheless, the period was still an optimistic one. In the

South, the schoolhouse stood as a gateway to freedom—the prob-lem was to open it equally to all. And even in the North, where overlooked neglect was now being uncovered, the issues were clear and the enemy, so it was believed, was identifiable. If black children in essentially black schools were being mistreated and miseducated by white, racist personnel, the solution was to inte-grate the schools and to change the personnel.

Granting the many strengths of the new criticism, its out-standing weakness has been the rather simplistic assumption that the source of the problem could be located in some quirk of personality on the part of individuals. When it was found that the teachers in a particular school were racist or that others were generally resentful of any expression of individuality, the implica-tion was that the problem had been explained. Unfortunately the new critics did not make a sharp distinction between the standards by which the competency of a teacher ought to be judged and the reasons why such standards are generally not operational—why teachers can get away without meeting them. If a teacher continu-ously discourages the expression of individuality or real creativity, or if he consistently treats black youngsters as inferior to whites, then there is good reason to question his general competence. If, in addition, he does these things and gets away with them, then there is a good reason to believe that the source of the problem lies in other areas.

The new critics were thus generally optimistic, believing that the problems could be handled by adjustments in personnel and/or curricula. If the problem was that children were breaking under too much direction, then make the classroom a great smorgasbord where each child could learn as little or as much as he liked in whatever area he chose. If the problem was that black children were being brutalized by white racist teachers, integrate the schools and children of both races would profit. Yet here, too, the results of implementing new measures did not result in any significant improvement in public schooling, and many of the critics are now expressing sympathy for proposals to disestablish the schools.

Perhaps more than the recent writers, the earlier critics of the progressive school recognized the interdependence that existed between the school and the society. Indeed, one of the pervasive themes of this group was that contemporary changes in the social structure required concomitant changes in the educational structure as well. This theme tied together writers as seemingly far apart as John Dewey and James Bryant Conant. Earlier, far-sighted scholars such as Confucius and Plato anticipated the use of public schools for filtering the social memory and thereby altering the consciousness of a people. This view deserves a fresh examination today.

SCHOOLS: THE MEMORY BANK

It is our contention not that the schools have failed in some way or another to achieve their ideal role, but rather that they have been eminently successful in accomplishing their "historical mission." To see how and why this is so it is necessary to discuss the function of education in any culture, and the specific functions of schools in industrial society.

Education involves the transmission of cultural norms and values, and the training of the young to take their place in the society. Thus by means of, for example, storytelling and ritual, children come to have certain images of their own society and certain attitudes toward the value of its preservation. At the same time they must be taught specific habits and skills important for that culture as prerequisite to social and occupational living. In most pre-industrial societies these functions are served by different agencies—the family, the priesthood, craftsmen, etc.—and although the division of educational labor is often not clear cut, there is a general reliance upon informal and personal relations to develop the abilities, beliefs, and continuities that are thought desirable. With the industrialization of the United States, however, and the coming to these shores of peoples of very diverse cultures it became necessary to melt individual and local differences into a more standardized society which was thought to be requisite for the continued growth of the capitalist economy; and public school proved an ideal pot. Because of its importance as an instrument of education and socialization the school has consequently reduced the influence of other and more personal agencies, sometimes consciously; as an instrument of the state it has attempted to shift loyalties on a large scale from personal and local groups to national ones.

The school has become the memory bank of modern industrial societies, serving to pass on to the young the social image, habits and skills that important segments of the society deem desirable.

As a social memory bank it serves not only to stamp into the young the correct attitudes, habits, and skills, but to stamp out others that are thought to be undesirable. Oftentimes what is stamped out is the result of "dysfunctional" attitudes such as those of the family, the church, and the local community.

Because a primary function of schooling is to shift loyalties from local to national groups, the content of its memory will change from one nation to the next (as witnessed by the different treatments given to the same event; read, for example, the different treatments of the American revolution given by British and U.S. textbooks). Nevertheless, the function of the schools for each nation remains essentially the same. The school serves to bridge the child's development as he or she moves from the private work of the family to the public, corporate domain, and it does this by substituting public and functional values for private and communal ones. Values that are expressive of the ideal family are not generally functional for the corporate society and must therefore be replaced by functional ones, e.g., substituting a principle of competence for acts of compassion and justice as the primary determinant of the distribution of goods.

The school functions as a memory bank in two quite different ways. In the first instance, like other institutions which have a socializing role, it is designed to establish a wider loyalty by teaching youngsters about the paramount value of their society. They are taught that injustice is caused by external forces, that destiny has mapped out the nation's past and future, and that good and wise intentions prevail among its leaders. Such teaching is a function of the content of the memory as it is developed through the articulated statements and visual materials that compose the curriculum of the school. Through the content of the memory, a youngster develops appropriate images of his or her society and of peoples' places in it. For the most part, but with some exceptions, the school serves to reinforce those images that are dominant in the society. Thus, the way in which the curriculum views the roles of men and women or of blacks and whites will generally mirror the roles that are socially acceptable.

The exceptions come about when for one reason or another the schools are used in a deliberate fashion to change a dominant image. However, such changes tend to be minor, altering the image only slightly. For example, curriculum reformers have pointed with some pride to the changes that have occurred in basic readers. Whereas previously such books presented only white children playing in their suburban or rural neighborhoods, now there are works that are specifically designed for ghetto youngsters, with pictures of black and brown children playing in an urban environment.That some of these books constitute an improvement over previous units is not at issue here. But even when a conscious attempt has been made to include the black child there is often a downplay of black culture. While the children are black, the authority figures—the teacher, the fireman, and the policeman—are usually still white. More important, and even more common, is the obvious downplaying of anything which might be associated as uniquely a part of the black culture. Black children, for example, are seen with neat, short cropped hair—rarely is it the Afro style which might be found among ghetto children. In other books, men, whether white or black, are rarely found with long hair. And women still wear kitchen aprons rather than surgical gowns. It is in terms of the content of the memory that children develop a sense of place and propriety.

In addition to appropriate images and attitudes, the public school is also the place where a child begins to learn the habits that are thought to be essential to the maintenance and the continuation of industrial society. These formal aspects of the social memory are taught by the school as behavioral norms which youngsters are expected to accommodate. If punctuality, obedience and a generally high toleration for meaningless tasks are more commonly found in the training of children than are rationality and insight, it is because punctuality, obedience, and a toleration of boredom are the first requirements of a large number of jobs in industrial society whereas rationality and insight are not.

The function that schooling serves in relation to the larger society accounts in some degree for the inability of recent critics to effect an improvement in the schools. Seeing bored children, for example, they have assumed that children ought not to be bored. However, many jobs in industrial society are in fact boring and thus people must be trained to tolerate boredom. Recent critics have also challenged the grading system, assuming that ranking is not an essential part of education. However, the belief that ranking was instituted, mistakenly or not, for educational purposes is clearly wrong. While ranking is a vestige of legitimate educational activities of appraising, evaluating and communicating, it clearly serves no significant educational purpose of itself, nor is it intended to. In part it is used to match ability and performance with an appropriate level of employment and in part it is used to mask the inequities of industrial society by teaching a youngster his place and position early and by establishing a general faith in the objectivity by which his place has been determined.

SCHOOLING AND SCHOLARSHIP

If the primary function of the public schools in the United States has been to socialize the young into a corporate, technologically complex society, then the primary function of a great many educators has been to develop, employ, and champion the physical and psychological controls that have or can facilitate the socializing and standardizing process. Too many educational philosophers, historians, psychologists, administrators, teachers, and technicians have accepted and usually applauded technological change as the main determinant governing our ideas of work and education. To accept technological development as the independent variable governing changes in work and in education is to sever these essentially human activities from their humanizing function. As a consequence, work continues to be evaluated first and foremost by stipulated requirements of production, and education is defined merely operationally as that which goes on in the schools.

The scholars, then, have tended to serve the corporate state well. When professors of educational administration began to model schooling after the efficiency reforms of the industrial factory, they initiated a movement that was to continue into the space age. The recommendations put forth by James Conant in the late fifties on the heels of the sputnik shock was (at that time) but the latest example of the use of schools to fill projected manpower needs of the industrial society and of the willingness of educators to define educational goals by the shifting requirements of industrial society. Even the "child-centered" reforms of the early progressive educators were developed in the context of an unbending and accepted technology and were often designed simply to soften some of its harsher effects.

Clearly there are different ways to look at these movements and different evaluations which could be made. Just as many industrial psychologists would claim that their purpose in serving the managers of industry was to make the work situation more pleasant, so too would many child-centered educators claim that their intent was to make schooling more pleasant. Whatever the intent of industrial psychologists may have been, however, they rarely functioned at the expense of efficient production; but they certainly served to retard the development of militant unions. Likewise, the reforms of the educators rarely functioned at the expense of the ever-intensifying division of labor.

An essential characteristic of social and behavioral engineering is that human concerns and problems be managed in such a way as not to interfere with what is accepted as the primary goal of an organization. All statements of concern must be redefined in a way that is consistent with the direction of the organization. Beginning with the crude techniques of the efficiency movement, industrial leaders have always recognized the benefits of engineering techniques and educational leaders have followed closely behind. The early techniques were crude because they failed to understand that man has a soul; they looked upon his essential body as merely an appendage to the machine. The engineering problem was to simplify and expedite his movements so as to achieve the maximum efficiency from the machine he was tending.

Despite the recent popularity of behavioral theory, actual practice has outstripped its theoretical expression. The discovery of the human soul has been the outstanding achievement of modern management. The soul, however, is not functionally distinct from the body, but rather it remains another element to be shaped, molded, and conditioned to the requirements of machine production. The modern manager has at his disposal the most advanced psychological and therapeutic techniques, all of which are employed to adjust human attitudes to the needs of the industrial process.

The essense of these new techniques, and of technology, is therefore not machines, but the control of both people and machines. One important prerequisite for such control is that issues become subordinated to the demands of technique itself, and the subordination can often be accomplished smoothly by applying the right definitions or giving new ones. The ends of such control may at times be laudatory, but in all cases rational arguments are undercut, and moral concerns are redefined in technological terms so that they may be resolved by technological means. Seen in this light no proposal is too radical for the educational manager if it allows the redefinition of moral problems in terms that are amenable to the efficient pursuit of institutional purpose. That is to say, moral passion can be a threat to technique insofar as it demands a fundamental rearrangement of priorities and values, but if the passion can be channeled acceptably by the technician it becomes consistent with the continued domination of technique. Thus technique does not begin with the machine, but with the way in which problems and passions are defined.

The impulse to define human concerns in "managerial" terms has become a standard theme of educational scholarship, expressed, among other places, in the appeal to behavioral techniques and objectives. It is no accident that the most educationally influential books on behavioral objectives take their examples from the military and from industry. Nevertheless, without the support of educational psychologists, school administrators, and other educational scholars, such techniques would be relatively harmless since most teachers are sufficiently perceptive to understand their limitations. What should be clear by now is that the editors of this volume—and most of the contributors—believe that education is far too important a human task to be given over to managers and experts.

SCHOOLS: THROUGH A GLASS, DARKLY

As noted earlier, most educational critics have assumed and/or argued that the schools have failed in carrying out their mission, and that therefore education was in need of radical change. The present volume, on the other hand, rests on the contrary assumption that the schools have succeeded well in their task, and that therefore it is society that is in need of radical change. The essays gathered here, then, begin where the most recent criticism has left off. For the most part they take up in greater detail themes that have been outlined in this Introduction. The aim is twofold: to show in some detail the functions schooling serves in modern industrial societies, especially the United States, pointing up the external (noneducational) factors that have influenced those functions; and to speculate about possible changes in the concept of work and education in a post-industrial age.

More specifically, James Anderson's "Education as a Vehicle for the Manipulation of Black Workers" shows not only that major industrialists turned to the issue of black education for economic reasons, broadly conceived, it also shows the extent to which liberal reformers of the late nineteenth century were unwilling to raise fundamental questions about the relation of public education to private economic interests even when it was obvious that the former was being employed, in the case of blacks, to establish and maintain a subordinate industrial caste.

An even more pervasive effort to subserve individual to socio-economic interests—and repressive ones at that—is seen by Joel Spring in "The American High School and the Development of Social Character." As the school came to replace the family as the basic socializing institution it obviously had to consider the issue of the sexuality of the young, and Spring takes up some of the theory and practice of solving this "problem," which could be taken humorously but for its all-too-often authoritarian and sadistic consequences.

The editors' "Training for the Welfare State: The Progressive Education Movement" attempts to reveal some of the basic attitudes and beliefs held by educational reformers toward workers in general, and minority groups in particular, and it argues that even though many of those reformers called themselves socialists, most of their proposals were altogether consistent with the welfare capitalism that was developing at that time.

The same theme is elaborated, and brought up to date by Herbert Gintis and Samuel Bowles in "The Contradictions of Liberal Educational Reform." With a good deal of documentation the authors show that now no less than during the Progressive Era the ideals of individual growth, social equality, and community have been sacrificed in the schools for the continuance of industrial capitalism.

In Kenneth Benne's "Technology and Community" the tone becomes less revisionist and more speculative. Benne begins from the fact that the benefits of technology have not been distributed equitably—either in the United States or around the world—and goes on to elaborate a concept of moral authority which would serve to govern the use and development of future technology.

The obvious abuses of technology have led many people to seek out art as an alternative. In "Art and Technology: Conflicting Models of Education?" Marx Wartofsky argues, however, that the concept of art thus advanced is usually seen to be an escape, a "cop out" from having to deal with the real problems that a rigid and mechanical work process brings to those who are unable to afford the luxury of such an escape. He also maintains that to divorce art from technology is to misperceive both, and that one of the essential functions of education must be to re-establish them in their mutual relationship.

In addition to the question of inequitable distribution, the problem of alienation is also raised in connection with technology. Don Ihde maintains that there is no necessary connection between the two in "A Phenomenology of Man-Machine Relations." He shows how different types of machines condition man's perceptions and experiences, with the implication that man is not essentially estranged from himself, nature, or anything else just because he is obliged to interact with technology and machines.

And finally Noam Chomsky, who educated an entire young generation to the evils of an arrogantly powerful state, articulates some of the basic assumptions about human nature that are involved in conflicting visions of work and education. "Toward a Humanistic Conception of Education" draws on Russell, von Humboldt, the early Marx, and Chomsky himself to suggest a view of human beings that focuses on their creativity and individuality, a view which is dangerous for education in a corporate state, but perhaps essential for the education system of any society that hopes to survive the closing decades of the twentieth century.

Education as a Vehicle for the Manipulation of Black Workers

James D. Anderson

The traditional liberal view which dominates historical scholarship on black education sees the rise of black schooling as the result of a humanitarian victory by a group of elite reformers over a reactionary white majority. The overriding conception which unites most of the histories of black education is that philanthropic men and women of the Northeast combined with southern reformers to help the ex-slaves transform their oppressive conditions. Standard historical opinion begins the story of black education by pointing out the repressive nature of the South at the turn of the century. It is argued that the bitter social pressures arising from the white supremacy movement of the late nineteenth century were leading toward the total destruction of black people. At this juncture historians introduce the northern philanthropists and the southern middle-class professional educators as the chief restraining forces to the white supremacy movement. These historians do not argue that the school campaigners sought to protect the political, social, civil, or human rights of black people in any direct manner; rather, they have painted a picture of patron saints from the industrial Northeast collaborating with southern reformers to sneak Horace Mann's school into the black community as the last avenue of advancement in an otherwise oppressive society.

For example, the studies of Louis Harlan, C. Vann Woodward, Horace Mann Bond, John Hope Franklin, and Henry Bullock all maintain that a group made up of northern philanthropists, southern reformers, and accommodationist Negroes helped the freedmen achieve a fuller freedom. Harlan contends that "The original purpose of the philanthropists was to cushion the Negro against the shock of racism and to keep public education open as an avenue of advancement."[1] The philanthropists and southern educators are cast as a class of persons who dedicated themselves to the ideas of protecting and elevating the ex-slaves. Harlan attributes humanitarian motives to the action of reformers and then portrays the black school as a saviour in a life or death social climate. He said that "the Negro schools occupied the zone between being kept deliberately poor but not destroyed."[2] Realizing the funda- mental shortcomings of the school system for black people, Harlan justifies the failures of the school campaigners by arguing that they "yielded reluctantly to the superior power of the white su- premacy movement, taking a middle path between equalitarian- ism and racism."[3] In short, the humanitarian zeal was trimmed largely for political expediency and not because of any lack of genuine commitment to meeting Negro aspirations.

Like Harlan, other historians of the South and of black educa- tion identify the men concerned with establishing a school system as the great moral forces in building a newer and better South. The southern educators, argued C. Vann Woodward, were "estimable gentlemen with high collars and fine principles, they were very much in earnest."[4] Further, they were "middleclass, professional people—schoolmen, churchmen, editors—inspired with humani- tarian zeal and a passion for uplift."[5] In essence there is no difference between Woodward's and Harlan's conception of the rise of black education and of the persons who led the movement. They both maintain that the zeal which animated the educational crusade in the South was a mixture of paternalism and *noblesse*

---

[1] Louis Harlan, *Separate and Unequal: Public School Campaigns and Racism in the Southern Seaboard States 1901–1915* (Chapel Hill: University of North Carolina Press, 1958), 1968 Atheneum edition, p. 82.

[2] *Ibid.*, p. 8.

[3] *Ibid.*, p. 92.

[4] C. Vann Woodward, *Origins of the New South 1877–1913* (Baton Rouge: Louisiana State University Press, 1967 edition), p. 397. Woodward realizes that the school campaigners did not seek any "basic alteration of social, racial, and economic arrangements" (*ibid.*). But this is a comment on other nonrevolution- ary vision, not on their motives and interests. As to the forces that moved them, he writes clearly, "The zeal that animated the education crusade was that mixture of paternalism and noblesse oblige which is the nearest Southern equiv- alent of Northern humanitarianism. The spirit was the most authentic heritage the dominant middle class got from the old ruling class" (*ibid.*, p. 401).

[5] *Ibid.*, p. 401.

oblige, representing the spirit of southern and northern humanitarianism respectively.

Horace Mann Bond, John Hope Franklin, and Henry Bullock, three black historians, all with basically different approaches to history, are united with Harlan and Woodward in sharing the assumption that the philanthropists and southern educators were simply humanitarians, paternalists, and builders of good will. Beyond that, they maintain, there was little or no interest in the schooling of blacks. Horace Mann Bond nearly credits the foundations with being the saviours of the black race in the South: ". . . the character, and almost all of the intelligence, of the present-day Negro can be traced back to the friendly intermediation of philanthropic persons of both races."[6] Of course he is on much safer ground when he includes both races. But he goes on to say that the foundations "developed leadership within the race, and provided physically and spiritually for the growth of opportunities for Negro children."[7] John Hope Franklin continued this line of argument in a short chapter on philanthropy and the Negro in his distinguished work, *From Slavery to Freedom.* Franklin realized that negative criticisms had been made of the foundations, but he maintained that black children benefited substantially from their generosity.[8] He continued the traditional conception of the relation between philanthropic individuals and the development of black education as the former being moved, largely by feelings of *noblesse oblige,* to uplift the latter from, social and economic deprivation. Henry A. Bullock, whose book on this subject won the Bancroft Prize in 1968, brought no new perspective on the philanthropic movement and its relation to the purpose of schooling in the black South. He argued that the philanthropists remained "personally aloof" from the racial conflict and adopted a policy of noninvolvement in racial matters.[9]

The approach to black education in the present work is entirely different. It does not deny altogether that paternalistic notions

[6] Horace Mann Bond, *The Education of the Negro in the American Social Order* (New York, 1934), p. 50.

[7] *Ibid.,* p. 150.

[8] John Hope Franklin, *From Slavery to Freedom* (New York: Alfred A. Knopf, Inc., 1947), 1967 edition, p. 386. Franklin anticipated vague popular criticisms of foundation work in the South but dismissed them, without investigation, as inappropriate.

[9] Henry A. Bullock, *A History of Negro Education in the South* (Cambridge: Harvard College, 1967), 1970 Praeger edition, p. 50.

inspired the crusade for black education. This approach argues that other concerns were more central and that the role of schooling in the black community is better understood when linked to larger social and economic questions. Specifically, this approach analyzes the institution of "Negro education" as a system deemed socially necessary for the development and maintenance of a particular form of economic order and white rule in the postwar South. The education of black people is seen as rooted mainly in exploitative economic and racial interests instead of in any humanitarian movement. Black public schooling is viewed as an institution forged from the interests and views of the industrial philanthropists of the Northeast and the reformers and emerging businessmen of the New South, who held corresponding interests in the industrial conquest and white dominance of the American South. The hegemony of the industrialists and the middle-class reformers over the structuring of the social arrangement in the postwar South dictated the institutional behavior of schooling in the black community. It was the understanding of this class that the social economy of the New South depended upon the proper socialization of the black population. We have, then, two different conceptions about the social purposes of schooling in the black South. The liberal view assumes that public schooling in the black South functioned historically as an institution of social, economic, and moral elevation. The argument here suggests the opposite—that the institution of black schooling was calculated to restrain black people and socialize them into a new form of subjugation, considered necessary because of the events of the Civil War and the interest in industrializing the postwar South.

The basic problem with the liberal approach is that its analysis of black education is narrowly based upon certain beliefs about the character and interest of a philanthropic elite and the southern reformers. The liberal scholars of this period, accepting the school campaigners at their most idealistic public rationalizations, have romanticized the school crusade to a point of serious historical distortion. The categorization of organized social philanthropy in the South merely as humanitarianism has led to the deliberate neglect of attempting to chart the rise of black education in terms of special social and economic interest. There are only a sprinkling of economic statements in the existing histories of black education. For the most part such evidence has been gathered to declare the irrelevancy of economic motivation rather than to connect the educational movement to specific class interests. This omission may continue so long as the leading historians of black education narrowly define economic interests as efforts for crude private benefits. In this framework economic factors apply only to the investor, a fact which thereby obscures social conceptions of economic order and concerns for racial dominance which carry very definite economic implications. Economic ordering need not only bring direct monetary returns, it may also lead to broader concerns, such as the realization of concepts of class rule and social order. A more important way to examine the economic and racial concerns which forged the crusade for black education is to explore the institutional role of schooling in socializing black people for particular roles in the social economy. Here one can identify the social purposes of black education with the economic and racial conceptions of the persons who exercised power in molding the character of black schooling.

The general historical view is that the southern white landowner and employer had little use for black literacy and the working class whites were supposedly afraid of the power that literacy would give black people. This view is probably most suggested by Louis Harlan. In one of his passages on the interest of owners and managers in the schooling of blacks, Harlan said: "Though there were personal exceptions, neither the northern investor nor the southern manager in these southern cheap-labor industries had an economic concern for a trained labor or citizenry."[10] Harlan was well aware of the interest of the business community, at least in the North, in the education of blacks. His contention, however, is that such interests were not economically based but were inspired by humanitarian zeal for uplift. Moreover, Harlan limits this concern to the businessmen of the Northeast. As to the South, he held that a distaste for literate blacks was "one of the few things upon which most whites agreed."[11] This view is held with virtual unanimity among historians of black education.

In contrast to the view of Louis Harlan and other liberal historians, southern manufacturers and northern investors and managers were very much interested in a trained black labor force and an educated citizenry. Furthermore, this concern was motivated

[10] Harlan, *Separate and Unequal*, p. 39.
[11] *Ibid.*, p. 40.

by economic concerns and a desire for the structuring of race relations. The movement for black education was not initiated to cushion black people against the shock of racism. Instead, both movements for and against the education of blacks were white supremacy movements, but with different social assessments as to what was necessary to prepare the black population for a role in the postwar South. Different attitudes toward education, labor policies, standards for race relations and such, grew out of different interests in economic development and the readjustment of the South to the rest of the nation. The South was never uniform in its conception of the ideal social economy and the differences become even sharper in the postwar period. As the industrialists came to power in the years following the war they introduced many new values of industrial capitalism. The concerns of industrialists had new implications for education and industry. Their attitudes were formed out of economic interests in the ability of the South's laboring population to develop the industrial natural resources left largely untouched because of the dominance of the plantation economy.

Interest in the training of a black industrial labor force had its origin in the Old South. By 1860 between 160,000 and 200,000 slaves (approximately 5 percent of the total slave population) worked in southern industries, and some of their training was already moving toward industrial literacy (i.e., functional literacy and rudimentary mechanical skills). Robert S. Starobin's useful study, *Industrial Slavery in the Old South*, points out that black slave managers were trained by their industrial enterprises to read, write, keep accurate accounts, and even collect and disburse money.[12] Starobin wrote that "Many slave engineers skillfully operated complicated industrial machinery."[13] Though the industrial movement was unable to develop and expand in the agricultural economy of the Old South, the businessmen engaged in iron works, lumber manufacturing, bridge building, etc., came to hold certain economic conceptions of black labor and its use in industrial development. A fundamental conviction was that black managers and black operators were less expensive to employ than whites, and that the reduction in labor cost increased the competi-

[12] Robert S. Starobin, *Industrial Slavery in the Old South* (New York: Oxford University Press, 1971), p. 169.

[13] *Ibid.*, p. 170.

tiveness of southern industries.[14] It was the belief of many of the owners that slave labor was an even greater advantage because it could be kept in stricter subordination and manipulated more easily than white labor. Starobin quoted one owner as saying, "there is no haggling or striking for wages, no contention about hours. Uniformity, obedience, and wholesome discipline, mark the [black] labor of the South."[15] Moreover, both planters and industrialists supported the view that black labor was as reliable and efficient as white labor, if not the best industrial force.

The events of the Civil War made it possible for those interested in the systematic training of the laboring population and the industrialization of the South to exert themselves in the Reconstruction years. Two factors which marked the emergence of the New South were the growth of industry and public education. Though agriculture was the first area reestablished in the postbellum South, industrial development was characteristic of the spirit of the period.[16] The renewed and more widespread interest in industrial development in the postwar South was accompanied by an intense interest in the conditions of the laboring population. Unlike their planter confederates, the postbellum industrialists desired a trained labor force and an "educated" black citizenry.

The early crusade for education in the South was undertaken by the northern-based Peabody Education Fund, established in 1867. The first general agent of that organization, Barnas Sears, noted as of 1880 the interest of southern industrialists in the promotion of the general education of the population.[17] Sears divided the South into three classes and assessed their impact upon efforts to establish a permanent public school system. To Sears, one-third of the population was in favor of public education and one-third was against; the other one-third he classified as neutral. The opposition class was described as the heirs of the plantation civilization who shunned public education and industry. Sears believed that they were upstart demagogues, "united by some common bond of sympathy, stung by wounded pride, and aroused to a high pitch of excitement by an appeal to their

---

[14] *Ibid.*, p. 172.

[15] *Ibid.*

[16] Woodward, *Origins of the New South*, pp. 113–15.

[17] The Peabody Education Fund, *Proceedings of the Trustees* (Cambridge, 1875–1916), Vol. I, p. 408.

prejudices and passions."[18] Sears believed that it was one of the fundamental goals of the agrarian South to "crush out the school system."[19] On the other hand, Sears praised the "enterprising character" of the industrialist wing and viewed its members as being in harmony with the interest of the industrial Northeast and receptive to the public school idea.

Testimony of southern industrialists helps to confirm the belief that in their role as investors and managers they were interested in the systematic training of the South's labor supply and held a special interest in the socialization of the black working class. The interests were ambiguous and contradictory at times but can be reduced to several consistent concerns. The industrialists were interested in raising the general efficiency of the black labor force, which they viewed as critical to the industrialization of the South. The industrialists were interested in education as a subtle and systematic form of coercion that would subjugate blacks and create an inexpensive labor force. Also, a key concern of the industrialists was to manipulate labor to their advantage through creating a docile, tractable black working force that would be insurance against the spread of unionized white labor.

All of these concerns were supported by the South's industrialists when they were investigated by a roving subcommittee of the Senate Committee on Education and Labor in 1883.[20] The subcommittee was charged to investigate the conditions for industrial development in the South and to focus specifically on the state of the laboring population. Interestingly, this was done in order to shed light upon the need for education and help the United States Congress act intelligently on the question of national aid to education. The measure then before Congress was the Blair Bill for national aid. The industrialists of the South gave lengthy and elaborate testimony revealing their perceptions of the requirements for industrializing the postwar South. Invariably they propagandized the traditional stereotypes about blacks as "lazy" and "shiftless" to rationalize the state of paternal despotism they envisioned for the black worker. Beneath this public rationalization, however, the industrialists expressed a firm belief that

[18] *Ibid.*

[19] *Ibid.*

[20] U.S. Senate Committee on Education and Labor, *Report of the Committee to Investigate the Relations between Capital and Labor*, 1883, Vol. IV (Washington, D.C., 1885).

black workers were imperative to the material prosperity of the South. To them, one of the first conditions for industrial growth and expansion was a reliable and trained labor force. An Alabama industrialist, Albert C. Danner, president of the Bank of Mobile and in the business of lumber manufacturing, viewed black workers as the primary laboring population. Danner said: "The black labor is about the only reliable labor that we have."[21] Danner considered black workers "the best laborers in the world."[22] A. S. Chamberlain, a Tennessee iron manufacturer, supported this view. Chamberlain asserted: "Colored men . . . are fully as good as white men; they are as steady . . . as reliable . . . and their product is fully as good as anything that we have got from white labor."[23] Many other industrialists, famous and little known, repeated these opinions. The point, however, is not to stress the competitiveness of black labor with white labor, for the industrialists had no plans of throwing them into competition for the same work. The critical point about black labor which held implications for the training of black workers was that the industrialists viewed it as essential and eventually sought to harness and control it through education. Surveys by the *Chattanooga Tradesman* concluded that Southern industrialists were satisfied with the performance of black laborers and regarded them as a necessary component of the southern working force.[24]

Out of the economic interests in black workers emerged a strong emphasis on education as a means of manipulating black people into the industrialists' scheme of material prosperity. Their advocacy of the systematic schooling of black youth was fundamentally a step toward securing control over black workers in that region. Their interest in supervising black youth was inspired generally by the feeling that they had lost control over the black workers because of the destruction of slavery. Though the end of slavery made it possible for the growth of industry, the loss of mastery over the living and working conditions of black workers was viewed as a disadvantage. Thus the industrialist's mission in the New South was aptly stated by the editor of the *New York Times*, who wrote that emancipation meant that southerners

[21] *Ibid.*, p. 102.
[22] *Ibid.*, p. 103.
[23] *Ibid.*, p. 46.
[24] Quoted in W. E. B. Du Bois, *The Negro Artisan*, Atlanta University Publication No. 7 (Atlanta: Atlanta University, 1902), p. 180.

would have to learn "the art of managing Negroes as paid laborers without the lash."[25] An Alabama iron manufacturer said of the relation between black labor and education, ". . . if the labor was better educated I am satisfied our labor here would be much more reliable."[26] Moreover, if black workers were to operate industrial machinery or be counted as an effective reserve force for skilled levels of work, it was considered that some form of industrial literacy was imperative.

The interest in harnessing a black labor force was further stimulated as southern industrialists became seriously concerned with blocking the spread of labor unions in the South. It was the general feeling that black workers could be used to undercut the power of labor unions. John W. Lapsley of the Shelby Iron Works in Alabama spoke for many of his fellow industrialists when he said: "I certainly do not think that the South is in any danger of any such war [between capital and labor] so long as the great staple of our labor is the negro. The negro will never combine against capital."[27] Industrialists provided numerous examples of employing black workers when they became dissatisfied with the white workers' demands for better wages and working conditions. Such interest led them to campaign persistently for control over the supervision of black youth. This was done expressedly at the expense of others who viewed education as a means of breaking the despotic state of wage slavery.

In order to see that not all blacks acceded to the economic and social ideas of the industrialists and school campaigners one simply needs to consult some of their prominent local educational leaders. Many of them who testified before the Senate Subcommittee on Education and Labor certainly did not hold the industrialists' views concerning the purpose of education and its relation to their social-economic position in the New South. Black educators spoke of schooling as a vehicle to instill equality and to launch black people into the political and professional levels; they were also interested in controlling black schools for the employment of black teachers. W. H. Spencer, a public school teacher in Columbus, Georgia, said that he felt black teachers were best

[25] Quoted in Nathan Huggins, ed. *Key Issues in the Afro-American Experience* (New York, 1971), Vol. II, p. 48.

[26] *Ibid.*, p. 462.

[27] U.S. Senate, *Report . . . Relations between Capital and Labor*, Vol. IV, p. 166.

for black schools because they understood the children better.[28] He said he would accept good white teachers, "provided that they would not teach us that we were inferior to them."[29] Spencer objected to a white woman teacher who called him a "nigger" and to a white male teacher because, "he would always teach the children that they were inferior to him."[30] Thomas S. Price, another teacher in Columbus, Georgia said he wanted education for black people so that they could have a "better conception of the value of their services" and not go to "work for nothing."[31]

The most consistent thought among the black educators was the idea of education as a means to teach self-respect, confidence and pride in being black. Tony Jenkins, a carpenter, said: ". . . speaking of education, I think the first thing they ought to learn, is to respect themselves, and then . . . they will certainly command respect from everybody else."[32] Another carpenter, V. J. Jones, identified himself and his people as "Colored" because "when I use the word 'Negro' I mean a slave."[33] Jones and Jenkins both were interested in building confidence in the black community by teaching that black people were the equals of all other human beings and could manage well for themselves. Jones remembered "when one white boy at the age of ten years could take the best and most responsible colored man and figure for him."[34] The purpose of schooling was to change this and create a "confidential people." Bishop Holsey of the Colored Methodist Church of America clearly stated the change which the educators wished to see. "My opinion," said Holsey, "is that whenever the day comes when our people can generally receive a good common English education there will be just as large a percent of them fitted to adorn society with industry and intelligence and integrity of character as will be found among any other race."[35] Holsey could certainly make such statements as he had made himself literate by studying graves in the woods during slavery.

Something must be said of an interview with R. R. Wright, the black educator of Augusta, Georgia, before turning again to

[28] *Ibid.,* p. 579.
[29] *Ibid.,* p. 580.
[30] *Ibid.*
[31] *Ibid.,* p. 620.
[32] *Ibid.,* p. 636.
[33] *Ibid.,* p. 626.
[34] *Ibid.*
[35] *Ibid.,* p. 777.

the plans of the white industrialists for educating the black man. Wright's own plans on this subject were very much like contemporary concerns for building race pride through a history of the black man's heritage. In speaking of the black man's heritage Wright said: "I think that about all the great religions which have blest this world have come from the colored races—all. I believe, too, that our methods of alphabetic writing all came from the colored race, and I think the majority of the sciences in their origin have come from the colored races . . . the first civilization of which we have record was in the Nile Valley, coming up from Ethiopia, and was a negro civilization."[36] Such rhetoric may be surprising for November 23, 1883, and coming from a black southerner. But clearly it was in great contrast to the views of the southern industrialists.

Even though such black voices were raised, their aspirations were set aside as the far more powerful industrialists pursued their own program of economic and racial exploitation. They were concerned that instruction for blacks inculcate in them values that would fit them to a subordinate role in the southern social economy. They did not want any education for blacks that would interfere with their prescribed roles as humble, obedient, inexpensive laborers in a system of exploitative industrial capitalism. Education which taught the equality of the races or encouraged politicization was frowned upon by the industrialists. They were especially on guard against the "higher branches" of knowledge which they thought encouraged blacks to avoid common labor. As one southern industrialist said, "This Greek and Latin business . . . really disqualif[ies] people for work and ought to be discarded in a scheme of education for the working classes and industrial instruction substituted."[37] To be sure, such statements also carried general implications for that portion of whites who comprised the white working class. It was not the feeling of the industrialists, however, that future white workers could be adequately identified, trained to docility, discouraged away from the ballot box, and kept out of labor unions. In fact, this problem made it more necessary to control black workers in order to check the power of white workers. Their organization could be checked by the "controlled" disorganization of the black workers. The Alabama iron and railroad industrialist J. W. Sloss said: "White

[36] *Ibid.*, pp. 813–14.
[37] *Ibid.*, p. 371.

men quit in a body and the negroes quit individually, each man, whenever he pleases."[38] The absence of collective labor bargaining among black workers was viewed as a credible deterrent to union activity among white laborers. Industrialists were interested in education as a vehicle for the maintenance of this special form of caste economy.

At the turn of the century, when the southern school campaign was most thoroughly organized, the concerns expressed by the industrialists came to form the ideological framework for black public schooling. Starting with the Conference for Education in the South, at Capon Springs, West Virginia, in 1898, northern philanthropists and southern reformers held many formal meetings to determine the type of schooling that would teach black people to know their place as cheap, nonunionized, nonpolitical, and socially segregated common laborers. The southern reformers were mostly middle class professionals, editors, ministers, and educators, who were passionately committed to maintaining white supremacy in the South and the nation and who were convinced that a southern alliance with the industrial Northeast was the proper path to reconstruction. These reformers, though not particularly seeking pure monetary rewards, were intensely concerned with establishing some form of white class rule and rebuilding the power of the white South; it was their conception of the good community and of what was necessary for southern material prosperity. Moved by their traditional racist mentality and their exaggerated fears of black political power, the professional reformers sought to relegate black southerners permanently to the bottom level of the South's social economy.

The northern agents, on the other hand, were mostly investors and entrepreneurs in southern industrial enterprises. As C. Vann Woodward put it, "Rockefellers and other capitalists monopolized southern monopolies."[39] The industrial magnates of the Northeast, John D. Rockefeller, Andrew Carnegie, J. P. Morgan, and Collis P. Huntington, were of course interested in the development of cottonseed oil, the mining of coal and iron, the manufacturing of steel, and the expansion of southern railroads. Black workers played an important role in the development of major southern industries. At the dawn of the twentieth century nearly one-third of the railroad firemen and brakemen and over

---

[38] *Ibid.*, p. 200.
[39] Woodward, *Origins of the New South*, p. 304.

half the track men were black. In Alabama over half the coal miners and more than three-fourths of the iron miners were black.[40] It was only natural for the capitalists who monopolized these industries at the national level to be concerned with their southern branches and the workers who kept them operating.

Prominent industrialists, however, were rarely active in the shaping of educational policy and ideology for black workers. Financial contributions to establish educational foundations and occasional speeches represented the extent of involvement by industrialists like Rockefeller, Morgan, Carnegie, and Huntington. The more intimate connections with the southern school crusade were made by their managers and friends who had more personal economic and social ties in the South. Morgan's southern manager, William H. Baldwin, Jr., was a rapidly rising railroad entrepreneur who had built the Southern Railway Company by using thousands of black workers.[41] Morgan had placed Baldwin as vice-president and general manager of the Southern Railway Company in 1894.[42] In the same year Baldwin became a trustee of Tuskegee Institute and worked closely with Booker T. Washington. Baldwin became a leading figure in the southern school campaign and was supported by other industrialists like George Foster Peabody and Robert C. Ogden. Peabody was from New York and became wealthy in banking and railroads.[43] Peabody was particularly interested in the growth of education and industry in the South because he was born and raised in Georgia and maintained close connections with the educational affairs of the State. He was a trustee of Fort Valley Industrial School in Georgia, a black industrial institute. Peabody was also a trustee of Hampton and Tuskegee Institutes, the two major centers for black industrial leadership. Robert C. Ogden's diligent work in leading the southern school campaign earned him the title of "Field Marshal." Ogden championed the southern education crusade through such various and influential positions as president of the Southern Education Board and president of the General Education Board, and he, too, was a trustee of both Hampton and Tuskegee institutes. He went South as a representative of Wana-

---

[40] Huggins, *Key Issues in the Afro-American Experience.* Vol. II, p. 52.

[41] Charles W. Dabney, *Universal Education in the South* (Chapel Hill: University of North Carolina Press, 1936), Vol. II, pp. 149–50.

[42] Woodward, *Origins of the New South*, p. 292.

[43] Louise Ware, *George Foster Peabody: Banker, Philanthropist, Publicist* (Athens: University of Georgia Press, 1951).

maker Clothing in New York and was interested in the manufacturing of cotton cloth and the use of black labor in the cotton and clothing industries.[44]

Until the Capon Springs Conference in 1898, most of these industrialists worked on the development of education in the South through institutions like Tuskegee, Hampton, and the Fort Valley State Industrial School. This conference, and others which followed, were largely the result of efforts by southern reformers, and they provided the opportunity to engage in the southern school campaign on a broader and more significant scale. The reformer most responsible for the first conference was Jabez Lamar Monroe Curry, the greatest educational statesman of the South.[45] Curry had moved into this influential position as general agent of the Peabody Fund in 1880 and later as trustee and general agent of the Slater Fund in 1890. In the last decade of the nineteenth century Curry was the sole agent of nearly all northern philanthropy in the South. In his position he worked with Baldwin, Ogden, Peabody, Booker T. Washington, and others seeking aid and advice for educational policy. By the time of the first Conference for Education in the South, Curry was an old hand at the promotion of southern education. Between 1881 and 1901 he spoke forty-seven times before southern state legislatures and many more times to educational associations on behalf of general education in the South.

The Conferences for Education in the South met annually from 1898 to 1914 at different locations in the South. After 1901 the members functioned mainly through the executive arm of the conferences, the Southern Education Board, which was established in that year. The conferences were mainly for propaganda purposes and are largely important for the resultant crystallization of thought among and between southern reformers and businessmen from both regions.

Historians like Bond, Bullock, Harlan, and Woodward have constantly misunderstood these conferences as the beginnings of a humanitarian movement in a period of pessimism. They view

[44] "The Ogden Movement," unpublished paper by Donald Spivey of the University of California at Davis, History Department. The paper is based on research in the Robert Ogden papers at the Library of Congress, Washington, D.C.

[45] William J. Lewis, "The Educational Speaking of Jabez L. M. Curry," Ph.D. dissertation, University of Florida, 1955. Lewis's dissertation is one of the best studies of Curry's thought and his public career.

the "official" launching of the educational crusade as a reaction to southern white oppression. Bullock analyzed the conferences thus: "Northern and Southern leaders, realizing that an equalitarian approach to the development of educational opportunities for the Negro American was not acceptable to white Southerners, joined forces to save for the former slaves what could be salvaged."[46] Harlan likewise saw the Conferences for Education in the South as a reaction to white oppression. He concluded that the philanthropists came forth to discuss the education of blacks in the South because they "were perturbed by the social and economic hindrances placed on Negroes by the sovereign whites."[47]

His conclusion suggests that the philanthropists and reformers were concerned about giving black people greater equality; but on the contrary, the persons who came together at the Conferences for Education in the South envisioned no place for blacks in the southern community above the level of certain forms of semi-skilled mechanical and agriculture labor. They sought to give them no more schooling than was needed to perform their menial function in the southern economy. It was not a movement to "salvage" a school system but a movement to gain the power to decide what kind of schools would exist in the South for blacks.

It was evident both from the personnel and from their discussions that the primary aims of the conferences were to bring about the realization of ideas about industry, education, and racial order expressed by southern industrialists, northern businessmen, and southern reformers. The careful restraint shown and the pretension to stay out of politics did not represent any fundamental compromise with the militant white supremacy movement. The concerns were more particular than that. The campaigns for industry and education had received some opposition from the agrarian South since the Reconstruction period. The conflict here was between those southern industrialists who felt that schooling was imperative to insure an orderly racial caste and material prosperity as opposed to the agrarians who believed that schooling raised "dysfunctional" expectations for blacks. Both camps, however, were champions of the white supremacy movement. On the other hand, the school campaigners were worried about the type of black educators mentioned earlier, who were interested in schooling as a vehicle for economic power, race pride, and social

---

[46] Bullock, *A History of Negro Education in the South*, p. 89.
[47] Harlan, *Separate and Unequal*, p. 78.

equality. Robert C. Ogden was thinking of these black educators and the agrarian faction when he wrote to Baldwin: "With southern prejudice on the one hand and Negro suspicion on the other, we have a delicate course to steer."[48] The school campaigners steered this course by making their position loud and clear on white supremacy and by courting an accomodationist Negro leadership, of which Booker T. Washington was the most well known.

The president of the Second Conference for Education in the South, J. L. M. Curry, became the number one spokesman for white supremacy. To Curry, the black man, "a stupid, indolent, shiftless laborer," was a "hindrance to southern wealth and development."[49] He therefore strongly advocated the industrial training of black workers. Scholars who have viewed this advocacy of Negro industrial training as a plea for black uplift often fail to see that the education of the black worker was to Curry a means to the continuation of white power. Curry made it clear that he expected the progress and wealth obtained from black labor to benefit a white ruling class. He defined the status of whites this way: "The white people are to be the leaders, to take the initiative, to have the directive control in all matters pertaining to civilization and the highest interests of our beloved land. History demonstrates that the Caucasian will rule. He ought to rule."[50] Curry, of course, held that "white supremacy does not mean hostility to the negro, but friendship for him."[51] (And he usually assumed this friendliness himself.) If white supremacy was a permanent fact of life then black people had to be prepared—in a friendly way—for their inevitable subordination. Curry thought that they should be systematically trained for this role. To him education was necessary because "the more debased, the less self-reliant, the more unskilled, the more thriftless and unemployed the race, . . . the more dangerous it will be, the less desirable as inhabitant, as laborer."[52] Thus Curry advocated the training of black workers for white economic prosperity and an orderly racial caste. He said: "In the name of the south-

---

[48] Letter from Robert C. Ogden to William H. Baldwin, Jr., Robert C. Ogden papers, Library of Congress.
[49] Lewis, "The Educational Speaking of Jabez L. M. Curry", p. 101.
[50] *Proceedings of the Second Conference for Education in the South* (Capon Springs, W.Va., 1899), p. 28.
[51] *Ibid.*
[52] *Ibid.*, p. 59.

ern white man . . . the Great White race . . . educate the negro."[53]
He felt that to neglect the training of the black masses would lead
to incalcuable injury to southern peace and prosperity.

Like Curry, the northern crusaders were interested in rebuilding the South under a class of white industrialists supported by a
submissive black laboring class. George Foster Peabody once
wrote to a friend:

> Have you the least doubt but that if the one million Negroes . . .
> were rightly educated . . . that they would be worth in dollars
> and cents three times their present value. If this be true, as I am
> positively sure that it is, and as the property of the State of
> Georgia is so largely owned by the white race, would not the
> gain to the white race, under present methods of distribution, be
> most incalculable in dollars and cents and far greater the quiet-
> ness and peace of life and harmony of conscience of the white
> governing citizen.[54]

As a key member of the southern school campaign Peabody
sought to impress upon the South the inseparable relation between
white material prosperity and the "right" education of the black
race. He told those fearful of education for black people that the
practical training of blacks would socialize them into a subordinate role and bring quietness to the South. In one letter Peabody
wrote: "Many of our southern people forget that he [the Negro] is
very amenable to teaching, and particularly the teaching of environment, and is ready to keep in his place, when given free opportunity to develop his capacity and all come to know what his true
place is."[55] Peabody, however, already "knew" what the black
man's capacity was and what kind of education was appropriate
to his capacity. As a trustee of Hampton Institute, Tuskegee Institute, and Fort Valley Industrial School, he constantly urged
blacks to accept the industrial curriculum in place of academic
work. To Peabody, even the music that black children learned
had to be practical. He objected to black people singing "the
classics" because he felt that such raised dysfunctional expectations. Whenever he encountered black people singing other than

---

[53] Newspaper clipping of a speech by Curry on November 5, 1901, J. L. M.
Curry papers, Library of Congress.

[54] George Foster Peabody to Colonel Smith (March 20, 1906), George
Foster Peabody papers, Library of Congress.

[55] George Foster Peabody to Henry R. Goethins (January 30, 1911), George
Foster Peabody papers.

spirituals he admonished them to change. The following reply from S. F. Harris, a black educator in Athens, Georgia, is just one example. Harris wrote to Peabody: "I beg to acknowledge the receipt of your letter . . . and to also express my appreciation of your kindly suggestions concerning the attention of our school to the music of the race, the Spirituals. I admit that the results from singing or trying to sing the classics are not *practical* and therefore as benefitial to my people as the "Spirituals." We shall give more attention to the "Spirituals."[56] It is important to note that Harris suggested that he was pressured into other types of academic work because Athens was "committed wholly to higher education for all the negroes." "This has made our problem of getting a foothold for Industrial education somewhat difficult," said Harris.[57] This was the idea that industrialists like Peabody worked so hard to destroy. Nothing was further from their idea of the orderly industrial South than the resistance to practical industrial training by blacks. This was not what Peabody had in mind when he said that the black man was "very ready to keep in his place." He was thinking of docile, tractable, moderately skilled laborers; contented, happily singing spirituals, and working faithfully for the "white governing citizen." Uppity blacks who shunned industrial training became the industrialists' nightmare.

It became the understood principle of the southern school campaign that the schooling of blacks was to be structured to mold them into economic servitude. There was probably no one in the school campaign who expressed this better than William H. Baldwin, Jr. Starting at the Second Conference for Education in the South in 1899, he always made it very clear that he wished blacks to serve as the cushion for industrial capitalism in the South. Baldwin put it this way:

> In the negro is the opportunity of the South. Time has proven that he is best fitted to perform the heavy labor in the Southern states. . . . The South needs him; but the South needs him educated to be a suitable citizen. He will willingly fill the more menial positions, and do the heavy work, at less wages, than the American white man or any foreign race which has yet come to our shores. This will permit the Southern white laborer to

---

[56] S. F. Harris to George Foster Peabody (July 16, 1906), George Foster Peabody papers.
[57] *Ibid.*

perform the more expert labor, and to leave the fields, the mines, and the simpler trades for the negro.[58]

In times of stability, periods without labor difficulty, Baldwin planned to keep black labor subordinate to white labor. In a crisis situation, however, he planned to use black workers to offset white workers and break the power of the trade unions. Baldwin said clearly, "The union of white labor, well organized, will raise the wages beyond a reasonable point, and then the battle will be fought, and the negro will be put in at a less wage, and the labor union will either have to come down in wages, or negro labor will be employed."[59] It would indeed demand a careful training of black workers to manipulate them back and forth to meet the demands of such schemes. It would require a separation of black labor and white labor. Black laborers would have to be trained to mark time in the menial jobs and move at Baldwin's notice into more skilled jobs. Moreover, they would have to be conditioned to give up "white jobs" when the labor crisis subsided, in order to return the society to stability (racial peace). In short, the black workers would have to be moderately trained, tractable, humble, and obedient.

Baldwin argued that the postwar southern economy, as the plantation economy, demanded the education of blacks in various arts and trades. The slave system of training was a perfect model, said Baldwin: "Each plantation had its own wheelwright and blacksmith, and carpenter and shoemaker. Each plantation was a small industrial school; but first, and most important of all, the negro was taught to work and was made to work."[60] He praised the "careful restraint" of this kind of education and pointed to its revival at Tuskegee Institute. He defined Tuskegee as an industrial school which primarily taught black youth "how to work with the hands" and the dignity of hard labor. Equally important, thought Baldwin, ". . . the Tuskegee student is taught . . . to have simple tasks and few wants . . . wants that can be satisfied."[61] Tuskegee was for Baldwin the proper solution to the South's racial and economic problems because it sought to fix blacks in a

[58] William H. Baldwin, Jr., "The Present Problem of Negro Education in the South," *Journal of Social Service*, Vol. 37 (December, 1899), p. 58.

[59] William H. Baldwin, Jr., to N. F. Thompson (April 15, 1900), Booker T. Washington papers, Library of Congress.

[60] *Proceedings of the Second Conference for Education in the South*, p. 67.

[61] *Ibid.*, p. 68.

subordinate racial class. In effect, he saw its existence as a means to increase the productive efficiency of the black laborers, to inculcate the consciousness which dignified labor, and to restrain the social and political wants of the black masses. Baldwin argued that industrial education carried with it a "moral teaching and practice," that "labor induces morality."[62] Out of this experience he said, "comes a modest air of hope, of ambition, and of zeal to work with the hands."[63] He constantly advocated the kind of training that would teach blacks to work hard and stay in "their place."

The educational reformers were very much concerned with instituting the kind of education that would adjust blacks to a subordinate role without raising dysfunctional expectations. Black workers were not expected to vote, organize for collective labor bargaining, or seek equality with whites. Their education was to restrain them peacefully in some sort of racial caste. In a very popular book, *Problems of the Present South*, Edgar Gardner Murphy, vice-president of the Conference for Education in the South, contended that black education, like slavery, was to serve as a system of restraint.[64] Murphy viewed the purpose of black education as that of arresting the upward and downward momentum of blacks. The education of blacks was defined as dangerous if it allowed them to descend into industrial inefficiency. Black schooling was viewed as equally dangerous if it encouraged blacks to desire the same economic, social, and political status as whites. The function of schooling was to exercise restraint.

Out of the Conferences for Education in the South came two educational boards that assumed general control over education in the South and especially over the education of blacks. The Southern Education Board was established in 1901 and the General Education Board in 1902. Robert C. Ogden was made president of the former and William H. Baldwin, Jr., became chairman of the latter. Ogden said that the Southern Education Board was established for "the maintenance of propaganda."[65]

---

[62] *Ibid.*

[63] *Ibid.*, p. 69.

[64] Edgar Gardner Murphy, *Problems of the Present South* (New York, 1904), pp. 163–64.

[65] Robert C. Ogden to Oswald Villard (March 11, 1905), Robert C. Ogden papers.

Ogden used his organization to propagandize education that would correspond to the interests of the industrialists of the South, who were bent on placing blacks in economic servitude. Ogden urged that the school crusaders bring the "whole subject of popular education before the businessmen of the South as a business proposition, touching very closely their individual and collective interest." [66] Ogden said that ". . . in the definite aims to be secured, the plain business man may often be the teacher of the teacher." [67] We have already seen the "collective interest" of southern businessmen with regard to black education and labor. It was probably Ogden's understanding of this interest that led him to say, "The prosperity of the South largely depends upon the productive power of the black man." [68] His willingness to allow the southern industrialists to shape the course of public education in the South evidences his commitment to their ideas of material prosperity and social order. He was convinced that the real value of providing education for the black man was the potential of schooling in the organization of the South's labor force. He wrote: "Negro progress is a white man's question." [69] In other words, the black man progressed for and according to the white governing class. To Ogden, this meant black common labor to operate white industries.

The crystallization of economic and racial concerns and the relationship of education to the realization of these aims led to organized action. William H. Baldwin, Jr., as chairman of the General Education Board, deliberately moved to gain control over all of northern philanthropy marked for southern education. Baldwin wrote to Booker T. Washington before the first meeting of the General Education Board under its national incorporation, and expressed satisfaction with his success in making the Board a national clearing house: "On Thursday next we have our first meeting under our National incorporation at Washington, D.C. and also we meet the Peabody Board. They have asked us to help them decide important questions and to cooperate with them. My hopes are being realized, General Education Board, Slater, and Peabody. It scares Mr. Murphy, but I am not afraid of the

---

[66] *Proceedings of the Third Capon Springs Conference for Education in the South* (Capon Springs, W.Va., 1900), p. 26.
[67] *Ibid.*, p. 27.
[68] Spivey, "The Ogden Movement," p. 6.
[69] *Ibid.*

results of concentration."[70] Baldwin had said as early as 1899, at the Second Capon Springs Conference, that it was imperative to "organize a general education board" for the selective distribution of philanthropy to "approved" black institutes. He asserted: "Now is the accepted time to concentrate with an organization that will be recognized by the whole country as a proper channel through which the negro industrial education can be reached successfully."[71] The establishment of the General Education Board in 1902 by John D. Rockefeller was an implementation of Baldwin's plans. As chairman, Baldwin eventually organized most of northern philanthropy under this board. His efforts were supported by Robert C. Ogden, chairman of the propaganda-generating Southern Education Board. Ogden appointed a subcommittee to make a comprehensive investigation of black schools. George S. Dickerman, chairman of the investigative subcommittee, said that the study was done to "increase the effectiveness of all faithful workers."[72] Both efforts sought to restrict the educational alternatives of blacks by monopolizing the distribution of funds, filtering them to those institutions with approved industrial programs which corresponded to the economic and racial interests of the school campaigners.

Another important step toward securing control of the training of black workers was to seek accommodationist Negroes who served, in effect, as industrial labor leaders of important black educational institutions. They found a ready partnership with Booker T. Washington and Tuskegee Institute. Robert C. Ogden, George Foster Peabody, and William H. Baldwin, Jr., were three of the four-member Tuskegee Committee for the Investment of Endowment Fund. Baldwin was the chairman of the Tuskegee Endowment Fund and the number one advisor to Washington. Booker T. Washington said that Baldwin was "always particularly interested and even anxious that in all my public utterances I should say the right thing, and above all, that I should say the helpful thing."[73] Baldwin and Ogden did not include Washington or any other accommodationist as an official member of the

---

[70] William H. Baldwin, Jr., to Booker T. Washington (June 23, 1903), Booker T. Washington papers.

[71] *Proceedings of the Second Conference for Education in the South,* p. 75.

[72] G. S. Dickerman, "The Conference for Education in the South, and the Southern Education Board," Report of the Commissioner of Education for 1907 (Washington, 1908), Vol. I, pp. 300–302.

[73] Booker T. Washington, *My Larger Education* (New York, 1911), p. 15.

General Education Board or the Southern Education Board. They did, however, place Washington on the payroll of the Southern Education Board as a field agent to survey the conditions of black education in the South. Washington was paid 83 dollars per month, whereas whites in similar positions were paid 145 dollars per month.[74]

Tuskegee became for Baldwin, Ogden, Peabody, and other school campaigners a major vehicle for achieving their goals of social, economic, and political subordination of black workers. The idea of the agrarian South—that blacks should be offered no schooling or only the lower grades of schooling—was thoroughly inconsistent with the industrialists' goals of isolating and manipulating the black labor force. Baldwin, Ogden, Peabody, and the southern reformers knew well that the black working population needed its own professionals for guidance in education, productive labor, and social life. As the slave-owners needed black drivers so did the industrial capitalists need a black manufactured elite to supervise and inform thousands of black workers and channel them into predetermined courses. This had been an idea of the school campaign since the first Conference for Education in the South in 1898. One reformer, after pointing out that "The masses of the race are to be tillers of the soil; toilers in our industries," proceeded to state, "Someone is going to lead the black industrial forces."[75] This economic consideration prompted the philanthropic leaders to provide for a small number of industrial institutes that would produce black industrial leaders. It is considered one of the "ironies of history" that Howard University, not Tuskegee, developed the first trade school. Tuskegee's lack of emphasis on skilled trades, however, is not so ironic given the interests of Baldwin, Peabody, Ogden, the southern reformers and the southern industrialists. They were more interested in people to propagandize certain political, social, and economic ideas. They considered the real value in Negro industrial training to be its potential for adjusting the race to servitude. Baldwin suggested the following principles for Negro industrial lessons: " 'Face the music'; avoid social questions; leave politics alone; continue to be patient; live moral lives; live simply; learn

[74] Robert C. Ogden to Edwin A. Alderman (June 3, 1903), Robert C. Ogden Papers (Letterbook, Box 13).

[75] *Proceedings of the First Conference for Education in the South* (Capon Springs, W. Va., 1898), p. 19.

to work and to work intelligently; learn to work faithfully; learn to work hard; learn that any work, however menial, if well done is dignified; . . . learn that it is a mistake to be educated out of your necessary environment; know that it is a crime for any teacher, white or black, to educate the negro for positions which are not open to him."[76] With the Southern Education Board checking for "sound" ideology and the General Educational Board controlling the purse strings, the above racial-economic philosophy was rigorously practiced until well into the twentieth century.

In conclusion, the southern school campaign was broad, the programs complex, and the political and economic connections were often very private. Consequently, it is difficult to get far beyond suggestive probes into alternative approaches without writing a full scale monograph.[77] Yet the studies of Harlan, Bond, Bullock, and others are inadequate for an understanding of the central concerns of the school campaigners. Perhaps this is so because the conceptions of education, labor, and social order employed by the school campaigners did not appear economically or socially rational to the historians. Harlan, for example, operated with the bias that public education inevitably improved wealth, freedom, and happiness and that schooling contained some magical force which liberated people toward human equality. Thus he could write that ". . . improvement of white education in the South has been one of the means by which Negroes of that region may expect eventually to secure their heritage of human rights."[78] What was it about southern white education that could lead Harlan to assume that it was a means to secure human rights for blacks? An even more important question is what led to the completely one-sided view that the school campaigners set out to cushion blacks against the shock of racism? It is difficult to see how the school campaigners set out to protect black people from a white supremacy movement by first declaring that they themselves believed in white supremacy, and then working diligently to keep black people out of politics, to make them accept the most menial jobs, to isolate them as an inexpensive labor

---

[76] *Proceedings of the Second Capon Springs Conference for Education in the South*, p. 74.

[77] This article is taken in part from my doctoral thesis, "Education for Servitude: The Social Purposes of Schooling in the Black South, 1870–1930," University of Illinois, 1973.

[78] Harlan, *Separate and Unequal*, p. 42.

force, and to engage them as a unit to depress wages for all workers, hurting mostly their own welfare. If this was, as Harlan claims, the middle ground between equalitarianism and racism, then what was racism? Moreover, the explicit and blatant racism of the school campaigners cannot be sufficiently explained by advancing the notion that the reformers yielded reluctantly to the power of white racism. Certainly, at no time did the likes of Baldwin, Ogden, Curry, Peabody, or their colleagues express either in writings, speeches, or letters, anything which indicated they thought black people to be the equals of whites. That is why neither Bullock, Harlan, nor Bond ever documented the view that the school reformers initially held such conceptions. On the contrary, the northern agents, southern industrialists and educators envisioned economic and racial advantages from an oppressed black population, an "inferior negro race"—disciplined, controlled, literate, and tractable. Those inclined to introduce arguments about the economic backwardness of the school campaigners' social views must be careful not to impose their notions of economic rationality on the reformers' conception of what was socially rational. A certain bias in historical scholarship has always maintained that no society is likely to tolerate, for reasons of economic prosperity and the protection of the government, an ignorant or poorly educated portion of its population. Holders of this view, therefore, cannot see why intelligent statesmen like Curry or practical businessmen like Baldwin urged a sharp limitation on the education of black people. William Taylor, in *Cavalier and Yankee*, shows that the slaveowners' attachment to the culture or mythical idea of the "cavalier" way of life was crucial in determining economic and political consequences, though such decisions are not considered economically rational. To overlook such social conceptions in human history is equivalent to overlooking American ghettos because "they don't make sense." The subjugation of blacks made sense to the school campaigners and so did the idea of "educating" them for their subjugated role.

The American High School and the Development of Social Character

Joel H. Spring

There is sometimes a great difference between what an institution intends to accomplish and the actual results of its activities. The American high school in the twentieth century has been organized as an agency of socialization to affect the character of American youth in a particular manner. One of the difficulties in measuring the results of this process is separating the influence of the school from that of other social organizations, such as the family and community. The simpler task, and the one of this essay, is to clearly define the intended effects of the organization of the school upon the social character of American youth and to judge their worth and meaning in the modern world. There is much evidence to show that the result of school socialization is the production of subservient, authoritarian personalities who function as well-hewn cogs of the corporate state. Could this result be accidental?

It was during the early part of the twentieth century that the institutional organization of the high school received its modern form and was directed toward the goal of producing particular effects upon the social character of American youth. This took place during a time when psychological beliefs and attitudes about the nature of civilization and adolescence created a feeling that the quality and future of modern civilization depended on the molding of the social character of youth. This framework of beliefs gave special meaning and direction to the social organization of the high school. The intent of this organization was to produce what Wilhelm Reich has called the armored character, a set of character traits typified by a love and a desire for authority, order, security, submission, bureaucracy, and a compulsive sense of duty. This set of character traits also displays a willingness to accept and perform work which is meaningless and repetitious, and an aggressive sense of nationalism and patriotism.[1] These were the character traits that the American high school was designed to produce.

The creation of these character traits depended on the channeling of the natural and spontaneous nature of youth into activities that would transform them into instruments of management control. The key to the control and shaping of adolescence was believed to be sexual instinct. Adolescence, a concept which did not fully develop in Western society until the nineteenth century,[2] was given its importance and definition by being considered the age of sexual maturation. The importance and concern given to this developmental stage occurred at two levels. In terms of the individual it was believed that excessive sexual activity, masturbation, and lust caused physical and moral degeneracy resulting in the individual being led down a path of crime or to the insane asylum. Adolescence was considered the crucial period for avoiding these problems by channeling interests into more "wholesome" activities. On another level it was believed that the social man was developed during the period of adolescence. The developing social instincts of youth were considered to be intimately related to the maturing sexual drives. This concept of social development and adolescence led to the belief that the quality of civilization and the social order depended on the proper channeling of the social-sexual drives of youth. G. Stanley Hall wrote in the introduction to his classic work on the psychology of adolescence published in 1904, "The whole future of life depends on how the new powers of adolescence now given suddenly and in profusion are husbanded and directed."[3] It was believed that the primary institution for the channeling of adolescent development for the good should be the high school. Of course the desire to

[1] See Wilhelm Reich, *The Discovery of the Orgone* (New York: Noonday Press, 1961), pp. 109–64.

[2] For some general statements on the development of a concept of youth see F. Musgrove, *Youth and the Social Order* (London: Routledge and Kegan Paul, 1964) and Philippe Aries, *Centuries of Childhood* (New York: Knopf, 1962), pp. 29–32.

[3] G. Stanley Hall, *Adolescence: Its Psychology and Its Relations to Physiology, Anthropology, Sociology, Sex, Crime, Religion and Education* (New York: D. Appleton and Co., 1904), Vol. I., p. xv.

control sexual behavior did not arise with the public school; but prior to industrialization and large-scale immigration from southern and eastern Europe it was felt that the mechanisms of control could be trusted to the informal devices of the family and the local community.

The idea of channeling the sexual drives of youth must be considered as one element of a broader concept of social control.[4] As the concept was defined and popularly used at the beginning of the twentieth century, social control meant the methods by which a society avoided chaos and achieved social stability. External control referred to the police, laws, direct authority, and other forms of control which directly confronted the individual. Internal control referred to conscience or the internalization of authority through institutions like the school, family, and church. The development of an internalized moral authority was favored because it was believed to be more effective than laws and police and because it did not appear to contradict the principles of democracy. Increasingly the school came to be viewed as the central institution for controlling beliefs and conduct and for maintaining the social order. It was in this context of commitment to social control that it was believed adolescent sexuality should be directed through some controlling social institution.

Since adolescence was defined in terms of the maturation of the sexual instincts, social attitudes toward sex and adolescence tended to be interwoven. Sometimes prescription for the treatment of sexual problems really meant the way all adolescents should be treated. The blending of these two themes created a sort of love-hate relationship toward adolescents. On the one hand, adolescent sexuality was linked to poetic romance, idealism, and social sacrifice. On the other hand, it was animallike, lustful, irrational, and the cause of social and mental degeneracy. In general, late nineteenth- and early twentieth-century Americans tended to view actual sexual activity as physically and mentally unhealthy. This belief was often reflected in an attitude that viewed adolescence as an unhealthy and unbalanced period of development.

As an internal form of social control the channeling of the sexual drives of adolescence was intended to develop a set of

---

[4] For a complete discussion of the concept of social control and education see Joel Spring, "Education as a Form of Social Control" (Cuernavaca: CIDOC, 1970); reprinted in C. J. Karier, P. Violas, and J. Spring, eds., *Roots of Crisis* (Chicago: Rand McNally, 1973).

character traits that would assure the continuance of the social order. It was believed that excessive sexuality caused both mental illness and those traits which led the individual to crime and social destruction. One study of the most popular sex manuals in North America which were published in the 1890s in Philadelphia found that excessive sexual activity was believed to cause mental illness, reduce physical and mental energy, and undercut the foundations of civilization. The manuals claimed that in marriage it was not necessary to limit sexual intercourse to once a month but that it could be performed once a week as long as the couple did not exceed that limit. One of the popular folk tales of the nineteenth century was that Newton's brilliance was related to his not having lost a drop of semen in his life. Interestingly, these manuals argued that nature had provided a natural check to male aggressiveness in female sexual passiveness.[5]

The concern about excessive sexuality was one of the central themes of Charles Eliot's introductory speech to the opening of the American Federation for Sex Hygiene at Buffalo, New York in 1913. Eliot's comments are important because of the vital role he played in the development of American educational institutions. In the 1890s he had chaired the important National Education Association's Committee of Ten, which dealt with the reorganization of the curriculum of the secondary school; he was president of Harvard and leading advocate of the elective system; and in the 1920s he was made president of the Progressive Education Association. As president of the American Federation of Sex Hygiene he told his audience in 1913 that the most important question confronting them was: "What forces can now be put into play against the formidable evils which gravely threaten family life, human happiness, civilization in general, and the very life of the race?" He defined the formidable evils earlier in the speech as the increasing sexual immorality in society caused by urbanization and industrialization. Eliot claimed that interest in sexual hygiene grew with "the many signs of physical deterioration among nations which suffer from the eager rush out of the country into the city, from the factory system, and from alcoholism and the sexual vices." He proceeded to list as signs of physical deterioration (1) "the diminishing size of young men"; (2)

5 Michael Bliss, "Pure Books on Avoided Subjects: Pre-Freudian Sexual Ideas in Canada" (paper presented to the Canadian Historical Association, June 4, 1970), pp. 3–5.

"rapid reduction . . . of the size of the family"; (3) "increasing physically and mentally defective children"; and (4) persons "who are practically unable to earn their livelihood."

Eliot proposed as a remedy for the formidable evils of modern civilization the attacking of the "three principal causes of the present evil conditions." These were the lust in men, the lack of moral principle in women, and those who made a profit out of commerce in "this licentious demand and supply." What Eliot proposed for male lust was full occupation of the mind and body in manly sports and in earning a livelihood. This was a rather standard prescription of the period, resting on the belief that hard work and sports would keep the mind from dwelling on sexual ideas. Eliot also recommended information on the good and evil in sexual relations, temperance in food and drink, and the "deliverance from mischievous transmitted beliefs, such as . . . the necessity of sexual indulgence for the maintenance of health and vigor in men." For strengthening the moral principle in women, Eliot recommended the weeding out of moral and mentally defective women and their segregation from the rest of society. He argued that the most important institution for segregating the morally and mentally defective was the public school. In his argument Eliot gave one of the most interesting recommendations for the extension of compulsory education. "Here is a great service," Eliot told the convention, "that the public schools can render to society, and here lies a strong argument in favor of the extension of attendance at school beyond the age of thirteen and fourteen. . . ." To attack commercialized vice he suggested greater police action and a strong stand against legalized prostitution.[6]

For adolescents, one important evil force leading to the destruction of civilization was believed to be masturbation. Even as late as 1929 writers on adolescent psychology were urging the use of methods to stop masturbation. Fowler D. Brooks, professor of education at Johns Hopkins University, in his textbook on adolescent psychology published in 1929 listed five major methods of controlling masturbation.[7] This list included the usual prescrip-

[6] Charles W. Eliot, "Public Opinion and Sex Hygiene," in American Federation for Sex Hygiene, *Report of the Sex Education Sessions of the Fourth International Congress on School Hygiene and of the Annual Meeting of Federation at Buffalo, New York August 27th and 29th, 1913* (New York, 1913), pp. 13–24.

[7] Fowler D. Brooks, *The Psychology of Adolescence* (Boston: Houghton Mifflin Co., 1929), pp. 507–12.

tions of the period. The first was preventing irritation of the genital nerve endings through cleanliness and the wearing of loose fitting clothes. It is interesting that cleanliness was associated with the control of sexual drives and the elimination of sexual stimulation. At the 1913 Buffalo meeting of the American Association of Sex Hygiene, Ella Flagg Young, superintendent of the Chicago public schools, argued that cleanliness was the first step in any sex hygiene program. She told the convention: "As I see it, instilling and developing a powerful, and when possible, a fine sense of the absolute need for keeping the body clean and pure should precede any spoken reference to sex relations or sex hygiene."[8] Brooks's list also included not giving children the opportunity for privacy; proper treatment of constipation and plenty of exercise; and warnings against the handling of sexual organs.

Brooks's fears and prescriptions for masturbation were mild compared to earlier pronouncements. Missing from his statements on masturbation were earlier beliefs that masturbation caused moral depravity and idiocy and drained the body of physical and mental energy. A Boston physician in a book titled *Satan in Society*, published in the United States in 1876, warned in an opening sentence of a chapter on male masturbation: "Viewing the world over, this shameful and criminal act is the most frequent, as well as the most fatal, of all vices." Masturbation before and after puberty, he argued, undermined the physical and mental health of the individual. The onanist could be identified by a countenance that was "pale, sunken, flabby, often leaden, or more or less livid, with a dark circle around the sunken eyes, which are dull, and lowered or averted." This physician listed some of the common physical complaints caused by masturbation as obscured vision, painful cramps, convulsive movements of epilepsy, fever, digestive derangements, vomiting, loss of appetite, and the appearance of pulmonary consumption.[9] G. Stanley Hall, in his classic work on the psychology of adolescence, argued that many of the sensational effects attributed to onanism were not as immediate or disastrous as represented in the popular literature. Hall then went on to state that the physical exertion of masturbation and the loss of sperm increased the possibility of physical infection, disease, traces of convulsions, epilepsy, optical

[8] "Discussion," American Federation for Sex Hygiene, *Report*, pp. 72–74.
[9] Nicholas Francis Cooke, *Satan in Society* (Cincinnati: C. V. Vent, 1876), pp. 91–105.

cramps, weak heart action and circulation, purple and dry skin, clammy hands, anemic complexion, dry cough, and digestive problems.[10] The previously cited study of late nineteenth-century sex manuals found the same links made between masturbation and the physical deterioration of the heart, complexion, digestive tract, and nerve system.[11]

Considered of more consequence than the actual physical effects of masturbation was the intellectual and moral damage. The Boston physician in the 1870s argued that onanism caused "loss of memory and intelligence, morose and unequal disposition, aversion, or indifference to legitimate pleasure and sports, mental abstractions, stupid stolidity, etc."[12] Intellectual dullness and possible idiocy and insanity were constantly stressed. One sex education program in Ontario between 1905 and 1911 which reached over thirteen thousand school boys stressed that the "Life Fluid" from the two "Life Glands" were needed to feed the brain and the nervous system. Boys attending these programs were warned that the draining of this fluid from the body could lead to death or in some cases a fate worse than death. The attending students were then told the story of a farm boy whose evil habits caused him to be placed in an insane asylum. Within the insane asylum the boy continued to drain away his life fluids until it was decided that the only means of saving his life was to cut off his two "Life Glands."[13] G. Stanley Hall's study of adolescence listed all of the major medical theories of the period dealing with mental disorders and masturbation. Some theories argued there was a masturbatic insanity which caused a range of symptoms from lethargy to destructiveness. Another argument held that masturbation was the product of a hereditary tendency toward nervous and mental disorders.[14] In either case masturbation was linked in some way to psychic disturbances.

The methods prescribed for controlling adolescent onanism and sexual lust reflected both a general belief about the personal habits required for a modern industrial state and the sadistic tendencies that are always present in attempts to repress sexual activities. Among the prescriptions were the cultivation of habits

[10] Hall, *Adolescence*, Vol. I, pp. 439–42.
[11] Bliss, "Pure Books on Avoided Subjects," p. 20.
[12] Cooke, *Satan in Society*, p. 100.
[13] Bliss, "Pure Books on Avoided Subjects," p. 20.
[14] Hall, *Adolescence*, Vol. I, pp. 445–48.

of industriousness, involvement in "worthwhile social activities," manly sports, and hard work for the channeling of sexual drives. Physical prescriptions for controlling sexual stimulation reflected the Protestant ethic of the period. Sex manuals suggested exercise, cleanliness, cold baths, the avoidance of stimulating foods and spices, regular evacuation of the bowels, reduced consumption of meat, and the avoidance of bedclothes stuffed with feathers. G. Stanley Hall's survey of the literature found similar recommendations for a balanced diet, exercises, hard beds, and loose clothes.[15]

Some suggestions for controlling sexual drives reflected an extremely sadistic attitude and a desire to crush any hope of sexual pleasure. One method was tying a towel around the waist with a knot on the back so that the individual would not sleep on his back. This supposedly would reduce nocturnal emission. There were also devices that could be bought for a similar purpose. G. Stanley Hall claimed that there were innumerable medical cures available for masturbation, including bromide, ergot, lupin, blistering, and clitoridectomy.[16] Kellogg, of cornflake fame, issued sex manuals from the Battle Creek Sanitarium which suggested methods such as circumcision, using metal cages, suturing the male foreskin shut, and applying carbolic acid to the female clitoris.[17] G. Stanley Hall also recommended circumcision because this reduced the excitability of the exposed surface.[18]

Of more importance than the physical methods of controlling onanism was the argument that the adolescent's mind and body should be kept occupied in wholesome activities. Charles Eliot's previously mentioned cure for lust through hard work and sports reflected the prevailing attitude of the period. Idle time allowed for thoughts to float onto ideas of lust. It was also believed that "wholesome" activities would be a way of draining energy from sexual instincts into other outlets. This argument was even given in reference to female onanism by a psychologist writing on the adolescent girl in the 1920s. She wrote, in reference to masturbation, "The broadening of interests during adolescence and association with the opposite sex are also outlets for energy and serve to direct attention away from herself into other channels."[19]

[15] *Ibid.*, pp. 468–71.
[16] *Ibid.*, p. 465.
[17] Bliss, "Pure Books on Avoided Subjects," p. 27.
[18] Hall, *Adolescence*, Vol. I, p. 467.
[19] Winifred Richmond, *The Adolescent Girl* (New York: Macmillan Co., 1925), p. 42.

The emphasis in terms of releasing sexual energy was on sports and other "wholesome activity." Wholesome activity was always contraposed to the unwholesome activities that appeared to be becoming a fixed part of the urban environment. At the 1913 meeting of the American Federation for Sex Hygiene, William T. Foster, president of Reed College, delivered one of the major addresses, with the interesting title "The Social Emergency," in which he warned, "Adolescent boys and girls spend most of their leisure time either in wholesome physical activity conducive to normal sex life or in various forms of amusement fraught with danger." He went on to list the dangerous amusements and temptations that acted as schools of sexual immorality: the list included billboards, picture postcards, motion pictures, modern fashion, saloons, billiard rooms, dance halls, ice-cream parlors, road houses, and amusement parks.[20] During the discussion at the end of this convention a physician from Evanston, Illinois, told the group that if they could solve the problem of immorality in the schools, "You have furnished the key to the possible recovery of a large portion of incurables . . . you have materially lessened the marriages from lust instead of love; you have corrected the various forms of venereal disease at their source and have opened the doors of a large percentage of the insane asylums and the jails."[21]

The concern about controlling and channeling sexual instincts was woven into the broader concept of adolescence. The social category of adolescence has only existed in Western society for about the last two hundred years. The development of a concept of adolescence has often been linked to the rise of national armies in the late eighteenth and early nineteenth century, a situation which defined a special age group for recruits, and to the displacement of youth from useful social roles by the rise of modern industrialization and urbanization. The picture of adolescence that emerged by the twentieth century was that of a period of development which was in turmoil by the storm and stress of rebellion, romanticism, poetic love, idealism, and chivalry. Philippe Aries, in his book on the history of childhood, wrote, "The first typical adolescent of modern times was Wagner's *Siegfried*: the music

[20] William T. Foster, "The Social Emergency," American Federation of Sex Hygiene, *Report*, pp. 45–54.
[21] "Discussion," *ibid.*, p. 78.

of *Siegfried* expressed for the first time the combination of (provisional) purity, physical strength, naturism, spontaneity and joie de vivre which was to make the adolescent the hero of our twentieth century, the century of adolescence." The century of adolescence brought together the themes of sexual and social development.[22]

The first important definition of adolescence given in modern times was by Jean Jacques Rousseau in his educational plan for *Emile*. In that classical work Rousseau defined adolescence as a period when the developing sexual drives caused a second birth that transformed the child into the social man. For Rousseau, in common with later writers on adolescence, the nature of civilization and the social order depended on how the sexual-social drives of adolescence were developed. Rousseau argued that before the period of developing sexual instincts the child was without ability to reason about moral and social matters. The child's world was dominated by a self-centered concern with preservation. The only things of use that could be taught the child before adolescence were those things that were necessary and useful for personal preservation. But, Rousseau argued, with the onset of sexual maturation the child was forced out of his self into the broader social world. What was originally just a concern for self-preservation was forced by the rush of new life into an empathy and sense of concern for the whole world. The sexual drives of adolescence created the social man.

The first major work on adolescence in the United States, G. Stanley Hall's *Adolescence*, gave the same emphasis to the relationship between the development of the sexual and social man. Hall wrote about the onset of adolescence, "The social instincts undergo sudden unfoldment and the new life of love awakens."[23] Hall's theory of adolescence was presented within an evolutionary framework which defined each stage of individual growth as a recapitulation of each stage of development of civilization. In other words, growth in childhood and adolescence recapitulated the history of the race. Hall defined childhood as the years between four and eight and related them to the cultural epoch when hunting and fishing were the main activities of man. From eight

[22] Aries, *Centuries of Childhood*, p. 30.
[23] G. Stanley Hall, "Childhood and Adolescence," in *Health, Growth, and Heredity*, ed. Charles E. Strickland and Charles Burgess (New York: Teachers College, 1965), pp. 99–113.

to twelve the child recapitulated the humdrum life of savagery. The passions of puberty began the development of the social person and in cultural terms the development of civilization.[24]

Hall's theory of recapitulation never received such wide support as did the idea of the importance of the sexual-social definition of adolescence. It was this sexual-social energy of youth, which, like masturbation and sexual lust, had to be controlled. The sexual-social concept of adolescence tended to create a highly romanticized view of the importance of this stage of physical development. Jane Addams, in a book first published in 1909, called the "divine fire" of youth "sex susceptibility which suffuses the world with its deepest meaning and beauty, and furnishes the momentum towards all art. . . ."[25] This romantic view of youth saw it as a time when the adolescent was swept along on a flood of contradictory emotions. The poetic nature of this inner turbulence was also reflected by the writings of Randolph Bourne, literary radical and education editor of the *New Republic*. Writing in the *Atlantic Monthly* in 1912 he tried to capture his idea of the spirit of youth by asking, "How shall I describe youth, the time of contradictions and anomalies? The fiercest radicalisms, the most dogged conservatism, irrepressible gayety, bitter melancholy—all these moods are equally part of that showery springtime of life."[26] The following year he called for a League of Youth to revitalize the cultural barrenness of America. The problem with civilization was that it was ruled by old men whose ideals and beliefs were outdated. "If we get few ideas after we are twenty-five, we get few ideals after we are twenty."[27] According to Bourne a man's ideals became outmoded by the time he was able to take the reins of social leadership.[28]

Like the problems of masturbation and lust, it was believed that problems of teen-age life and those of American culture could not be solved by mere suppression of the sexual-social instincts. Masturbation and sexual drives, it had been argued, could be controlled by draining off youthful energy into sports

[24] *Ibid.*

[25] Jane Addams, *The Spirit of Youth and the City Streets* (New York: Macmillan Co., 1909; reprinted, Urbana: University of Illinois Press, 1972), p. 16.

[26] Randolph Bourne, "Youth," in *The World of Randolph Bourne*, ed. Lillian Schissel (New York: E. P. Dutton and Co, 1965), pp. 3–15.

[27] *Ibid.*

[28] *Ibid.*

and "wholesome" activity. The sexual-social concept of youth stressed that the solution to social problems depended on directing instinctual developments into socially acceptable and useful channels. G. Stanley Hall believed the future of civilization depended on giving the proper direction to the instincts of youth. Hall contended that all art, literature, religion, and science could be linked to the reproductive instincts. He used the image of social acts moving out in concentric circles from a center of sexual energy. His emphasis on instinctual behavior, unlike Freud's use of repression, led to an interpretation of all acts as having a direct natural basis. He argued that things like poetry and courtship could be viewed as a natural accompaniment to the sexual drives and believed that romantic actions existed either to intensify the sexual act or as a higher expression of love. For example, he argued that the entire momentum of growth and completeness of development depended on the intensity of the act of impregnating the ovum. He wrote, "To make this intense and give an inheritance that is all-sided and total, nature seems to require, in ways and for reasons which biology does not yet fully understand, special prenuptial activities known as courtship, wooing, charming, falling in love, etc." Higher levels of love, he argued, are reached directly from the reproductive instincts. The final stage of this direct progression he defined as a "love of being or of all that exists, visible and invisible."[29]

The problem as Hall saw it was directing these natural adolescent instincts into proper forms of action. The ability to fulfill this function, he argued, should become the means by which social institutions are evaluated. Placing his belief in the proper training of adolescents as the panacea for social problems he wrote that the "womb, cradle, nursery, home, family, relatives, school, church, and state are only a series of larger cradles or placenta as the soul . . . builds itself larger mansions, the only test and virtue of which is their service in bringing the youth to ever fuller maturity."[30] In this sense Hall argued that social life should be organized around the adolescent like a placenta, to protect him from the "unnatural" influences of modern civilization, and to nurture him in proper ideals. He recommended the organization of boys' clubs under the guidance of adults. These social organizations were to utilize the natural instincts of youth and "so direct

[29] Hall, *Adolescence*, Vol. II, pp. 120–40.
[30] *Ibid.*, p. 125.

intelligence and will as to secure the largest measure of social service, advance altruism and reduce selfishness, and thus advance the higher cosmic order."[31]

The argument that natural instincts are good when properly harnessed explains why the great apostle of youth culture, Randolph Bourne, would publish in 1916 a book in praise of the Gary, Indiana, public school system. The goal of this system was to institutionalize as much of the life of the children and adolescents of Gary as was possible. Bourne, like Hall, was concerned with the effects of modern urban life upon the child. Bourne resented the "wasted street and alley time of the masses of city children."[32] What appealed to Bourne was the attempt by the Gary schools to provide pupils with a total community life. School vacations were reduced, the school day was lengthened, and an attempt was made to provide for all activities within one institutionalized structure. The organizaion of the Gary public schools was based on the idea of replacing a lost community education. The superintendent wrote: "The school must do what the school, home, and small shop formerly did together."[33] It was this community idea that appealed to Bourne. The Gary schools were to provide all activities in the form of work, study, and play. The activities of the workshops included both training and maintenance of the school plant. Vocational training directly connected to the life of the school was to show the student the usefulness and meaning of labor. Play instincts were channeled through supervised playgrounds and the organized social life of the school. Ideally, Superintendent Wirt of the Gary schools hoped, one school would become a total community of children and youth by including in one educational plant all grades from kindergarten to the second year of college. It was this totally institutionalized life that the fire-brand of youth culture advocated as a "practical working-model for imitation and adaptation in other communities, large and small."[34]

Natural instincts were therefore conceived of as being directable but unchangeable. To cultivate the good youth and the good man it was necessary to properly channel natural impulses. To

---

[31] *Ibid.*, p. 432.
[32] Randolph S. Bourne, *The Gary Schools* (Boston: Houghton Mifflin Co., 1916), p. 38.
[33] *Ibid.*, p. 40.
[34] *Ibid.*, p. 177.

produce the good social man required surrounding the growing social awareness of youth with the right environment. This was the conclusion that Jane Addams arrived at as she viewed the tawdry life of Chicago. One major problem with society as Jane Addams saw it was that the spirit of youth was being seduced by the flashing lights and cheap dance halls of modern cities. In her 1909 book she argued that it was the "fundamental susceptibility of sex which now so bewilders the street life and drives young people themselves into all sorts of difficulties. . . ."[35] Sex drives, Jane Addams argued, could not be suppressed but could be directed. It was in the proper utilization of these sexual energies that Jane Addams placed part of her hope for the reform of society. She felt that Americans had been too unwilling to talk about this fundamental instinctual drive. This instinct growing and permeating the life of youth had to be recognized and used for the betterment of society. She proposed that parks, playgrounds, parades, education, and national ceremonies should take the place of cheap dance halls and movie houses. The "divine fire" of youth, Jane Addams believed, should be directed toward the problems of the world. The youthful quest for beauty and impatience with the world's wrongs would purify the social order. The spirit of youth recaptured from the shoddy commercialism of modern society could be properly tended "into a lambent flame with power to make clean our dingy streets."[36]

The schools were considered the ideal institution for harnessing and directing the sexual-social instincts of adolescents. The National Education Association's 1911 report of the Committee on a System of Teaching Morals in the Public Schools gave special consideration to the child development argument. The methods proposed for social education in the high school grades were distinctly different from those of the grammar school grades. The report suggested that the social training methods in the high school include student self-government and a curriculum geared to showing the social relationships between the individual and society. The committee proposed that the grammar school grades emphasize the inculcation of good moral habits. For instance, instructions for the second grade recommended training in obedience by "obeying directions given in reference to conduct and school work." The report advocated two different methods of

---

[35] Addams, *The Spirit of Youth*, p. 20.
[36] *Ibid.*, p. 162.

training based on age groups because it placed the development of social instincts at adolescence. The report described the high school age as "the time of life when passion is born which must be restrained and guided aright or it consumes soul and body. It is the time when social interests are dominant and when social ideals are formed."[37]

The effect on the high schools of considering adolescence the social age was an emphasis on a social education that included clubs, group activities, and student goverment. These social activities, it was felt, would give a healthy outlet and guidance for developing adolescent interests. Irving King, professor of education, and social education advocate at the University of Iowa, argued in 1914 that a high school education must provide the adolescent with the opportunity for social service. He wrote that at sixteen "youth emerges from the somewhat animal-like crassness of the pubertal years and begins to think of his social relationships, his duties and the rights and wrongs of acts."[38] King believed that the high school should guide the romance and idealism of youth into socially useful activities. In the same spirit as Hall, Addams, and Bourne he wrote: "Every youth is . . . an incipient reformer, a missionary, impatient with what seem to him the pettiness and the obtuseness of the adult world about him."[39] This same sentiment was echoed by Michael V. O'Shea, professor of education at the University of Wisconsin, who wrote that the "reformer . . . realizes that if he would get his cause adopted he must appeal to youth . . . youth longs for a new order of things. . . ."[40]

As junior high schools developed after 1910 they also claimed the function of guiding and directing awakening social instincts. In 1916, Joseph Abelson, writing in *Education* on the benefits of the junior high, argued that one of the serious defects of the present educational system was the beginning of the high school education after the social instincts had already begun to develop. "To remedy this evil," he wrote, "the Junior High School takes

[37] "Tentative Report of the Committee on a System of Teaching Morals in the Public Schools," *National Education Association Proceedings* (1911), pp. 354, 360.

[38] Irving King, *The High-School Age* (Indianapolis: Bobbs-Merrill Co., 1914), p. 80.

[39] *Ibid.*, p. 106.

[40] M. V. O'Shea, *The Trend of the Teens* (Chicago, F. J. Drake and Co., 1920), p. 13.

the pupil under its roof at the age of twelve, which is a period of 'fulminating' psychic expansion."[41] He went on to claim that psychologists and educators agreed that secondary education should begin at the beginning of adolescence. The junior high school, by providing differentiation and selection of courses, would take account of the "nature and upheaval which makes the pubescent ferment."[42]

One interesting thing about Abelson's argument was that not all psychologists and educators would have agreed that the age of twelve marked the beginning of adolescence. G. Stanley Hall had placed the beginning of pubescence at thirteen with girls and at fourteen with boys. Youth proper, he stated, extended "from sixteen to twenty in boys and perhaps fifteen to nineteen in girls; and a finishing stage through the early twenties."[43] In 1921 Ella Lyman Cabot, a popular writer on children's ethics, tried to find the starting points of the various stages of child development by constructing a chart based on popular works by educators and psychologists. The chart attests to the complete lack of agreement about the age at which early adolescence began. The majority of the texts used in the chart agreed that adolescence, or as Cabot called it, "The Age of Romance," began at between fifteen or sixteen. The beginning of the stage of child development labeled in various fashions as the paradoxical age, gang period, early teens, age of chivalry, and pubertal years, was placed at ten, eleven, twelve, and thirteen depending upon the source.[44] Contrary to Abelson's argument, there was a great lack of clarity and confusion about the limits of this stage of pre-adolescent development.

What the junior high school movement did by adopting a psychological argument was to impose defined age limits on this pre-adolescent period. Proponents of the junior high school defined the crucial age of early adolescence as between twelve and fourteen and adopted the psychological argument to promote a general program of social education. Early differentiation would provide for future social specialization, while social education would provide for social unity and cooperation. Thomas Warrington

[41] Joseph Abelson, "A Study of the Junior High Project," *Education* (September, 1916), p. 11.

[42] *Ibid.*

[43] G. Stanley Hall, *Health, Growth and Heredity*, p. 128.

[44] Ella Lyman Cabot, *Seven Ages of Childhood* (Boston: Houghton Mifflin Co., 1921), p. xxvi.

Gosling of the Department of Public Instruction in Madison, Wisconsin, wrote in the *Educational Review* that in the junior high school a new spirit would pervade: "This spirit will be the spirit of cooperation, the spirit of service and of sacrifice for the common good." He supported this by stating, "Those who know the nature of children are aware that the junior high school period coincides with the time when the social instincts begin to assert themselves with great force."[45]

It was in this manner that the social-sexual concept of youth influenced the development of the junior high school and contributed to the argument for expanding the high school into a mass institution. It was a society that was fascinated and frightened by the sexuality and poetry of youth. The fear of adolescence was reflected in the concern about controlling and repressing sexuality as a necessary way of avoiding social chaos, criminal actions, and insanity. This often led to the perpetration of physical cruelty and anxiety such as that exhibited in the more extreme methods of controlling masturbation. The high school must be viewed in terms of a love-hate relationship. On the one hand, the high school in the twentieth century became a temple of worship of the golden adolescent. The high school became the hope for the future and for civilization. On the other hand, the high school became a place where youth was institutionalized out of fear that if its social development was left without strict control, the very foundations of civilization would begin to crumble.

The American high school was developed as a mass institution designed to shape the social character of youth through the repression and channeling of sexual drives. The high school was to manufacture character traits that would reflect self-sacrifice, industriousness, and other virtues associated with capitalism. These character traits reflected what Wilhelm Reich called the armored character and it is Reich's model which most clearly explains the relationship of the character development within the high school and the modern industrial state. Reich argued that modern authoritarian societies depended on the creation of an authoritarian structure within the personality of the individual. The key to the creation of this structure was the repression and inhibition of sexual drives. By sexual, Reich meant a person's general ability

[45] Thomas Warrington Gosling, "Educational Reconstruction in the Junior High School," *Educational Review* (May, 1919), pp. 384–85.

to experience pleasure. Genital sexuality was the central drive for pleasure. Reich argued that sexual repression caused pleasure anxiety and an inability to experience pleasure. The desire of one individual to repress the sexuality of another reflected a sadistic desire to deny pleasure. One can see this evidenced most directly in the instruments and methods used for controlling masturbation. From this perspective one view of the high school can be that of a sadistic institution designed to inhibit and rob youth of its general ability to experience pleasure.[46]

Of more importance here are what Reich sees as the consequences of the pleasure anxiety produced by sexual inhibition. Fear and anxiety about pleasure drives a person to seek secure and well-ordered activities. One source of security is the acceptance of authority and a sense of duty. Another source is in monotonous, routine, and joyless work. In a broader social context an armored individual seeks and accepts the security of well-ordered bureaucratic institutions and the patriotic nationalism of the modern state. The insecurity of the individual results in aggressive and sadistic actions toward free and spontaneous actions of others. It also results in a highly developed sense of morality. Reich believed that these were the character traits that supported the exploitive forms for modern capitalism. In its more extreme form the armored character supported fascism and totalitarian governments.[47]

Reich's model puts the goals inherent in the high school in a much harsher light. In fact, Reich would have agreed that if one wanted a generation with character traits that reflected a high sense of morality and duty, sexual desires should be controlled through some social institution. In the same manner one could produce individuals willing to sacrifice themselves to the common good and the nation-state and willing to perform meaningless jobs in the bureaucratic structures of modern capitalism.

Placed within the Reichian model the goals for character development inherent in the early shaping of the high school as a mass institution become quite clear. This does not mean that these goals lasted nor that they were effective, but they did exist

[46] Reich, *The Discovery of the Orgone*, pp. 109–64.

[47] See Wilhelm Reich, *The Mass Psychology of Fascism* (New York: Noonday Press, 1970) and *The Sexual Revolution* (New York: Noonday Press, 1962).

as goals in the very foundation of the structure: the American high school was to be an institution of sexual repression, simultaneously shaping a social character that would submit to the authority and goals of a capitalist society and would seek the security and order of a role within the bureaucratic enterprise.

Training for the Welfare State: The Progressive Education Movement

Walter Feinberg and Henry Rosemont, Jr.

In 1892 when the journalist and educational commentator John Maynard Rice toured the nation's schools for the upper-middlebrow journal *The Forum* he found them to be with few exceptions the most dehumanizing and depressing of institutions. Describing one such school in New York he said:

> The spirit of the school is, Do what you like with the child, immobilize him, automatize him, dehumanize him, but save, save the minutes. In many ways the minutes are saved . . . Everything is prohibited that is of no measurable advantage to the child, such as the movement of a head or limb, when there is no logical reason why it should be moved at the time. I asked the principal whether the children were not allowed to move their heads. She answered "Why should they look behind when the teacher is in front of them?"—words too logical to be refuted.[1]

In 1970 after a similar tour of the nation's schools for the upper-middlebrow Carnegie Foundation Charles Silberman wrote *Crisis in the Classroom*, in which statements like the following are common:

> In that same school system, the principal of the elementary school serving the city's wealthiest neighborhood insists that all students carry their books in their left hand when going from room to room. Asked why, the principal looks surprised, and

NOTE: Walter Feinberg is grateful to the University of Illinois Research Board for awards which permitted him to conduct some of the research presented herein.

[1] J. M. Rice, "The Public School System of New York City," *The Forum* Vol. 14 (January, 1893).

after some hesitation and fumbling, explains that the children need to have their right hand free to hold on to the banisters to avoid falling when going up or down stairs. And besides, he adds, if children were permitted to carry books in their right hand, they might bang them against, and thus damage, the steel coat lockers that line some of the halls. (The students are also required to walk only on the right side of the corridors and stairs.) [2]

Clearly the descriptions (and recommendations) of Rice and Silberman are essentially the same; it is difficult to detect a temporal difference of three-quarters of a century between these accounts. Both men were critical of the extant educational structure, both believed the schools could be renewed by a pedagogy which would loosen the structure of the classroom to include more opportunities for children to learn from their own interests. And last but not least, both saw the schools as a major vehicle for the trip to the Promised Land: the technological society.

Rice and Silberman may be seen as the historical poles of the progressive education movement,[3] and from their views—and the views of the progressives who came between them—it can also be seen that the movement was made up of reformers, not radicals. This is not to say that their visions of a munificient Tomorrow did not include significant changes from the world of the present; rather it is to point up their concerted beliefs (and actions) to the effect that such changes must come about through developments in science and technology instead of through the sustained social and political efforts of human beings.

It will be argued herein that despite a few radical moments the progressive movement moved in place politically and socially, serving in the end the *status quo ante,* and, more important, enhancing the position of those who controlled it. The basically conservative nature of their educational critiques and programs stemmed from the mistaken assumption that inadequate pedagogic techniques and classroom procedures were and are the root

---

[2] Charles Silberman, *Crisis in the Classroom: The Remaking of American Education* (New York: Random House, 1970), p. 131.

[3] Silberman makes a number of distinctions between his own reforms and those of the progressive era which are generally accurate. Nevertheless, the tone of his critique and the nature of his recommendations allow him to be placed most naturally in the progressive movement. Of significance is his attempt to join the impulses of the child with the structure of knowledge and his seeing the teacher as an orchestrator of the learning environment.

causes of continuing educational problems. Both the old and the new progressivism hold that the basic goals of education are to be determined by the functional requirements of a sophisticated industrial society, and that therefore the problems of schooling can best be analyzed by identifying their dysfunctional products and correcting them. Occasionally this approach results in an analysis of the society's institutions—as, e.g., when Dewey and others criticized laissez faire capitalism—but more commonly this approach identifies rigid and archaic attitudes as the causes of educational and social discontent. Thus Silberman locates the cause of the rigidly structured classroom and teacher-imposed discipline on the "mindlessness" of teachers and administrators, implying that once these people reflect on what they are really doing they will quickly move to eliminate the horrors most of his book is devoted to cataloging.[4] In this way Silberman's work diverts attention away from the more probable causes of the sicknesses of the schools, namely the inequities in the larger society; what is wrong with public schools is almost surely not endemic to the schools themselves but rather is the result of the gross mal-

---

[4] Silberman's belief that "mindlessness" is a basic cause of the "failure" of schooling is evident throughout *Crisis in the Classroom*. The following is but one of many examples: "Schools fail, however, less because of maliciousness than because of mindlessness. . . . Educators and scholars, frequently with the best of intentions, have operated on the assumption that children should be cut or stretched or otherwise 'adjusted' to fit the schools, rather than adjusting the schools to fit the children." Although Silberman challenges the efficiency of *existing* work norms in guiding schooling, he does not challenge the belief that work norms, broadly defined, should determine the form and contents of schools. This is evident from the following passage: "For children who may still be in the labor force in the year 2030, nothing seems more wildly impractical than an education designed to prepare them for specific vocations or professions or to facilitate their adjustment to the world as it is. To be 'practical' an education should prepare them for work that does not yet exist and whose nature cannot even be imagined" (ibid., pp. 113–14). Although Silberman eschews modeling schools after existing work norms and argues that the only proper kind of education for the work of the future is one that teaches the intellectual disciplines that can be applied to new problems as they arise, he does little to show that rigid mind-deadening work will disappear or that society's more odious labors will be reasonably shared. Given the probability that such tasks will continue to exist even in light of Silberman's utopian suggestions, it is not unlikely that some parents, sharing the belief that schooling should follow work norms, will continue to demand mechanical rigor and routine for their children. And, given the ethical structure of present day society, a structure that Silberman does not challenge, along with the likelihood that their children will be performing such work, their demands are not unreasonable.

distribution of wealth and power in the United States. Against this background it does not appear overly radical—or even innovative, for that matter—for Silberman to suggest the importation of British infant school reforms to American classrooms as a way of directly improving the quality of American education.

Moreover, current suggestions for implementing what are essentially progressive reforms of three decades ago may be misleading historically as well as politically because such suggestions imply that the older progressive movement was ultimately a failure, not changing the basic features of American educational institutions. There is much evidence, however, to show that the progressives were more successful than even many of them dared hope, and that their impact has been significant and enduring. If their results are difficult to see today it is because we tend to look in the wrong direction; progressive education was not fundamentally concerned with classroom reform (although such reform was important to the movement.) It was first and foremost designed to develop the skills, work habits, and social attitudes that were required by the changing nature of work in the United States during the early decades of this century, and second, it was designed to rationalize the processes of production and education. In these aims the movement was largely successful. Thus if the "new progressives" now perceive an increasing discrepancy between the world of work and the school house it can only mean that the nature of work is changing yet again as a transition is made from an industrial to a post-industrial political economy.

The success of the earlier progressivism can be seen in a number of different areas. Many of Silberman's proposals were also proffered by Rice in 1892, and have been in effect for some time; indeed, even at that early date Rice was praising the public school systems of St. Paul and Minneapolis for their forward-looking direction.[5] In 1916 progressives like Bourne and Dewey also praised the schools in Gary and Indianapolis, Indiana (three years before the founding of the Progressive Education Association (1919–55). By the 1930s progressive educators had captured sizable grants from the Carnegie and Rockefeller foundations, and in the 1940s the Life Adjustment Movement was being

[5] See Joseph M. Rice, "The Public Schools of Minneapolis and Others," *The Forum*, Vol. 15 (May 1893), pp. 362–76. Also, J. M. Rice, "The Public Schools of Chicago and St. Paul," *The Forum*, Vol. 15 (April 1893), pp. 200–215.

heavily funded by the Office of Education.[6] When many people were attacking the schools in the 1950s for failing to keep pace with the nation's scientific needs it was progressive educators—and their foremost theoretician John Dewey—who received the greatest vilification. The attacks on progressive education by Hyman Rickover, Dwight Eisenhower, Joseph McCarthy, the American Legion, etc., all attest to the movement's importance.

Further, progressive reforms influenced much more than educational rhetoric; they have also affected classroom procedures and educational evaluation on a major scale. Teachers, for instance, are now serving more facilitative and less didactic functions than before, field trips are a commonplace, students engage in more individual and group projects, and art, music and other aesthetic activities are taught for their expressive role as well as for their academic significance. As Lawrence Cremin has correctly observed:

> There is a "conventional wisdom," to borrow from John Kenneth Galbraith, in education as well as economics, and by the end of World War II progressive education had come to be that conventional wisdom. Discussions of educational policy were liberally spiced with phrases like "recognized individual differences," "personality development," "the whole child," "the needs of learners," "intrinsic motivation," "teaching children, not subjects," "adjusting the school to the child," "real life experiences," "teacher-pupil relationships," and "staff planning." Such phrases were a cant, to be sure, the particular jargon of the pedagogs. But they were more than that for they signified that Dewey's forecast of the day when progressive education would eventually be accepted as good education had now finally come to pass.[7]

So then, to whatever extent Silberman and other contemporary critics suggest that the progressive movement did not measure up, it is clear that they are using the wrong measuring rod. Further, because the progressives did advocate, attempt, and utilize many

---

[6] For examples of the type of support and sponsorship granted to progressive type educational reform by the Carnegie Foundation and the General Education Board, and by the U.S. Office of Education, see Lawrence A. Cremin, *The Transformation of the School: Progressive in American Education 1876–1957* (New York: Vintage Books, 1961), pp. 257, 333–37.

[7] *Ibid.*, p. 328. We are indebted to Herbert Gintis and Samuel Bowles for bringing this particular passage to our attention.

of the same reforms later proposed by Silberman, their history provides evidence to justify skepticism about the worth of such proposals today.

In the first place, it is not all clear that the difference between a good classroom and a poor one can always be traced solely, or even primarily, to variations in pedagogical style. There remain many classrooms where, by any criteria, meaningful learning takes place, and where youngsters seem to be genuinely happy with the activities of the school. Some of these classrooms will employ the "open" techniques advocated by Silberman, but others will not. A number of fine music programs, for example, are often carried out voluntarily after regular school hours, and the primary pedagogy in these programs remains imitation and drill. On the other hand there have been open-classroom situations where students seemed to learn less than they would on the streets. In short, progressive or open-classroom techniques are not of themselves either necessary or sufficient conditions for worthwhile education.

Another and more important reason for skepticism regarding Silberman's critique is that it mistakenly attributes the rigidity of many classrooms to the mindlessness of teachers. Mindlessness is perhaps best contrasted with minding, and if some educators have ignored progressive pedagogical principles, they have paid fairly close attention to the desire for structure and discipline on the part of many members of the P.T.A. There is little evidence to support the view that the general public wants more open classrooms; on the contrary, the evidence shows that many parents want more discipline, more structure, and more rote learning than do most teachers, and therefore a so-called mindlessness may be more accurately seen as the minding of the desires of many parents.[8]

Even sensitive critics outside of the educational establishment

----

[8] Indeed if any information can be gained from surveys on this matter it is that teachers are far more favorably inclined toward progressively directed reform than are parents. In a 1969 poll, for example, 62 percent of the parents indicated that "maintaining discipline is more important than student self-inquiry." Only 27 percent of the teachers indicated the same attitude. In the same survey 70 percent of the parents expressed the belief that "homework requiring memorizing is good and useful" while 46 percent of the teachers expressed the same attitude ("Discipline is a big issue—for parents," *Life*, Vol. 66, No. 19, May 16, 1969, p. 29).

have had difficulty accounting for the resistance to some progressive reforms. To a person like John Holt, for example, the logic was so perfectly clear that the choice was obvious:

> The idea of painless, non-threatening coercion is an illusion. Fear is the inseparable companion of coercion, and its inescapable consequence. If you think it your duty to make children do what you want, whether they will or not, then it follows inexorably that you must make them afraid of what will happen to them if they don't do what you want. You can do this in the old-fashioned way, openly and avowedly, with the threat of harsh words, infringement of liberty, or physical punishment. Or you can do it in the modern way, subtly, smoothly, quietly, by withholding the acceptance and approval which you and others have trained the children to depend on; or by making them feel that some retribution awaits them in the future, too vague to imagine but too implacable to escape. You can, as many skilled teachers do, learn to tap with a word, a gesture, a look, even a smile, the great reservoir of fear, shame, and guilt that today's children carry around inside them. Or you can simply let your own fears, about what will happen to you if the children don't do what you want, reach out and infect them. Thus the children will feel more and more that life is full of dangers from which only the goodwill of adults like you can protect them, and that this goodwill is perishable and must be earned anew each day.

> The alternative—I can see no other—is to have schools and classrooms in which each child in his own way can satisfy his curiosity, develop his abilities and talents, pursue his interests, and from the adults and older children around him get a glimpse of the great variety and richness of life. In short, the school should be a great smorgasbord of intellectual, artistic, creative, and athletic activities, from which each child could take whatever he wanted, and as much as he wanted, or as little.[9]

But for too many lower-class children this type of schooling can seem almost cruel, for when they enter the time-clock world of the assembly line they will not be able to take whatever they want, or as much as they want. They will have to take whatever is given to them at giving time. In the context of contemporary American society Holt's programs are only appropriate for certain middle-

---

[9] John Holt, *How Children Fail* (New York: Delta Books, 1965), pp. 179–80.

class families—in whose suburbs open classrooms have fairly wide support—for the children from these families are not believed to be headed for laboring tasks as much as for middle-management positions; that is, they will fill those positions which require the independence, self-discipline, cooperation, and so on that is fostered in the schools that Holt favors. Thus both the ghetto and the suburban parent have the correct instincts about the proper schools for their offspring, and the differences in the schools will be no less striking than the differences in their homes, or more important, than the differences in their probable futures.

The extent to which there is a parallel between parental perceptions of the schools and their beliefs about child-rearing practices in general has been poignantly summarized by the psychiatrists Grier and Cobbs, who focused specifically on blacks, but whose point is general:

When black men recall their early life, consistent themes emerge. For example, the mother is generally perceived as having been sharply contradictory. She may have been permissive in some areas and punitive and rigid in others. There are remembrances of stimulation and gratification coexisting with memories of deprivation and rejection. There is always a feeling that the behavior of the mother was purposeful and deliberate. . . .

The black mother shares a burden with her soul sisters of three centuries ago. She must produce and shape and mold a unique type of man. She must intuitively cut off and blunt his masculine assertiveness and aggression lest these put the boy's life in jeopardy.

During slavery the danger was real. A slave boy could not show too much aggression. The feelings of anger and frustration which channeled themselves into aggression had to be thwarted. If they were not, the boy would have little or no use as a slave and would be slain. If any feelings, especially those of assertive manhood, were expressed too strongly, then that slave was a threat, not only to himself and his master but to the entire system as well. For that, he would have to be killed.

The black mother continues this heritage from slavery and simultaneously reflects the world she now knows. Even today, the black man cannot become too aggressive without hazard to himself. To do so is to challege the delicate balance of a complex social system. Every mother, of whatever color and degree of proficiency, knows what the society in which she lives will require of her children. Her basic job is to prepare the child for this. Because of the institutionalization of barriers, the black mother knows even more surely what society requires of *her* children. What at first seemed a random pattern of mothering has gradually assumed a definite and deliberate, if unconscious, method of preparing a black boy for his subordinate place in the world.[10]

Faced with these realities it is little wonder that families with lower-class backgrounds do not applaud uniformly the progressive or open-classroom reformers. Parents who are more concerned with a no-nonsense inculcation of the three R's than with programs which supposedly bring joy and delight to their children show thereby a recognition of the fact that joy and delight are not highly valued as work norms. But this situation places the liberal —and many radical—educators in a painful dilemma: on the first horn, if they want to overhaul the schools in an effort to bring more justice to the larger society, educators can only do so against the wishes of many of those most unjustly treated at present; on the other horn, respecting the wishes of those for whom the American dream is still more of a nightmare requires educators to maintain institutions which reinforce some of the most unjust features of the society. The plight of the poor is so immediate that many reform or radical educators opt for the second alternative, with statements like the following from Michael B. Katz as typical: "Educational radicalism has been offered as a cure for the pathology afflicting the education of the urban poor. . . . In fact, I suspect that what the poor want for their children is affluence, status, and a house in the suburbs rather than community, a guitar, and soul. They may prefer schools that teach their children to read and write and cipher rather than to feel and to be."[11]

Katz's observation will seem perfectly straightforward—and morally commendable—to most noneducators; to the professionals it is very difficult to accept when phrased in this manner because it requires the explicit admission that existing work norms should continue to govern the character of education, and adoptive preparation for the work place is not what most of them have been thought to have meant by the term "education." The same admission was made by the progressives four decades ago, but before turning directly to an examination of their views on this

---

[10] William H. Grier and Price M. Cobbs, *Black Rage* (New York: Bantam Books, 1969), pp. 51–52.

[11] Michael B. Katz, *Class Bureaucracy and Schools: The Illusion of Educational Change in America* (New York: Praeger, 1971), p. 139.

issue it will be useful first to develop the concept of "work norm" in somewhat greater detail.

The Protestant ethic has been so pervasive in Europe and the United States for the last century that it is difficult to see that there is not a single, consistent set of work values that does, or should, accompany all engagements in labor. That the schools have been fashioned to inculcate such habits as punctuality, speed, "stick-to-itiveness," and industry among many children is due to the common belief that these values are the norms which should govern the behavior of all work activity—from farming, to the assembly line, to the research laboratory. But this belief is mistaken; work norms appropriate to a largely agrarian political economy are often dysfunctional when applied in an urban industrial setting.

For example, the farmer training his offspring does not have to expend much time or effort inculcating punctuality or speed. If they sleep in one morning until 6 A.M. instead of getting up at 5, it simply means that the family will work that evening or the next until 8 P.M. instead of 7. To be sure, the product itself demands punctuality at times—as, e.g., when the hay is ready to be cut—and consequently there are limits to such temporal self-regulation; but the limits are usually reckoned more in days and weeks than in hours and minutes. To children who will go to work in an assembly plant, on the other hand, it is necessary to learn the difference between being in your seat when the bell rings, rather than at 9:02; on the assembly line, no one can work until all workers are in their proper place.

The converse of this example is equally illustrative of the non-unitary nature of work norms. A farming family must teach its young to see their jobs through, and thus "stick-to-itiveness" will be inculcated, and highly valued. One cannot stop feeding the chickens because it is 5 P.M., and planting must continue until it is completed. The reward for perseverance is of course the pride that can be taken in a job well and completely done. Unfortunately this sense of accomplishment is lost on the assembly line— and lost absolutely because of the nature of the process—as each automobile worker fastens two fender bolts to the chassis that pass by every fifty-two seconds. Perseverance then, will not be highly valued in the working-class urban school, and an acceptance of fragmentary tasks will instead be developed by such devices as subject departmentalism: drawing does not stop when the picture is completed, it is stopped when art period is over.[12]

Seen in this light (and many others as well) the black and white families who migrate from the still-agrarian South to urban industrial centers are surely not "culturally deprived"; rather they hold a set of norms that are for the most part inappropriate for the factory work they have left the land to seek. Moreover, this phenomenon is not confined to those who have traveled the Mississippi-to-Michigan route in the last decades; the overwhelming majority of all immigrants to the United States for the last hundred years have come from the rural and not the urban areas of their homelands. And if agrarian work norms thus dominate family life among most of the poor, it follows that their children will be almost wholly dependent on the public schools for acquiring the means to escape from poverty—unless, of course, there are radical changes made in the political economy.[13]

Returning now to the progressives, it is clear from their proposals and programs that they did not contemplate seriously any radical political and economic changes. The commonly held view of progressive educational reform is that it was intended to divorce schooling from work, largely by designing education around the developmental requirements of the child rather than around the rigid, mechanical requirements of the factory assembly line. Much of progressive literature lends support to this view,[14] but it does not credit the reformers with sufficient insight into the nature of twentieth century technology. The progressive educators, and Dewey especially, saw clearly that the continued development of technology would one day render obsolete the factories of the 1930s, and consequently that another set of work

---

[12] Report cards generally do take some note of perserverance, but are written as: "completes assignments *on time*".

[13] This argument is not vitiated by the recent work of Christopher Jencks, who does not examine the impact of schooling or socialization for work (Christopher Jencks et al., *Inequality: A Reassessment of the Effect of Family and Schooling In America* (New York: Basic Books, 1972).

[14] One of the most well-known statements of the need to relate the curriculum to developmental aspects of the child was provided by Dewey in *The Child and The Curriculum*. For example: "Development is a definite process, having its own laws which can be fulfilled only when adequate and normal conditions are provided" (John Dewey, *The Child and The Curriculum and The School and Society*, Chicago: University of Chicago Press, 1962, p. 17. While Dewey's emphasis is not on the same chronological stages as found in Piaget, to whom Silberman appeals, there are nevertheless many similarities.

norms would have to be taught to many of those who would be in the labor force during the 1960s.[15] And the new work norms were best inculcated in a child-centered ("open") classroom curriculum; rather than learning to accept external constraints many of the children of post-industrial society would have to learn to constrain themselves through internalizing the newly appropriate norms.[16]

A fundamental weakness of the progressives is thus their almost tunnel-vision view of technology as the touchstone for the good society, for they were thereby unable to see clearly enough that it is people and not machines who hoard wealth and wield power. By not being basically concerned to alter the extant distribution of that wealth and power the progressives could not but serve the wealthy and the powerful. Moreover, it is not relevant to point out in rebuttal to this criticism that many progressive reforms were and continue to be justified in the abstract by values that are at odds with the mind- and body-deadening norms re-

[15] In response to David Snedden, Dewey argued against a vocational education system that would simply adjust workers to the existing industrial regime. See John Dewey, "Education vs. Trade Training," *The New Republic*, Vol. 2, No. 27 (May 8, 1915). In this critique of Snedden, Dewey expressed the belief that vocational education ought to help alter the existing industrial system rather than simply reflect it. While Dewey's proposal has a certain radical flavor to it in contrast to Snedden's views, the nature of the changes he envisaged were not spelled out. Nevertheless, in the course of time the tie between work norms and schools as envisaged by progressives became less and less radical sounding as progressive schooling was justified as the most effective way to adjust youngsters to the new requirements of work. For example:

"Writing in *School and Society*, Dwayne Orton . . . emphasizes that the evidence from exhaustive studies 'calls for more attention to the development of psychological skills, such as resourcefulness, cooperativeness, adjustability, responsibility and reliability' in vocational education. . . .

"What is important, regardless of the nature of job opportunities open to youth at a given period or in a section of the country, is the fact that advancement for the individual in the vocational field, broadly conceived, turns more and more upon qualities of character, a capacity for creative relations with people, general intelligence, and education and less exclusively than was once the case upon prior training of a technical character.

"And because rapid changes occur in vocational as well as in professional practice, education for a vocation should enable the individual to meet the experiences of a life with flexibility, to possess himself of a basic knowledge that has application to families of occupations" (V. T. Thayer, *The Role of the School in American Society*, New York: Dodd, Mead and Co., 1960, pp. 103, 127).

[16] John Dewey, *Human Nature and Conduct* (New York: Modern Library, 1957).

quired on the assembly line. What is important is that none of those reforms is at odds with the demands of a system of production which requires compliance with those killing norms as prerequisite for escaping from poverty and the more overt forms of oppression; the assembly lines are staffed almost solely by those for whom the work is a step upward both socially and economically.[17]

Admittedly, some progressives discussed the poor and the dispossessed in detail, and may seem to be more radical in their views than is being suggested here. In 1932, for example, George Counts shocked the education establishment by declaring that the progressive movement, which previously had served the children of middle-class parents, must come to identify with and aid the poor peoples of not only the United States, but the whole world:

> The weakness of progressive education thus lies in the fact that it has elaborated no theory of social welfare, unless it be that of anarchy or extreme individualism. In this, of course, it is but reflecting the view point of the members of the liberal minded upper class who send their children off to the progressive schools.
>
> If progressive education is to be genuinely progressive, it must emancipate itself from the influence of this class, face squarely and courageously every social issue, come to grips with life in all its stark reality, establish an organic relation with community,

---

[17] The reluctance to deal with the mind-deadening nature of work is revealed by, among other things, the response of management to industrial unrest resulting from the nature of work. Recently, for example, General Motors has experienced labor trouble at its Vega plant at Lordstown, Ohio. The new plant was designed to meet the foreign small car competition by turning out one hundred cars each hour (instead of the normal sixty), and every thirty-six seconds the worker meets a new Vega. In the best spirit of industrial "efficiency," the assembly line has been planned to eliminate all unnecessary movement so that a worker's entire activity is spent in performing his stipulated task, and the automobile itself is designed with the requirement of production speed foremost in mind such that "each part could be added in thirty-six seconds by a diligent unskilled worker" (Rothschild; see below for source).

The plant has experienced a series of wildcat strikes, and what the management regards as sabotage. Workers have complained about both the speed and the monotony of the line, and management has responded to these complaints by instituting counseling sessions and encounter groups in an attempt to calm the situation. They steadfastly deny, however, the workers charge that monotony is the problem. As one manager responded: "Monotony is not quite the right word. There is a great deal of misunderstanding about that, but it seems to me that we have our biggest problem when we disturb that 'monotony.' The workers may complain about monotony, but years spent in the factory lead me to believe that they like to do their jobs automatically" (Joseph E. Godfrey, head of the GM Assembly Division, quoted in Emma Rothschild, *New York Review of Books*, Vol. XVIII, No. 5, March 23, 1972).

develop a realistic and comprehensive theory of welfare, fashion
a compelling and challenging vision of human destiny, and become less frightened than it is today at the bogeyes of imposition
and indoctrination.[18]

By the end of the 1930s, however, Counts and many other progressives were spending more of their time trying to expel Communists from the teachers' union than educating the poor, and
by the late 1940s most of Counts's writings were devoted to
singing the praises of America the Beautiful while heaping scorn
on Ivan the Terrible. The personal history of Counts is mirrored
by the institutional history of progressive education from 1932 to
1952, turning as it did from radical reform programs for restruc-
turing society to much tamer proposals for adjusting youngsters
to the pressures of the technological U.S.A.[19]

Although progressives like Counts and Dewey sometimes spoke
of themselves as radical and as socialists and although they were
"red baited" during the 1930s and after, these facts tell us more
about the climate of American public opinion than they do about
the policies and programs of these men in particular or progressive
reforms in general. For example, while Dewey embraced the
socialist label during the depression, he stopped short of calling
for a drastic redistribution of wealth or a sharing of the necessary
but onerous work of a society. Dewey's socialist manifesto, *Individualism Old and New*, written during the depths of the depression, called for such ameliorative reforms as the progressive
income tax and expansion of federal control commissions.[20] Perhaps his most "radical" proposal was for a coordinating economic
council composed of people from both labor and business. The
remainder of this book was devoted to exploring the cultural lag
that existed in an America that had become corporately integrated
in form but not in consciousness or spirit and by calling for
greater incorporation Dewey's book can easily be construed as
an appeal to close the gap in the direction of the corporations.

Dewey, Counts, and other early progressives achieved their
radical reputation during the late 1920s and the 1930s because

---

[18] George S. Counts, *Dare the Schools Build a New Social Order?* (New
York: John Day Co., 1932), p. 4.

[19] See George S. Counts, *The Country of the Blind: The Soviet System of
Mind Control* (Boston: Houghton Mifflin, 1949), and Nucia Lodge, *Education
and the Promise of America* (New York: Macmillan Company, 1945).

[20] John Dewey, *Individualism Old and New* (New York: Capricorn Books,
1962).

of their flirtation with Marxist philosophy and because of their praise of the political and educational experiments carried out in the Soviet Union. What attracted them to Marxism and to the Soviet Union at that time was not primarily the attempt to close the gap between wealth and poverty, but rather the vision of education used for molding and moving a large population toward a common end. Dewey's essentially laudatory description of Soviet education is perhaps indicative of his more general attitudes about control:

> Nowhere else in the world is employment of it [progaganda] as a tool of control so constant, consistent and systematic as in Russia at present. Indeed, it has taken on such importance and social dignity that the word propaganda hardly carries, in another social medium, the correct meaning. For we instinctively associate propaganda with the accomplishing of some specific ends, more or less private to a particular class or group and correspondingly concealed from others. But in Russia the propaganda is in behalf of a burning public faith. One may believe that the leaders are wholly mistaken in the object of their faith, but their sincerity is beyond question. To them the end for which propaganda is employed is not a private or even a class gain, but is the universal good of universal humanity. In consequence, propaganda is education and education is propaganda. They are more than confounded; they are identical.[21]

The Soviet Union during the late 1920s was for Dewey the exemplar of the controlled corporate society that he believed America was (and ought to be) becoming. But it was not only the masses that had to be bent to the social will; the new society demanded new roles for everyone and if control was to be complete, even the intellectuals—who had traditionally been defined as being at least partially outside of society—must now enthusiastically find their place within it. *Individualism Old and New* lamented and deplored the fate of the artists whom Dewey believed remained unincorporated and outside the mainstream of American society. The Soviet Union therefore provided an even more important object lesson. One intellectual,

> not a party member, told me that he thought those intellectuals who had refused to cooperate wherever they could with the new government had made a tragic mistake; they had nullified their

---

[21] John Dewey, *Character and Events*, ed. Joseph Ratner (New York: Henry Holt and Co., 1929), Vol. 1, p. 399.

own power and had deprived Russia of assistance just when it was most needed. As for himself he had found that the present government cleared the way for just the causes he had had at heart in the old regime, and whose progress had always been hopeless compromised by its opposition; and that, although he was not a communist, he found his advice and even his criticism welcomed as soon as the authorities recognized that he was sincerely trying to cooperate. And I may add that, while my experience was limited, I saw liberal intellectuals who had pursued both the policy he deplored and the one he recommended. There is no more unhappy and futile class on earth than the first, and none more fully alive and happy—in spite of narrowly restricted economic conditions, living quarters, salaries, etc.—than the second.[22]

The question of social control was thus not an issue for progressive educators, self-styled radicals or otherwise; everyone applauded an affirmative answer. But another aspect of Marxism was an issue, namely, the appropriateness of a class analysis for understanding the dynamics of society in the United States. Arguing for such an analysis were George Counts, John Childs, and Theodore Brameld. Arguing against it stood Dewey, R. B. Raup, W. H. Kilpatrick, and H. Rugg. More than an indication of the radicalism of the movement the debate signaled the passing of the short-lived radical phase. Dewey's own ambivalence toward class analysis had been expressed a year earlier in *Liberalism and Social Action*, and the position taken by him in 1936 served only to crystallize his opposition and to help establish as appropriate the view that American society was composed of a conglomeration of pressure groups each vying with each other for favors and power. As Dewey put it: "Any one habituated to the use of the method of science will view with considerable suspicion the erection of human beings into fixed entities called classes, having no overlapping interests and so internally unified and externally separated that they are made the protagonists of history—itself hypothetical."[23]

[22] *Ibid.*, p. 404.
[23] John Dewey, *Liberalism and Social Action* (New York: G. P. Putnam's Sons, 1935), p. 80. At the time of the writing of this work, Dewey's attitude was perhaps still more ambiguous than the above passage reveals. Note, for example, a somewhat contrasting passage from the same work: "The actual corrosive 'materialism' of our time does not proceed from science. It springs from the notion, sedulously cultivated by the class in power, that the creative capacities of individuals can be evoked and developed only in a struggle for material possessions and material gains" (*ibid.*, p. 89).

Although Dewey would occasionally slip into the language of class antagonism, once the spectre of science was raised against such an analysis the slips were explicitly recovered. Even though a few progressives like John Childs continued to argue for the viability of a class analysis, by 1936 the battle had been won by others and, except for a general acceptance of the need for strong social control, Marxism was not especially welcome in the Progressive camp. In its place stood a pressure-group theory of American society serving ultimately to rationalize the broad outline of American economics and politics, and simultaneously serving as theoretical foundation for advocating the need for strong (albeit subtle) measures of social control by the schools.[24]

Commentators have traced the fall of progressive educational reform as it moved from a "radical" social reconstructionist view in the 1930s to a "life adjustment" approach to schools in the 1940s.[25] They have quite properly noted that the life adjustment movement implicity accepted the basic structural elements of American society while teaching youngsters the skills that would

---

[24] Our own views on the "pressure-group theory" are outlined more fully in "Aesthetes and Experts: For Whom Does the Bell Toll?" in the *Journal of Aesthetic Education*, Vol. 6, Nos. 1–2 (January–April, 1972). For the progressives, it is significant to note that among the major arguments used against the class analysis was the contention that Americans simply did not perceive themselves as members of any specific and clearly identifiable class but rather identified much more strongly with different groups, each bidding for favors. Accepting this argument, it was then concluded that social change would come about not by playing upon class differences, but rather by building through education consent among the various groups. The critique, however, begged a rather significant question. Presumably, if one believed that America was really governed by a ruling class in its own self-interest and against the interest of the vast majority, then the first element of strategy would be to bring the majority to a perception of what was really the case; i.e., to make them class conscious. Thus to argue that American society was not amenable to a class analysis because the majority of people did not perceive themselves to be members of any particular class was simply to beg the question. Putting the issue of class consciousness aside, progressives themselves had frequently cited evidence which would have lent credence to a class analysis. There is of course reason to believe, given the disproportionate distribution of wealth, power, and influence that the class analysis was dismissed too quickly. In any event, its dismissal by progressives in the late thirties goes a long way toward explaining the general enthusiasm with which many progressives greeted the tame, status quo oriented life adjustment movement of the 1940s. For a more detailed statement of this issue, see Walter Feinberg, *Reason and Rhetoric: The Intellectual Foundations of Twentieth Century Liberal Educational Policy* (New York: John Wiley and Sons, 1975).

[25] A number of books document the different phases of progressive education. The most often cited is Cremin's *Transformation of the Schools*.

allow them to accommodate themselves to life in an industrial, welfare-state America. The description of the life adjustment movement is accurate, but the idea that progressive education in fact moved from one position to another is not. As maintained earlier, it was rather a movement that was basically designed to develop the skills, work habits, and general social attitudes that were required by the changing nature of work. Both poverty and laissez-faire capitalism were important issues, not basically because of their immoral nature, but because in their more extreme forms they were a threat to the stability required for continued techno-logical growth. When laissez-faire capitalism turned into a welfare-state capitalism which promised to end poverty while enhancing stability, socialist alternatives were no longer considered by "radi-cal" progressives.

Poverty was, of course, a persistent theme of the educational reformer as it was with the social reformer in general and they both tried to alleviate some of its harsher effects. But their per-ceptions were generally guided by a very cautious view of what was possible, and as often as not their efforts served to appease and comfort the impoverished rather than aid them in changing the social factors which caused their poverty. The progressive historian James Harvey Robinson wrote when proposing a history curriculum for the children of the industrial laborers: "The goal of history for the child of the industrial laborer is to teach him to become 'influential in bettering the lot of himself and his fellow workers without seriously diminishing the output.' It is the function of such a history to allow these children 'to see the significance of their humble part in carrying on the world's work, to appreciate the possibilities of their position and to view it in as hopeful a light as circumstances will permit.' "[26] It is noteworthy that Rob-inson traced his intellectual roots back to Marx, but certainly the captains of American industry did not have a great deal to worry about from that kind of Marxism. To advocate altering the attitudes of the impoverished working class, rather than striving to eliminate their poverty, is a program to which John Rockefeller would surely have contributed a few of his famous ten-cent pieces. Progressives like Robinson and Dewey often justified their argu-ment for social control by claiming that control was inevitable and that the only real issue was the direction it would take—

[26] James Harvey Robinson, *The New History: Essays Illustrating the Modern Historical Outlook* (New York: Macmillan Company, 1922), p. 142.

democratic or totalitarian.[27] Except for some rather vague and general notions about democratic controls, the nature of the proposed direction is only suggested. Robinson's attitude toward the industrial worker is rather typical, suggesting that reformers did not envisage any drastic redistribution of power or of economic rewards.

The views of Dewey and his disciples are not fundamentally different. The advocacy of social welfare programs and other reforms is not particularly significant for the working class if the import of the programs is merely to defuse explosive industrial situations. Where Dewey and all of his progressive confreres stopped short was at the edge of advocating the sharing of the necessary but unpleasant mind-killing work of a society, or advocating the principle that any increase in wealth for the richest members of the society be preceded by a greater increase for the poorer members. Industrial unrest and not socioeconomic inequity was the real problem as defined by the progressives, and Dewey made this point rather clearly in the confidential document that he submitted to Woodrow Wilson's military officer General Churchill during World War I. This document resulted from a study of the Polish community during World War I and it shows remarkably little concern for the conditions of the Polish working class; it does show, however, considerable concern for the effects that alienation and unrest might have on the American war effort and upon industrial growth after the war is over:

> The great industrial importance of Polish labor in this country must be borne in mind and the fact that there will be a shortage of labor after the war and that there is already a movement under foot (which should be carefully looked into) to stimulate the return of Poles and others of foreign birth in Southeastern Europe to their native lands after the war. With the sharp commercial competition that will necessarily take place after the war, any tendency which on the one hand de-Americanizes and

---

[27] It was argued that the complexity of technology had established such total interdependence that the absence of large-scale controls would result in sheer chaos and social anarchy, and further that the end result would be some form of fascism. This argument was used repeatedly to discourage action from the more radical left as self-defeating. The argument itself, drawn partly from the German experience, had some degree of historical validity. It also had a strong self-fulfilling quality about it, as it removed the element of moral responsibility from the activity of the right, making the left the sole initiator of social events. It suggested that they alone were responsible for whatever events might follow their initial acts.

on the other hand strengthens the allegiance of those of foreign birth to the United States deserves careful attention.[28]

From statements like this it is clear that Dewey's progressive educational reform was a response to a nation moving into an age of technology and that it rested on the assumption that science and technology alone could properly determine the appropriateness of human values and human institutions; the Polish workers themselves were not asked their opinion on these matters.

The essence of contemporary educational reform, then, lies in technology and machinery and not in pedagogic techniques.[29] Progressive educators gave much theoretical attention to the relationship between man and machine in an attempt to discredit more traditional approaches to societal change. But that relationship had been fundamentally altered by the Industrial Revolution in ways that the progressives do not seem to have fully appreciated. Before the eighteenth century, technology and machinery were basically extensions of the bodies of human beings who were not estranged from the natural and social world about them. Pulleys, plows, levers, saws, etc. made much physical labor easier; they did not obviate the need for that labor nor the need to have that labor take place in a genuine community. By the mid-nineteenth century, however, machines stood clearly between man and nature, and people became more dependent on oil than their ancestors had been on rainfall. Moreover, the machines now replaced rather than assisted men and women in their labors, and consequently a dependency relation grew and intensified that had been almost totally absent in the past, accompanied by a breaking of social bonds.

[28] John Dewey, "Conditions Among the Poles in the United States: Confidential Report," 1917, p. 73. For a more complete description of the report and of Dewey's perceptions of minority groups in general see Walter Feinberg, "Progressive Education and Social Planning," *Teacher's College Record*, Vol. 73, No. 4 (May, 1972) pp. 485–506.

[29] Thus the progressive movement was far more than a set of pedagogic techniques, but it is easy to overlook the extent to which the reforms were geared in the first instance to technological demands rather than to human aspirations, because many of the more obvious and direct applications of technology to education—IQ tests, teaching machines, etc.—were not greeted with enthusiasm by many progressives, nor were they incorporated into the curricula of many progressive schools. It is a mistake, however, to draw conclusions of significance from this reaction because the essence of twentieth century educational reform does not, as maintained here, lie in the development of any specific educational technique but rather in the way in which educators came to look at the relationship between man and machine.

This view of pre-industrial man-machine relations is not intended as a paean or a defense of the Luddites; there are surely many plagues from which humankind is now relatively free due to the development of science and technology. Rather it is an attempt to point out an increasing discrepancy between long-established and cherished goals of human life and the modern means of their achievement; something is lost in the translation from "a loaf of bread/a jug of wine/and thou" to Wonder bread, Boone's Farm, and I Love Lucy.

The progressives thus did not address a fundamental problem with respect to technology (any more than it is being addressed today by most champions of technology and technological expertise): it not only serves in the attainment of ends, it influences significantly one's appreciation of them. By not attending to this problem the progressives could and did assume that technology was only benign—a needed assumption for the advocacy of man's subservience to its requirements. But such advocacy *eo ipso* served to remove from ethical and aesthetic (or spiritual) considerations those manifold areas of human experience which were altered or lost by the subservience. It was clear to the progressives that once-stable families and communities developed and enhanced attitudes which were often dysfunctional in the industrial setting, and consequently these social groups could no longer carry out the essential training of the young, and their socializing roles came to be, for many immigrant offspring, reduced to insignificance. Many traditional (and perhaps instinctive) sources of human satisfaction were lost by these dislocations, and it was surely mistaken to believe that equivalent sources could be found in the public schools.

By accepting the dictates of technology in this way the progressive educators were obliged to attempt only those reforms which were necessary for, or at least consistent with, continued economic development, ignoring reforms based on principles of equity which might threaten social stability and technological growth.[30] As

---

[30] It is primarily for this reason that the early progressives could overlook the education of the American black for so long a time and why they were unable to challenge the industrial interests which were directing black schools in a way which would establish a shadow labor force that would keep industrial wages depressed. See James Anderson, "Education For Servitude: The Social Purposes of Schooling in the Black South," Ph.D. dissertation, University of Illinois, 1973. The limits that a commitment to technological growth placed on educational reform in the progressive era of American educational develop-

part of a large-scale effort to adjust institutions and attitudes to a continuously evolving technology, progressive education was also part and parcel of the scholarship of the times, and it is no accident or coincidence that theoreticians like Dewey are so closely associated with it.

The educational philosophy elaborated by Dewey expressed a concept of human nature and freedom which was uniquely consistent with the requirements of the new industrial age, at the same time challenging only minimally the existing distribution of wealth in the society. Further, Dewey's progressive scholarship elaborated a concept of vocation that maintained the existing structure of work while rationalizing vocational education as a legitimate and worthwhile project for the public schools. One consequence of this move was to ultimately support the complacency of union members toward their own status and the eventual abandonment of the principle of equity that spirited some of the earlier phases of the labor movement.

Similarly, Dewey's philosophy of education advocated a child-centered pedagogy, largely because he believed that it was the most effective way of inculcating the norms required by the increasingly more sophisticated technology that would soon augment the production of the assembly line: "When we look at the problem as one of an adjustment to be intelligently attained, the issue shifts from within personality to an engineering issue, the establishment of arts of education and social guidance."[31]

To Francis W. Parker, whom Dewey referred to as the father of progressive education, the child was the archetypal man, possessing the grace, poise, and intellect that all artists and scholars attempted to emulate. The romantic side of the movement insisted that the integrity of childhood be recognized without central consideration to the specific skills that the child might need in adult society; for in a world of changing technology many of the needed skills could not even be predicted. In this way the rigor and discipline that was felt to be too often imposed by the teacher came

---

ment can also be seen operating today in those developing areas which, having made a commitment to maximize technological growth, are attempting to use schools to smooth over the dislocations which have thereby resulted. For an analysis of this problem, see Walter Feinberg's forthcoming article, "Educational Equality under Two Conflicting Models of Educational Development," in the journal *Theory and Society: Renewal and Critique in Social Theory* (Amsterdam, Elsevier Publishing Co.).

[31] Dewey, *Human Nature and Conduct*, p. 10.

to be thought of as dysfunctional to the educational process and generally harmful to the child. Instead of the impositions of external discipline, progressives developed a theory of pedagogy whereby discipline was to be a natural outgrowth of the child's interest and whereby much of the educational program of the school was to be joined with play activity. Thus they argued that play was not to be thought of as antagonistic to education nor even as a necessary respite to the rigors of learning. Play was an integral aspect of education, being the first activity where the child voluntarily disciplined his own interests toward the completion of some projected end; and again, the end for the progressives was the internalizing of the requisite norms and values.

Play was not, however, to be totally spontaneous; rather it was to be directed toward an appreciation of the machine and of the complexities of industrial civilization. The romanticism of progressive educators was not confined to their views of childhood alone. If the child symbolized the new man, the machine symbolized the possibility of a new age, an age of material abundance, social harmony, and man's ultimate control over the forces of nature. In order to control nature, however, man first had to learn to control himself and to recognize the limits that technology placed on his freedom.[32]

It was the belief in the total control of nature by benign technology which made progressivism the education for the new age, and this belief was shared by people of many political persuasions. Frank Parsons, an avowed socialist and one of the founders of the vocational guidance movement, could envisage a day when every aspect of an individual's personality could be tested, making possible the proper educational and vocational fit.[33] The psycholo-

---

[32] Dewey puts this point emphatically: "The machine is the authentically embodied *Logos* of modern life, and the import of this fact is not diminished by any amount of dislike to it" (John Dewey, "Philosophy," in Charles Beard, ed., *Whither Mankind*, New York: Longsmans, Green and Co., p. 317). Perhaps the classic statement of this point of view is to be found in William Fielding Ogburn, *Social Change* (New York: Delta Books, 1966), originally published in 1922. Ogburn argues that social crisis results when changes in technology are not adequately accompanied by changes in values.

[33] For a detailed analysis of Parsons's ideas and influence on vocational guidance see Eleanor Feinberg's "Frank Parsons and the Role of Vocational Counseling in Education," Ph.D. dissertation, University of Illinois, 1974. Also, from a generally different point of view, but with adequate material to substantiate the concern for control, see Howard V. Davis, *Frank Parsons: Prophet, Innovator, Counselor* (Carbondale: Southern Illinois University Press, 1969).

gist E. L. Thorndike was not at all antagonistic to capitalism, but could envisage and applaud the coming of that very same day.[34] David Snedden, the efficiency-minded educator criticized by Dewey for supporting the industrial status quo, cited the total control of the reform school as the ideal educational environment.[35] And Randolph Bourne, who criticized Dewey for the latter's stance on World War I, cited the schools of Gary for their effectiveness in reducing the influence of alien community and civic groups on children in the public schools.[36] Some educators believed that the schools should take their cues from the business leaders of the society, and they proposed that tests and the curricula be designed to fill the industrial needs as perceived by businessmen. Others were less certain. Dewey, for example, argued that the business structure itself was too loosely planned and that more control had to be exerted upon the manufacturing and distribution of goods as well as upon their consumption. He was critical of educators who mindlessly took their cues from the business establishments, because business itself was symptomatic of inadequate controls.[37] Dewey's contribution to the question of

[34] The extent of Thorndike's interest in the total control of human activity can be illustrated in a number of ways. Among the most revealing is his belief that "The man of amateurish semi-knowledge is a 'public danger' since he is likely to try to understand the specialist instead of obeying him and thus does not know his place intellectually" (Edward L. Thorndike, "Intelligence and Its Uses," *Harper's Monthly*, May, 1922). For a discussion of the ideology behind the early testing movement see Clarence J. Karier, "Testing For Order and Control in the Corporate Liberal State," in C. J. Karier, P. Violas, and J. Spring, *Roots of Crisis* (Chicago: Rand McNally, 1973, pp. 108–37).

[35] For a detailed description of Snedden's career see Walter H. Drost, *David Snedden and Education for Social Efficiency* (Madison: University of Wisconsin Press, 1967).

[36] Randolph Bourne, *The Gary Schools* (Boston: Houghton Mifflin Co., 1916).

[37] For an elaboration of the varied avenues that the drive for control took among liberals see Clarence J. Karier, "Liberalism and the Quest for Orderly Change," *History of Education Quarterly*, Vol. XII, No. 1 (Spring, 1972). Karier's emphasis is on the impulse for control among liberals in general. While this was an important element tying together various shades of liberalism, there are differences as well. Whenever social control is initiated it is because someone believes that some goal needs to be accomplished, and that its accomplishment will require more than one person. Using this as a paradigm, then all acts of control involve three functions: first a decision as to the goal, second the act of controlling human activity toward the goal, and third the act that results from being controlled. Precisely how these functions are distributed determines to some extent the kind of control that is being exerted. To some educators there was a clear division of labor whereby some group (oftentimes the business establishment) would decide as to the goal (such as the manpower

control is to be found superficially in his elaboration of the requirements of corporate, technological society, but more deeply it is found in his reinterpretation of, or failure to fully appreciate, traditional concepts of human nature and morality.

The classical philosophical treatises on ethics generally have in common the attempt to find some criteria by which moral standards could be applied to human activities. Where they tended to differ in the past was not with respect to the legitimacy of the quest itself, but about the nature of the standard. Plato could elaborate a theory of social harmony defined as justice, and declare it to be the standard against which a society was to be measured. Kant developed a set of moral laws placing the locus of morality in the university of the will and Bentham countered by developing a calculus of pleasure and pain which then placed the standard in the measured consequences of the act. With Dewey, however, the quest for a standard was of secondary consideration: "Morality is largely concerned with controlling human nature."[38] To a large extent, the moral problem was a problem of technique, of "modifying the factors which now influence future results," and of "changing the working character or will" of another person.[39] Thus while Dewey vigorously opposed a *narrow* vocational

---

needs at the time) and another (often the educators) would decide upon the best technique to achieve it, and then the techniques would be applied on people who had little say either about the nature of the goal, or the application of the technique. On the other hand, educators like Dewey had some commitment to the idea that these three functions should not be so rigidly separated and argued that those affected by an act should have a part in deciding the goal. Indeed one of the reasons Karier's article is significant is because of the element of surprise that is aroused when he shows that such was often not the case. The reason that the two patterns of control become blurred among educators as different as Dewey and Thorndike is in an ambiguous commitment on Dewey's part to scientific decision making. Whereas to someone like Thorndike science rather clearly meant "correct" decisions made according to certain specified procedures and consistent with the efficient management of society, Dewey's meaning was less clear. Science is often defended as the best means to make the alternatives and methods public and therefore to establish some kind of social consensus. It was because of this argument, for example, that Dewey could conclude that there was an essential connection between science and its public characteristics on the one hand, and the requirements of a democratic society for decision making procedure that are reasonably open on the other. There was, however, another sense to Dewey's use of the term "science," one that was associated better with scientific management and social coordination and Karier is quite correct in asserting that when push came to shove Dewey and other liberals were much more likely to opt for this kind of "science."

[38] Dewey, *Human Nature & Conduct*, p. 1.
[39] *Ibid.*, p. 19.

emphasis on education, he provided intellectual support for the belief that morality and education were but special cases of social engineering in general.

In the same vein, freedom too was essentially an engineering problem. Human freedom was to be found by locating and working within the dominant forces of the times. It was concerned with the techniques by which habits once attached to the traditions and institutions of a prescientific and pretechnological age would be brought into conformity with the "new forces generated by science and technology."[40] The goal of freedom became the liberation of the potential latent in the machine, and because technological development requires coordinated efforts of different people from different cultures, the issue of freedom shifted back and forth between an individual concern and a social one. At best it was simply assumed that as technology was forced from the antiquated attitudes of another age, human freedom and justice would also be enhanced.

The role of the teacher as orchestrator of the learning environment rather than as pedagogue cramming knowledge down the child's throat can similarly be understood more easily against the backdrop of the progressives' larger concept of freedom. While the emphasis on the relationship between the child's play and the child's education may or may not have been good pedagogy, it certainly was a recognition that the school was coming to encompass more and more of the child's life and that each and every aspect of childhood activity was useful material for the leaning which was now primarily to take place in the school.

Play did not mean only games, however; it meant organizing the active energies of children toward the performance of a common activity and the appreciation of a common goal. In other words, the activity of the school was designed to resurrect the commonality of purpose and tradition which technological society so much needed but had so badly abused. The goal was "to make each one of our schools into an embryonic community life, active with types of occupations that reflect the life of the larger society."[41] The goal would be accomplished when each child, realizing that modern civilization, composed of an intricate network of mutually serving roles, is the product of a long history of human

---

[40] Dewey, *Liberalism and Social Action*, p. 75.

[41] John Dewey, *The School and Society in the Child and the Curriculum* (Chicago: University of Chicago Press, 1956), p. 29.

progress, became saturated with the "spirit of service."[42] This general characterization is especially true of Dewey's laboratory school at the University of Chicago, where the aim was to show the mutual dependence of one occupation upon another and to create in the schoolhouse the harmonious community that Dewey hoped might eventually exist outside of it. This aim could be realized by the development in each youngster of an appreciation for the interrelationship of roles in an industrial society, as well as developing general understanding that present day society is the culmination of a long process of human activity and progress. The children of the laboratory school came mainly from upper–middle-class families and their own role in industrial society would perhaps not be obviously inconsistent with the lessons that Dewey taught them. The accuracy of the lesson for children of the industrial class is not quite so obvious.

Dewey's views on vocational education are complex and too easily oversimplified. The favorable commentaries usually afforded his view are probably justified when contrasted with recommendations put forth by Snedden and others, for his view on education in general and vocational education in particular are indeed easily distinguished from those of Snedden. Dewey was vigorously opposed to modeling the school after the needs of the business community and of confining vocational education to the learning of specific industrial skills. Moreover, he was a critic of the uses to which intelligence tests were being put—sorting youngsters in order to train them for different roles in the industrial system. His arguments for vocational education expressed as much interest in the needs of the individual and the nature of education as they did in the needs of the society. All of these points are correctly stressed by Dewey's commentators, and each of these points sets off Dewey and the progressives who followed him from a sizable number of educators of his time.

But what is not emphasized in the commentaries is the extent to which Dewey was willing to accept the inequitable distribution of work of the status quo, with many people destined to live much of their lives performing unpleasant, odious labors while society's more interesting work was reserved for the few who were chosen by inheritance or, better, by education. Indeed Dewey's awareness of the possibly disruptive effects of this division can be seen in his proposals for vocational education. Unable or un-

[42] *Ibid.*

willing to advocate a more equitable distribution of work, he saw, as did Robinson, the solution lying in the development of new attitudes about work. Indeed Dewey's awareness of the possibly disruptive effects of this division can be seen in his proposals for vocational education. If the chores of the laborer were potentially alienating and thereby would disrupt the efficient workings of technology, the solution was to teach laborers' children the value of the work performed and about the vast network of interrelated and supporting roles:

> Work is essentially social in its character, for the occupations which people carry on are for human needs and ends. . . . Everything about this scheme is dependent upon the ability of people to work together successfully. If they can do this a well-balanced, happy, and prosperous society results. Without these occupations, which are essentially social life—that is human life—civilization can not go on. The result is a sort of social education by other individuals and to whole communities. When it is left to circumstances this education, although necessary, is haphazard and only partial.[43]

The above passage introduces the section on the Gary schools in John and Evelyn Dewey's *Schools of Tomorrow*. It is interesting not because of the sentiment it expresses (it is certainly not unreasonable to want people to work together successfully or for society to be well balanced and happy), but rather because Dewey believed that this was actually happening in Judge Gary's steel town. *Schools of Tomorrow* and the treatment of Gary in it provide some remarkable insights into the goals of progressive education. Dewey was impressed by the Gary schools for two reasons. He was impressed first by the efficient use of the school plant—especially in light of Gary's average tax base—and second he was impressed by the nature of Gary's vocational education programs. The presence of the huge steel plants in Gary should have given Dewey pause to ask why the schools were supported by only an average tax base. But he did not dwell any longer on this issue than he did on the applicability of a class analysis to American society. Disregarding this oversight, however, Dewey's analysis of the vocational education program is even more instructive.

He observed with some enthusiasm that children were not

[43] John and Evelyn Dewey, *Schools of Tomorrow* (New York: E. P. Dutton, 1915), p. 121.

being trained for specific industrial roles, but were developing a general understanding of shopwork in many of its aspects. Included in this understanding was some knowledge of the general scientific principles behind industrial work along with an awareness of the historical and social context in which the work was carried out. One of the indexes of the success of the Gary schools was the retention rate—fewer students than in other school districts left before completing high school. Success here, however, is not due solely to the innovative curriculum, but depends in part on the fact that children are brought to a sharp awareness of the relation between their work in school and their eventual employment outside of it. Businessmen, reports Dewey, "come to the schools and tell the students what the chances for graduates and nongraduates are in their business and why they want better educated employees." Moreover:

> Since the first day the Gary child began going to school he has seen boys and girls in their last year of high school still learning how to do the work that is being done where, perhaps, he expects ultimately to go to work. He knows that these pupils all have a tremendous advantage over him in the shop, that they will earn more, get a higher grade of work to do, and do it better. . . . He is familiar with the statistics of workers in that trade, knows the wages for the different degrees of skill and how far additional training can take a man. With all this information about, and outlook upon, his vocation it is not strange that so few, comparatively, of the pupils leave school.[44]

With so much of the school geared to developing the work norms of industrial life it seems to be in the interests of apology for Dewey to write that "The industrial features . . . were not instituted to turn out good workers for the steel company, nor to save the factories the expense of training their own workers, but for the educational value of the work they involved."[45]

Precisely what such educational value might be is unclear, but Dewey does note, after describing the differences and similarities between the curriculum of the college and the factory-bound child that "It is just as valuable for the man who works with his brains to know how to do some of the things that the factory worker is doing, as it is for the latter to know how the patterns of the machine he is making were drawn, and the principles that govern the power

[44] *Ibid.*, pp. 138, 190.
[45] *Ibid.*, p. 129.

supply of the factory."[46] Dewey was obviously not advocating that knowledge of the power supply of the factory might come in handy in case of a strike. The point was rather that such mutual understanding would help bring about the "well-balanced, happy, and prosperous society" which he envisaged. Judge Gary would surely have agreed, enthusiastically.

The Deweys' laudatory description of this part of the teacher's role is peculiarly reminiscent of John Dewey's own activity in the Polish community of Philadelphia where he took it upon himself to become the arbiter of the moral values of the community. He writes of the teacher's role:

> They [the immigrant parents] are naturally suspicious of government and social authority . . . and it is very important that their children should have some real knowledge on which to base a sounder judgment. Besides giving them this, the schools try to teach American standards of living to the pupils and so to their parents. On entering school every pupil gives the school office, besides the usual name, age, and address, certain information about his family, its size, its resources, and the character of the home he lives in. This record is kept in the school and transferred if the child moves out of the school district. . . . By comparing these with any family record, it is a simple matter to tell if the family are living under proper moral and hygenic conditions.
> . . . If bad conditions are due to ignorance or poverty, the teacher finds out what can be done to remedy them, and sees to it that the family learns how they can better themselves. If conditions are very bad, neighborhood public opinion is worked up through the children on the block.[47]

If any parent had doubts about the validity of their instinctive distrust of public authority, Dewey's description of the role of the teacher would surely have reassured them that their doubts were firmly based in reality.

There is another dimension of *Schools of Tomorrow* which commentators simply overlook, but which is probably more indicative of the general perspective of progressive than almost anything else. The book was written by Dewey and his daughter Evelyn in 1915 to describe some of the developments in both private and public progressive schools. Each chapter begins with

[46] *Ibid.*, p. 191.
[47] *Ibid.*, pp. 147–48.

a description (primarily written by John Dewey) of the philosophy underlying the school and then a description (primarily written by Evelyn Dewey) of the school itself. In general, Dewey's educational philosophy was critical of any pedagogy that abstracted one aspect of human development and treated it as if it were the whole of learning. This accounts to a large degree for his criticism of the overly "bookish" learning of many of the schools of his time, and he constantly advocated the work of the mind being joined with the work of the hand. In *Schools of Tomorrow* he describes a number of schools in which this preferred kind of learning is taking place. There is, however, a real difference in the activities of different kind of schools and of Dewey's reporting of them. When he is describing the schools which have middle-class children as clients the activity curriculum he outlines is not at all designed for specifically vocational purposes: the object is to develop motor, perceptual, and problem-solving skills and general awareness of aspects of life and nature. When his description turns to those public schools catering primarily to children from lower-class homes the activity curriculum takes on quite a different meaning: here the object is basically vocational and is designed to develop the work norms of the modern factory. Dewey, perhaps unwittingly, affirmed the distinction very well. After describing an all-black vocational school in Indianapolis in which black youngsters learned motor skills and some trades, but had little in the way of intellectual studies, he suggested this kind of education as especially promising for children of colored and immigrant parents.[48]

The misperception of progressive reform has been followed by erroneous judgments about its place in American society and about its value. That progressive education was a series of proposals designed for society in a state of transition from one mode of production to another is too often overlooked, as is the general structure of the society around which it molded its pedagogy. Any evaluation of progressive education is therefore conditioned at least in part by one's historical perspective. If it is assumed that the nature of work, the division of labor, and the allocation of rewards are irrevocably set, then it is perhaps also reasonable to praise this type of educational reform as historically and metaphysically valid. If, on the other hand, one believes that the several facets of labor and its distribution are alterable and that it is

[48] *Ibid.*, pp. 151–52.

desirable to alter them in certain directions, then progressive reforms will not constitute an education for all seasons. And if the desired direction is toward equity and equality there is little reason to believe or hope that Silberman and other progressive-like critics of the present will be of any more assistance in pointing out the way than their predecessors.

It has been written in defense of Dewey in particular and in praise of progressive education in general:

> His point was that in the urban community individuals would be removed from direct participation in producing life's goods. In order to make sense out of a world they could only experience in fragments, they would have to be helped to see it conceptually, and to understand that the intricate superstructure of specialized processes was an elaboration of means related to fundamental human needs. . . . The new complexity was the result of man's intellectual leap forward and the present task was to become thoroughly familiar with the intellectual skills, and with the content and habits of men that had transformed the banks of the Chicago river—and might eventually transform the face of the moon. The task of the liberal educator was to give the young an understanding of their place in the scheme of things. . . . Consequently they might avoid feeling alienated by the rush of the city's streets; they might feel that they could share in the processes that were contributing to the improvement of life.[49]

We endorse the above as a description of the progressive education movement but we have stood on the banks of the Chicago River in the 1970s, and we have watched the rush of that city's streets; and we have not been able to avoid feeling both alienated and nauseated by the American processes, educational and otherwise, that have transformed not only the moon, but the face of Indochina as well.

[49] Arthur G. Wirth, *John Dewey as Educator: His Design for Work in Education* (New York: John Wiley and Sons, 1966), p. 292.

The Contradictions of Liberal Educational Reform

Herbert Gintis and Samuel Bowles

I. INTRODUCTION

The bloom is off the liberal educational reform movement. The social scientists who provided the intellectual impetus and rationale for compensatory education, for school integration, for project Headstart and Title I are in retreat. In the state and national legislatures as much as intellectual circles, the mood of the reformers is one of retrenchment and retraction. In less than a decade, liberal hegemony in the field of educational theory and policy has been shattered. How did it happen?

The 1960s and early 1970s have witnessed a sustained political assault against economic inequality in the United States. Blacks, women, welfare recipients, and young rank-and-file workers have brought the issue of inequality into the streets, forced it onto the front pages, and thrown it into the legislature and the courts. The dominant response of the privileged has been concern, tempered by a hardy optimism that social programs could be devised to reduce inequality, alleviate social distress, and bring the nation back from the brink of chaos. This optimism has been at once a reflection of and rooted in a pervasive body of liberal social thought, as codified in modern mainstream economics and sociology. At the core of this conventional wisdom in the social sciences is the conviction that in the advanced capitalist system of the United States, significant progress toward equality of eco-

A version of this essay will appear in the authors' forthcoming book, *Educational Capitalism in the United States* (New York, Basic Books).

nomic opportunity can be achieved through a combination of enlightened persuasion and social reforms, particularly in the sphere of education and vocational training.

The disappointing results of the War on Poverty, and, in a larger sense, the persistence of poverty and racism in the United States have dented the optimism of the liberal social scientist and the liberal policy maker alike. The record of educational reform in the War on Poverty has been nothing short of catastrophic. Thus, for example, Averch et al. could conclude their survey of the efficacy of educational programs with: "Virtually without exception all of the large surveys of the large national compensatory education programs have shown no beneficial results on average."[1] The publication of the results of the Office of Education's *Survey of Educational Opportunity*—"The Coleman Report"— did nothing to bolster the fading optimism of the school reformers.[2] For while Coleman and his associates did identify positive effects of a few aspects of the school, such as teacher quality, the weight of the evidence seemed to point to the virtual irrelevance of educational resources or quality as a determinant of educational outcomes. Studies by economists in the late 1960s revealed the tenuous or even nonexistent relationship of schooling to economic success for blacks.[3] By 1972 a broad spectrum of social scientists and the public were ready to accept the view put forward by Jencks that a more egalitarian school system would do little to create a more equal distribution of income or opportunity.[4]

The massive statistical studies of the last ten years—the Coleman report, Jencks's study, the evaluation of compensatory education and others—softened the liberal position for the conservative counterattack. Most notable has been the resurgence of the genetic interpretation of IQ. Sensing the opportunity afforded by the

[1] Henry Averch et al., "How Effective Is Schooling? A Critical Review and Synthesis of Research Findings" (Santa Monica: Rand Corporation, 1972), p. 125.

[2] James S. Coleman et al., *Equality of Educational Opportunity* (U.S. Government Printing Office, 1966).

[3] See for example Randall D. Weiss, "The Effect of Education on the Earnings of Blacks and Whites," *Review of Economics and Statistics* 52 (May 1970); and Bennett Harrison, "Education and Underemployment in the Urban Ghetto," *American Economic Review*, Vol. 42, No. 12 (December 1972), pp. 796–812.

[4] Christopher Jencks et al., *Inequality: A Reassessment of the Effect of Family and Schooling in America* (New York: Basic Books, 1972).

liberal debacle, Arthur Jensen[5] began his celebrated article on the heritability of IQ with "Compensatory education has been tried, and apparently it has failed." In the debate that has ensued, an interpretation of the role of IQ in the class structure has been elaborated: the poor are poor because they are intellectually incompetent; their incompetence is particularly intractable because it is rooted in the genetic structure inherited from their poor and also intellectually deficient parents.[6] An explanation of the intergenerational reproduction of the class structure is thus found in the heritability of IQ. The idea is not new: an earlier wave of genetic interpretations of economic and ethnic inequality followed in the wake of the purportedly egalitarian but largely unsuccessful educational reforms of the Progressive era.[7]

Others, such as Banfield[8] and Moynihan,[9] have located the failure of liberal reform not in the genes, but in the attitudes, time perspectives, family patterns, and values of the poor.

In order to grasp why the recent statistical studies showing the impotence of education as an instrument for equality constituted such a blow to the liberal position, and why the conservative reaction has proved so successful, we must consider the place of liberal educational theory in the larger body of social science thought concerning the workings of the advanced capitalist economy.

The long-term development of capitalist society is governed by its fundamental economic institutions: markets in land, labor, and capital; private ownership of the means of production; the control of technology, production, and capital accumulation, ac-

[5] Arthur R. Jensen, "How Much Can We Boost IQ and Scholastic Achievement?" *Harvard Educational Review*, Reprint Series No. 2, 1969, pp. 126–34.

[6] The most explicit statement of the genetic interpretation of intergenerational immobility is Richard Herrnstein, "IQ," *Atlantic Monthly* Vol. 229, No. 9 (September 1971), pp. 43–64.

[7] Michael Katz notes the historical tendency of genetic interpretations of social inequality to gain popularity following the failure of educational reform movements. See Katz, *The Irony of Early School Reform* (Cambridge, Mass.: Harvard University Press, 1968). On the rise of the genetic interpretation of inequality toward the end of the Progressive era, see Clarence J. Karier, "Testing for Order and Control in the Corporate Liberal State," in C. V. Karier, P. Violas, and J. Spring, *Roots of Crisis* (Chicago: Rand McNally, 1973) pp. 108–37.

[8] See Edward Banfield, *The Unheavenly City* (New York: Little, Brown and Co., 1968).

[9] See Daniel P. Moynihan, The Negro Family: The Case for National Action (Cambridge, Mass.: MIT Press, 1967).

cording to ownership of factors of production. It has been long recognized that the unfettered operation of these institutions leads to undesirable outcomes. Among these are the fragmentation of communities, the deterioration of the natural environment, alienated work and inhuman working conditions, insufficient supplies of necessary social services, and an unequal distribution of goods and services among individuals. As these problems have appeared in increasing severity through the years, an alternative to classical laissez-faire liberalism has been embraced by all but the most dogmatic defenders of the capitalist faith.

This alternative, progressive liberalism, does not question the fundamental rationality of capitalist economic institutions. Rather it treats troublesome social problems as aberrations which may be alleviated by means of political and social correctives. Among these correctives, two have stood out: education and state intervention in economic life. Both have been evident in embryo since Adam Smith, both have been essential (though often unacknowledged) instruments of capitalist growth, and have become ever more powerful with the increasing extension of market and profit-oriented activities into all areas of social life. Both, it is thought, can serve as powerful compensatory and ameliorative forces, rectifying social problems and limiting the human costs of capitalist expansion.

The importance of education and state intervention as complements to the normal operation of profit-oriented production in the context of markets in land, labor, capital, and commodities is no longer open to question. The capacity of capitalist society to reproduce itself in expanded form from period to period rests squarely on the role of the state and the educational apparatus. Nevertheless, these correctives have not resolved the problems to which they have been directed. Inequality, class stratification, destruction of community and environment, and alienating, bureaucratic, and fragmented jobs all exist in unattenuated form. Rising per capita income has, if anything, heightened dissatisfaction over these flaws to the point of unleashing a veritable crisis of values in the advanced capitalist societies in Europe and America.

Thus the thrust of many modern radical critics of capitalism is not to berate the operation of its economic institutions per se, but to question the limits of education and state policy within the framework of a profit-oriented market system. The liberal position is, of course, in clear continuity with its historical development: [10] insofar as *any* reform is possible, it is possible within the market system, and can be effected through enlightened policy. The only points of contention within the progressive liberal tradition concern the technical limits of the possible in any materially productive society.

In this paper we shall confine our analysis to the educational system, maintaining that within the logic of a capitalist system the range of effective educational policy is severely limited by the functional role of schooling in the reproduction of an adequate labor force in a hierarchically controlled and class stratified production system.

Our argument proceeds as follows. In Section II we shall present two versions of progressive liberal educational theory. The first—the "democratic" version ably defended by John Dewey— asserts that as a necessary consequence of developing a citizenry adequate to the economic and political roles it must assume in a democratic economy, the educational system must promote healthy individual psychic growth and equality of opportunity.[11] The second—the "technocratic-meritocratic" version favored by contemporary social scientists and policy makers—asserts only the compatibility of these various functions of the educational system, based on the assumption that the central economic function of schooling is the generator of those cognitive and psycho-motor skills required of workers.

In Section III, we shall present empirical anomalies in the predictions based on these views. We shall first show that despite rapid economic development and vast extensions of formal education, the contribution of schooling either to healthy psychic development or equality of opportunity or outcomes has not manifested itself. Nor, as we shall show, is this due to the lack of commitment on the part of progressive liberal reformers. Indeed,

---

[10] The emphasis that progressive and liberal educators placed on state planning and on schooling as a more rational means than the market for the selection of talent is not at all antagonistic to capitalism, but is rather consistent with the form that capitalism must take in its advanced stages.

[11] During certain phases of his career, Dewey identified his own position with socialism. His emphasis, however, was less on the just distribution of social goods than it was on the function of the state in rationalizing production and consumption, and therefore his "socialism" was easily compatible with the corporate capitalism that developed.

the history of Progressivism leads us to postulate underlying difficulties, based on the incompatibility of the Progressive ideal with the operation of basic capitalist economic institutions. In Sections IV, V, and VI, we shall subject both versions of modern liberal theory to critique, arguing their inadequacy on both theoretical and empirical grounds. Its failures in practice, we shall argue, flow naturally from these inadequacies. A humane and equal educational system, we conclude in Section VII, requires the replacement of the hierarchical division of labor on which capitalist production is based.

II. DEMOCRACY AND TECHNOCRACY: LIBERAL THEORIES OF EDUCATION

Two questions may be raised concerning the limits of educational policy. The first concerns the compatibility of the various functions schools are supposed to perform. The second concerns the power of schooling to perform these functions. We will deal with each in turn.

In the eyes of most liberal reformers, the educational system must fulfill at least three functions. First and foremost, schools must produce the kind of individuals capable and willing to staff the various occupational, political, and other adult roles required by an expanding economy and a stable polity. "Education," says John Dewey in *Democracy and Education* (probably the most important presentation of the liberal theory of education in its progressive form) "is the means of [the] social continuity of life."[12] We refer to this process as the expanded reproduction function of education.

Second, while inequality in economic and social outcomes is allegedly necessary and in the interests of all in any advanced economy, the equalization of opportunity is desirable from the point of view of both equity and efficiency. Dewey is representative of a much larger body of liberal thought in asserting the role of the school in this process: "It is the office of the school environment . . . to see to it that each individual gets an opportunity to escape from the limitations of the social group to which he was born,

---

[12] John Dewey, *Democracy and Education* (New York: Free Press, 1966), p. 22.

and to come into living contact with a broader environment."[13]

Last, education is a major instrument in promoting the psychic and moral development of the individual. A person's happiness depends in large part on the extent, direction, and vigor of development of his or her physical, cognitive, emotional, aesthetic, and spiritual potentials. If the educational system has not spoken to these potentialities, it has failed utterly. Again quoting Dewey, "The criterion of the value of school education is the extent to which it creates a desire for continued growth and supplies the means for making the desire effective in fact. . . . The educational process has no end beyond itself; it is its own end. . . ."[14] The compatibility of these three functions—expanded reproduction, equalization, and self-development—derives from two basic assumptions underlying Dewey's version of liberal theory: first, that the positions that require staffing in capitalist society are best served by individuals who have achieved the highest possible levels of personal development; and second, that a free and universal school system can ensure that opportunities for self-development are rendered independent of one's race, ethnic origins, class background, and sex. The expanded reproduction and self-development functions of schooling are not only compatible, they are necessarily coextensional. Dewey himself is very clear on this: "If education is growth, it must progressively . . . make individuals better fitted to cope with later requirements. . . ."[15]

But why may this be so? Dewey gives us a first indication in his criticism of Rousseau, "who has marred his assertion that education must be a natural development and not something forced or grafted upon individuals from without, by the notion that social conditions are not natural."[16] Dewey then locates the "naturality" of democratic institutions in their reliance on democratic principle, which "repudiates the principle of external authority . . . in favor of voluntary disposition and interest," thus requiring a "liberation of powers" on the part of the individual:

---

[13] *Ibid.*, p. 20. The Classical liberal statement advancing the school as the agent of equality of opportunity is found in W. Lloyd Warner, Robert J. Havinghurst, and Martin B. Loeb, *Who Shall Be Educated?* (New York: Harper and Bros., 1944).

[14] *Ibid.*, pp. 50–53.

[15] *Ibid.*, p. 56.

[16] *Ibid.*, p. 60.

The devotion of democracy to education is a familiar fact. . . . A democracy . . . is primarily a mode of associated living. . . . The extension in space of the number of individuals who partici- ipate in an interest so that each has to refer his own action to that of others to give point and direction to his own, is equivalent to the breaking down of those barriers of class, race, and national territory which kept men from perceiving the full import of their activity. These more numerous and more varied points of contact denote a greater diversity of stimuli to which an individual has to respond. . . . They secure a liberation of powers which remain suppressed as long as the incitations to action are partial. . . .[17]

For Dewey, the essence of self-development is the acquisition of control over the personal activity; and in this process education plays a central role: "Education is that . . . reorganization of experience which adds to the meaning of experience, and which increases ability to direct the course of subsequent experience."[18] It follows as a matter of course in liberal theory that expanded reproduction and self-development are uniquely compatible with equality of opportunity in a democratic setting. In Dewey's words:

The intermingling in the school of youth of different races, differing religions, and unlike customs creates for all a new and broader environment. Common subject matter accustoms all to a unity of outlook upon a broader horizon than is visible to the members of any group while it is isolated. . . .

. . . A society which is mobile and full of channels for the distribution of a change occuring anywhere, must see to it that its members are educated to personal initiative and adaptability.[19]

Whereas Dewey argues the necessary association of expanded reproduction, equality of opportunity, and individual growth, a more modern liberal perspective argues only their mutual com- patibility. This conviction stems from characterizing productive enterprises as fundamentally technical systems, where job ade- quacy is essentially grounded in technical competence. The struc- ture of economy, according to this view, is basically a reflection of a hierarchically stratified order of cognitive and psycho-motor competencies. Indeed, in the words of a foremost sociologist proponent, Otis D. Duncan, "We suggest . . . that 'intelligence' is

[17] *Ibid.*, p. 87.
[18] *Ibid.*, p. 76.
[19] *Ibid.*, pp. 21, 88.

a socially defined quality and this social definition is not essentially different from that of achievement or status in the occupational sphere."[20] The more successful individuals, according to this view, are the more skillful and the more intelligent. Since cognitive and psycho-motor development are vital and healthy components of individual psychic development, and can be provided equally according to the "abilities" of the students upon their entering schools, the compatibility of functions of the educational system in capitalism becomes a scientific proposition.

The prevalence of this perspective can be gleaned from the policy-maker's reaction to the "rediscovery" of poverty and inequality in America during the decade of the 1960s. Inequality of opportunity for education and training was quickly isolated as the source of the problem. Moreover, in measuring the efficacy of the educational system, both of preschool enrichment and of the public school programs, measures of cognitive outcomes have provided the unique criteria of success.[21] Finally, the failure of educational policies to improve significantly the position of the poor and minority groups has, among a host of possible reappraisals of liberal theory, raised but one to preeminence: the nature-nurture controversy as to the determination of intelligence.[22]

This "technocratic" view of schooling, economic success, and the requisites of job functioning, supplies an elegant and logically coherent (if not empirically compelling) explanation of the rise of mass education in the process of industrial development. Because the Industrial Revolution, according to this view, entails the application of increasingly complex and cognitively demanding operational technologies, industrialization requires an increasing level of cognitive competence on the part of the labor force as a whole. Formal education, by extending what had been throughout human history the privilege of the few to the masses, opens the upper levels in the productive hierarchy to all with the ability and willingness to attain such competencies. Hence the observed statistical correlation between education and economic

[20] Otis Dudley Duncan, David L. Featherman, and Beverly Duncan, *Socioeconomic Background and Occupational Achievement: Extensions of a Basic Model*, Final Report, Project No. 5–0074 (EO–191), Contract No. OE–5–85–072 (Washington, D.C.: U.S. Department of Health, Education, and Welfare, Office of Education, Bureau of Research, 1968), p. 90.

[21] See Averch et al., "How Effective is Schooling?".

[22] See Samuel Bowles and Herbert Gintis, "IQ in the U.S. Class Structure," *Social Policy*, Vol. 3, Nos. 4–5 (January–February 1973), pp. 65–96.

status reflects the success of a fundamentally egalitarian school system in promoting and making widely available the opportunity for cognitive growth.

According to this view, the natural egalitarianism of schooling is complemented by the meritocratic orientation of industrial society. Since ascriptive differences are minimized in favor of actual achievement in the criteria for access to occupational roles, since ability is fairly well distributed across social classes, and since whatever differences based on social class exist in an individual's "natural" aspirations to social status are minimized by the competitive orientation of schooling, the increasing economic importance of schooling represents a potent instrument toward the efficient and equitable distribution of jobs, income, and status. If certain social class or other social inequalities remain at the end of this process, they must simply be attributed to inevitable human differences in intellectual capacities or to patterns of free choice based on class, racial, sexual, or other differences in motivational patterns.

Thus as long as schooling is free and universal, the process of economic expansion will not only be consistent with the use of education as an instrument for personal development and social equality; economic expansion, by requiring educational expansion, will necessarily enhance the power of education to achieve these ends.

Given the compatibility of various functions of education, a second group of questions concerning the limits of educational policy deals with the power of schooling to perform the three functions outlined above. Since the educational and state apparatuses are the central social corrective mechanisms, the issue of their potential efficacy is crucial to the establishment of the liberal outlook. Dewey does not withdraw from this issue: "The school environment . . . establishes a purified medium of action. . . . As a society becomes more enlightened, it realizes that it is responsible not to transmit and conserve the whole of its existing achievements, but only such which make for a better future society. The school is its *chief agency* for the accomplishment of this end" (emphasis added).[23]

But such generalizations cannot substitute for direct confrontation with the thorny and somewhat disreputable facts of industrial life. Self-development may be compatible with ideal work

[23] Dewey, *Democracy and Education*, p. 20.

roles, but can constructive education change the seamy realities of the work-a-day world? Equality may be compatible with the other functions of education but can the significant and pervasive system of racial, class, and sexual stratification be significantly modified by "equal schooling"?

Early liberals did not shy away from the dehumanizing conditions of work. Adam Smith himself notes: "In the progress of the division of labor, the employment of the far greater part of those who live by labor . . . comes to be confined to a few very simple operations. . . . But the understandings of the greater part of men are necessarily formed by their ordinary employments . . . [a man thus employed] generally becomes as stupid and ignorant as it is possible for a human creature to become." [24] But he did believe that the state could successfully counter the deleterious effects on individual development: "His dexterity in his own particular trade seems . . . to be acquired at the expense of his intellectual, social and martial virtues. But in every improved and civilized society this is the state into which the laboring poor . . . must necessarily fall, unless government takes some pains to prevent it." [25]

James Mill proclaimed even more positively the corrective power of education: "The minds . . . of the great body of the people are in danger of really degenerating, while the other elements of civilization are advancing, unless care is taken, by means of the other instruments of education, to counteract those effects which the simplifications of the manual processes has a tendency to produce." [26] But modern liberal commentary has been less sanguine, and has rather preferred to argue that proper education could improve the work environment directly by supplying experts with "well balanced social interests," to use Dewey's phrase.

> Much is said about scientific management of work. It is a narrow view which restricts the science which secures efficiency of operation to movements of the muscles. . . . The tendency to reduce such things as efficiency of activity and scientific management to purely technical externals is evidence of the one-sided stimulation of thought given to those in control of industry— those who supply its aims. Because of their lack of all-round and

---

[24] Adam Smith, *The Wealth of Nations* (New York: Modern Library, 1937), p. 734.

[25] *Ibid.*, p. 735.

[26] James Mill, "Education," *Encyclopedia Britannica*, 4th ed., 1924.

well balanced social interests, there is not sufficient stimulus for attention to the human factors in relationships in industry.[27]

This balance would be supplemented by the natural "desire and ability to share in social control" on the part of educated workers:

> a right educational use of [science] would react upon intelligence and interest so as to modify, in connection with legislation and administration, the socially obnoxious features of the present industrial and commercial order. . . . It would give those who engage in industrial callings desire and ability to share in social control, and ability to become masters of their industrial fate.[28]

This approach became a fundamental tenet of educational reformers in the Progressive era. Thus the power of the schools came to be seen in their ability to fuse the motivation and activities of work and play in the citizen:

> Psychologically, the defining characteristic of play is not amusement nor aimlessness. It is the fact that the aim is thought of as more activity in the same line, without defining continuity of action in reference to results produced. Activities as they grow more complicated gain added meaning by greater attention to specific results achieved. Thus they pass gradually into work. Both are equally free and intrinsically motivated, apart from false economic conditions which tend to make play into idle excitement for the well to do, and work into uncongenial labor for the poor. Work is psychologically simply an activity which consciously includes regards for consequences as a part of itself; it becomes constrained labor when the consequences are outside of the activity as an end to which activity is merely a means. Work which remains permeated with the play attitude is art—in quality if not in conventional designation.[29]

Education, according to Dewey, could promote the natural movement of industrial society from less to more fulfilling types of work, hence bringing the needs of expanded reproduction and self-development increasingly into a harmonious union.

To complete our exposition of liberal theory, it remains to describe its perspective on the power of the educational system to promote social equality. For Dewey, of course, this power derives from the necessary association of personal growth and

---

[27] Dewey, *Democracy and Education*, p. 85.
[28] *Ibid.*, p. 320.
[29] *Ibid.*, p. 206.

democracy—whose extension to all parts of the citizenry is a requisite of social development itself.

In the technocratic version of liberal theory, however, the egalitarian power of the educational system is contingent on proper social policy rather than a necessary by-product of the economic development process itself. This power derives in the first instance from the alleged central role of education in promoting cognitive development. Were economic success dependent on ascriptive criteria such as race or sex or upon deeply rooted differences in human character, the power of schooling to reduce the transmission of economic status from generation to generation would of course be minimal. But, according to the liberal-technocratic view, this is not the case. The primacy of schooling in generating cognitive skills and the putative importance of intellectual abilities in the allocation of high status or well-paid jobs renders social policy toward the equalization of educational access particularly potent. If simply equal access is not sufficient, then enlightened policy might devise special programs for the education of the poor: job training, compensatory education, and the like. Thus in an essay entitled "Investing in Poor People," T. W. Schultz, the father of the economics of education in the United States, writes: "Much of the remaining poverty in the U.S. is, I believe, a consequence of low earning capabilities which in turn is in large part a result of a lack of schooling. Thus interpreted, it represents past mistakes, ex-post malinvestment, underinvestment at the time the particular persons who are now twenty-five years of age and older attended school. Now look at the Negroes as a group in the same way. Their low earning capabilities . . . are in part to be viewed here as the result of historical malinvestment."[30] He concludes his case for expanded educational and training programs for the poor with the statement: "It is precisely in poor people in the United States where the best unexhausted opportunities to invest exist."[31]

Poverty and inequality, in this view, are characteristics of individuals and the product of past mistakes, not the normal outgrowths of a set of economic institutions. The problem, clearly, is to fix up the people, not to change the economic structures

---

[30] T. W. Schultz, "Capital Formation by Education," *Journal of Political Economics*, Vol. 68, No. 6 (December 1960), p. 573.

[31] *Ibid.*, p. 574.

which regulate their lives. This, indeed, is the meaning of the "social power" of schools toward equalization.

Despite persistent failures, the liberal faith in the equalizing power of schooling has dominated the intellectual scene and has provided the theoretical basis for state social policy. Education has been considered not only a powerful tool for self-development and social reproduction; it has been seen at least since Horace Mann coined the phrase well over a century ago as the "great equalizer." In the next section, we shall document the extent of these failures.

III. THE THEORY IN PRACTICE: ANOMALIES IN THE LIBERAL OUTLOOK

The record of actual successes and failures of public education is not sufficient either to accept or to reject the liberal outlook. However, it must be a point of departure in any sincere inquiry into its potential contribution to reform in an age of growing upheaval and social disintegration.

Considering first the objective of expanded reproduction, there can be little doubt that U.S. education has performed well its function of preparing future workers for effective performance in an expanding economy. Increased schooling has been identified as a major contributor to the economic growth of the United States. Edward Denison, in his path-breaking study, *The Sources of Economic Growth in the U.S.*, concluded: "The education that the U.S. labor force has received has increased at a rate that can only be described as phenomenal. . . . With such enormous advances it is not surprising to find that improved education has made a major contribution to economic growth. By my calculations, from 1927 to 1957 . . . education contributed 42 percent of the . . . growth rate in product per person employed."[32]

Turning to the other two objectives of schooling, the overall assessment of liberal reform is far from sanguine. First, despite the concerted efforts of progressive educators of three generations, and despite the assimilation of its doctrine by the National Education Association, schools by and large remain hostile to the

[32] Edward F. Denison, *Sources of Economic Growth in the U.S. and the Alternatives before Us* (New York: Supplementary Paper No. 13, Committee for Economic Development, 1962).

individual's needs of self-development. Education seems quite capable of preparing people for economic life—fulfilling its function of expanded reproduction—without producing the full Deweyian "person." Second, despite the universalization and quantitative extension of education, there is little indication that this movement has led to the reduction of class stratification and income inequality, or to an increase in social mobility. And in spite of vigorous efforts of reform, schooling remains a weak instrument in promoting "full participation" of racial minorities in the United States—indeed, even the expensive pilot projects in this direction seem to have failed rather spectacularly. We shall discuss each of these problems in turn.

The failure of schools to provide a liberating education owed not to the lack of effort of its progressive humanizers. "The problem of the twentieth century," wrote Frank Tracy Carleton in 1908, "is to make education an engine of social betterment. Hitherto educational progress has been conditioned by economic and social changes. Have we advanced far enough on the path of civilization to make it, in a measure, a directive agent?"[33] Evidently not. Sixteen years before Carleton wrote, Joseph Mayer Rice bemoaned the political and unprofessional control of the schools, of "political hacks hiring untrained teachers who blindly led their innocent charges in sing-song drill, rote repetition, and meaningless verbiage."[34] Sixty-two years and a vigorous reform movement later, Charles Silberman, an editor of *Fortune* magazine and author of a highly touted three-year Carnegie Foundation study of American education, is pained to find "the grim joyless places most American schools are, how oppressive and petty are the rules by which they are governed, how intellectually sterile and aesthetically barren the atmosphere, what an appalling lack of civility obtains on the part of teachers and principals, what contempt they unconsciously display for children as children."[35] Silberman goes on to criticize "the slavish adherence to the time-table and lesson-plan, the obsession with routine *qua* routine, the absence of noise and movement, the joylessness and

---

[33] Frank Tracy Carleton, *Education and Industrial Evolution* (New York, 1908), p. 17. Cited in Lawrence Cremin, *The Transformation of the School* (New York: Random House, 1964), p. 86.

[34] Cited in Cremin, *The Transformation of the School*, p. 5.

[35] Charles E. Silberman, *Crisis in the Classroom* (New York: Random House, 1970), p. 83.

repression, the universality of the formal lecture or teacher-dominated discussion."[36]

We doubt that the official professional teachers' reply to Rice, that "if the schools produced results, that was all that was asked of them,"[37] can be defended in terms of "realities" of learning theory. In 1897 Rice himself demonstrated statistically the poor showing of rote learning even in such a cut and dried area as spelling proficiency. The progressive schools of the first decades of the twentieth century, dramatically described in John and Evelyn Dewey's *Schools of Tomorrow*, certainly worked, as testified by extensive statistical testing of achievement outcomes in 1942.[38] And in 1970, Silberman could say with authority: "There is clear evidence that schools can be humane and free without in any way sacrificing intellectual development. . . . Secondary schools tend to be even more authoritarian and repressive than elementary schools; the values they transmit are the values of docility, passivity, conformity, and lack of trust. These unpleasant attributes might be tolerable if one could view them, so to speak, as the price to be paid for 'a good education'—and good, that is to say, in academic terms. Such is not the case."[39]

If not forced upon educators by the requirements of effective learning, can the structure of schooling be justified by the task of training a democratic citizenry? Hardly. Silberman merely echoes the voice of many, saying "The most important characteristic that nearly all schools share is a preoccupation with order and control . . . how can a group 'achieve enough maturity to keep itself under control' if its members never have an opportunity to exercise control? Far from helping students develop into mature, self-reliant, self-motivated individuals, schools seem to do everything they can to keep youngsters in a state of chronic, almost infantile, dependency."[40]

Silberman, like most liberal critics of modern education, tends to attribute the oppressiveness of schooling to simple oversight and irrationality: "What is mostly wrong with public schools is not due to venality or indifference or stupidity but to mindlessness . . . it simply never occurs to more than a handful, to ask why

---

36 *Ibid.*, p. 83.
37 Cited in Cremin, *The Transformation of the School*, p. 7.
38 *Ibid.*, pp. 251–57.
39 Silberman, *Crisis in the Classroom*, p. 323.
40 *Ibid.*, p. 103.

they are doing what they are doing, to think seriously or deeply about the purposes or consequences of education."[41] Yet, as we will show, the history of the progressive education movement attests to the intransigence of the educational system to "enlightened change" within the context of corporate capitalism.

Progressivism as the keynote of modern educational theory embraced such pillars of intellect and influence as John Dewey, Charles W. Eliot, Alfred North Whitehead, William James, and G. Stanley Hall. The birth of the Association for the Advancement of Progressive Education in 1918 was merely the political codification of an already active social movement whose aim, in the words of its founder Stanwood Cobb, "had little of modesty . . . we aimed at nothing short of changing the entire school system of America."[42] Subscribing to Dewey's dictum that "education is the fundamental method of social reform," the statement of principles of the Association for the Advancement of Progressive Education held its aim to be "the freest and fullest development of the individual, based upon the scientific study of his mental, physical, spiritual, and social characteristics and needs."[43] However "vanguard" today's liberal educationists feel themselves to be, they envision little more than did the Progressives in the dawning years of the century. Schooling was to provide the child with the freedom to develop "naturally" with a teacher as guide not taskmaster. Intrinsic interest, not external authority, was to motivate all work. The leitmotif of the day was "taking the lid off kids," and the aim was to sublimate natural creative drives in fruitful directions rather than to repress them. Emotional and intellectual development were to hold equal importance, and activity was to be "real-life" and "student-directed."

The mass media dramatically attest to the ideological victory of the progressives: professional journals, education textbooks, and even the various publications of the Office of Education mouthed the rhetoric of Progressivism. As Lawrence A. Cremin, the foremost historian of the Progressive Movement in education, notes:

> There is a "conventional wisdom" . . . in education . . . and by the end of World War II progressivism had come to be that conventional wisdom. Discussions of educational policy were

[41] *Ibid.*, ch. 2.
[42] Quoted in Cremin, *The Transformation of the School*, p. 241.
[43] Quoted in *ibid.*, p. 240–41.

liberally spiced with phrases like "recognized individual differences," "personality development," "the whole child," "the needs of learners," "intrinsic motivation," "persistent life situations," "bridging the gap between home and school," "teaching children, not subjects," "teacher-pupil relationships," and "staff planning." Such phrases were a cant, to be sure, the particular jargon of the pedagogs. But they were more than that for they signified that Dewey's forecast of the day when progressive education would eventually be accepted as good education had now finally come to pass.[44]

Yet the schools have changed little in substance.

Thus we must reject mindlessness along with venality, indifference, and stupidity as the source of oppressive education. The fact that repressive and authoritarian education persists does not seem to impair the reproduction function of the educational system, and hence represents a glaring anomaly for the liberal outlook.

The record of education as a promoter of social equality is no more encouraging than its performance as an instrument for individual self-development. Our free and public system of education has never been particularly egalitarian in its actual operation; it appears to be no more equal now than it was a generation ago. Moreover, current research strongly suggests that even in those cases where education has been used as an equalizing instrument, its role in promoting economic and social equality is meager at best. Let us look at the evidence.

Because of the relative ease of measurement, inequalities in years of schooling are particularly evident. If we define social class standing by the income, occupation, and educational level of the parents, a child from the 90th percentile in the class distribution may expect on the average to achieve over four and a half more years of schooling than a child from the 10th percentile.[45] As can be seen in Table 1, the number of years of schooling attained by an individual is strongly associated with parental socioeconomic status. This table presents the estimated distribution of years of schooling attained by individuals of varying socioeconomic backgrounds. The data in the table indicate, to take an extreme example, that an individual in the highest socioeconomic

[44] *Ibid.*, p. 328.
[45] See Samuel Bowles, "The Integration of Higher Education into the Wage Labor System," *Review of Radical Political Economics*, Vol. 4, No. 2 (Spring 1974).

Table 1. Estimated Probability of Attainment of Different Levels of Education for Individuals of Different Socioeconomic Background

	Socioeconomic Background (deciles)									
X \ Y	10	9	8	7	6	5	4	3	2	1
10	39.7	23.0	14.5	9.4	6.0	3.7	2.1	1.1	0.4	0.1
9	21.3	20.4	16.7	13.3	10.2	7.5	5.2	3.3	1.7	0.4
8	13.3	16.6	15.9	14.3	12.2	10.0	7.8	5.5	3.3	1.1
7	8.6	13.1	14.2	14.1	13.2	11.8	10.0	7.8	5.2	2.0
6	5.5	10.1	12.2	13.2	13.4	12.9	11.8	10.0	7.5	3.5
5	3.5	7.5	10.0	11.8	12.9	13.4	13.2	12.2	10.1	5.5
4	2.0	5.2	7.8	10.0	11.8	13.2	14.1	14.2	13.1	8.6
3	1.1	3.3	5.5	7.8	10.0	12.2	14.3	15.9	16.6	13.3
2	0.4	1.7	3.3	5.2	7.5	10.2	13.3	16.7	20.4	21.3
1	0.1	0.4	1.1	2.1	3.7	6.0	9.4	14.5	23.0	39.7

Years of Schooling (deciles) (left axis, Y)

Data refer to "non-Negro" males from "non-farm" backgrounds aged 35–44, reported in full in Bowles and Nelson, "The Genetic Inheritance of IQ and the Intergenerational Reproduction of Economic Inequality" (1973). The data presented here are calculated from a simple correlation between years of schooling and a composite index of parental background (father's occupation, father's educational level, parents' income). Taking account of errors in reporting data, this correlation is estimated as .66.

decile has 397 times the probability (39.7 percent) of ending up in the highest education decile as does an individual from the lowest socioeconomic decile (0.1 percent).[46] Table 2 draws attention to one aspect of qualities: the relationship between family income and college attendance. Even among those who had graduated from high school, children of families earning less than $3,000 per year were over six times as likely *not* to attend college as were the childern of families earning over $15,000.[47]

Not surprisingly, the results of schooling differ greatly for children of different social classes. Most easily measured but probably of limited importance are differences in scholastic achievement. If we measure the output of schooling by scores on nationally stan-

[46] The correlation for the 35–44 year age group on which table 1 is based is .66. Analogous correlations for age groups 25–34, 45–54, and 55–64, are respectively, .64, .67, .63. Thus choosing a different age group will not appreciably alter the degree of inequality indicated by the table.

[47] For recent evidence on these points see U.S. Bureau of the Census, *Current Population Reports*, Series P–20, Nos. 183 and 185 (1969). Also, J. Karabel, "Community Colleges and Social Stratification," *Harvard Educational Review*, Vol. 42, No. 4 (November 1972), pp. 521–62.

Table 2. College Attendance in 1967 among High School Graduates, by Family Income[a]

Family Income[b]	Percentage who did not attend college
under $3,000	80.2
$3,000 to $3,999	67.7
$4,000 to $5,999	63.7
$6,000 to $7,499	58.9
$7,500 to $9,999	49.0
$10,000 to $14,999	38.7
$15,000 and over	13.3

[a] Refers to individuals who were high school seniors in October 1965 and who subsequently graduated from high school. Based on U.S. Department of Commerce, Bureau of the Census, *Current Population Report*, Series P–20, No. 185 (July 11, 1969), p. 6. College attendance refers to both two- and four-year institutions.

[b] Family income for 12 months preceding October 1965.

dardized achievement tests, children whose parents were themselves highly educated outperform the children of parents with less education by a wide margin. Data collected for the Coleman report reveal, for example, that among white high school seniors, those whose parents were in the top education decile were on the average well over three grade levels ahead of those whose parents were in the bottom decile.[48]

Given the great social class differences in scholastic achievement, class inequalities in years of educational attainment are to be expected. Thus one might be tempted to argue that the data in Table 1 are simply a reflection of unequal intellectual abilities, or that the data in Table 2 are the consequence of differing levels of scholastic achievement in high school and do not reflect any additional social class inequalities peculiar to the process of college admission.

This view, so comforting to the admissions personnel in our elite universities, is unsupported by the data, some of which is presented in Tables 3 and 4. Table 3 indicates that even among children with identical IQ test scores at age 6 to 8, those with rich, well-educated, high-status parents could expect a much

[48] These calculations are based on Coleman et al., *Equality of Educational Opportunity*, and Samuel Bowles and Valerie Nelson, "The Genetic Inheritance of IQ and the Intergenerational Reproduction of Economic Inequality," unpublished MS., Harvard University, May, 1973.

Table 3. Estimated Probability of Attainment of Different Levels of Education for Individuals with Similar Childhood IQ but Different Socioeconomic Background[a]

Years of Schooling (deciles)	Socioeconomic Background (deciles)									
X / Y	10	9	8	7	6	5	4	3	2	1
10	30.9	19.8	14.4	10.9	8.2	6.1	4.4	3.0	1.7	0.6
9	19.2	16.9	14.5	12.4	10.5	8.7	7.0	5.4	3.6	1.7
8	13.8	14.5	13.7	12.6	11.4	10.1	8.7	7.1	5.3	2.8
7	10.3	12.4	12.6	12.3	11.7	11.0	10.0	8.7	7.0	4.1
6	7.7	10.4	11.4	11.7	11.8	11.5	11.0	10.1	8.7	5.7
5	5.7	8.7	10.1	11.0	11.5	11.8	11.7	11.4	10.4	7.7
4	4.1	7.0	8.7	10.0	11.0	11.7	12.3	12.6	12.4	10.3
3	2.8	5.3	7.1	8.7	10.1	11.4	12.6	13.7	14.5	13.8
2	1.7	3.6	5.4	7.0	8.7	10.5	12.4	14.5	16.9	19.2
1	0.6	1.7	3.0	4.4	6.1	8.2	10.9	14.4	19.8	30.9

[a] See notes to Table 1.

These data are calculated from the estimated standardized regression (β) coefficient of socioeconomic background in an equation using this variable as well as IQ measured at age 6–8 as independent variables. For this table $\beta=.56$. See Bowles and Nelson, "The Genetic Inheritance of IQ and the Intergenerational Reproduction of Economic Inequality."

higher level of schooling than those from less-favored origins. Table 4 shows that access to a college education is highly unequal, even for children of the same measured "academic ability."

The social class inequalities in our school system and the role they play in the reproduction of the social division of labor are too evident to be denied. Defenders of the educational system are forced back on the assertion that things are getting better; the inequalities of the past were far worse. And, indeed, there can be no doubt that some of the inequalities of the past have been mitigated. Yet new inequalities have apparently developed to take their place, for the available historical evidence lends little support to the idea that our schools are on the road to equality of educational opportunity. For example, data from a recent U.S. Census survey reported in Table 5 indicate that graduation from college has become no less dependent on one's class background. This is true despite the fact that the probability of high school graduation is becoming increasingly equal across social classes. Additional

Table 4. Probability of College Entry for a Male Who Has Reached Grade 11

		Socioeconomic quartiles[a]			
		Low			High
		1	2	3	4
	Low 1	.06	.12	.13	.26
	2	.13	.15	.29	.36
Ability					
quartiles	3.	.25	.34	.45	.65
	High 4	.48	.70	.73	.87

[a] The socioeconomic index is a composite measure including family income, father's occupation and education, mother's education, etc. The ability scale is a composite of tests measuring general academic aptitude.

Based on a large sample of U.S. high school students as reported in John C. Flannagan and William W. Cooley, *Project TALENT, One-Year Follow-Up Studies,* Cooperative Research Project No. 2333 (Pittsburgh: School of Education, University of Pittsburgh, 1966).

ble 5. Among Sons Who Had Reached High School, Percentage Who Graduated from College, by Son's Age and Father's Level of Education

			FATHER'S EDUCATION					
	Likely dates of		Some high school		High school graduate		Some college or more	
on's age n 1962	college graduation[a]	<8 years	Percentage graduating	Ratio to <8	Percentage graduating	Ratio to <8	Percentage graduating	Ratio to <8
25–34	1950–59	07.6	17.4	2.29	25.6	3.37	51.9	6.83
35–44	1940–49	08.6	11.9	1.38	25.3	2.94	53.9	6.27
45–54	1930–39	07.7	09.8	1.27	15.1	1.96	36.9	4.79
55–64	1920–29	08.9	09.8	1.10	19.2	2.16	29.8	3.35

[a] Assuming college graduation at age 22.
Based on U.S. Census data as reported in William G. Spady, "Educational Mobility and ccess: Growth and Paradoxes," *American Journal of Sociology,* Vol. 73, No. 3 (November 67).

data confirm this impression. The strength of the statistical association (the coefficient of correlation) between parents' social status and the years of education attained by the children for people now 55–64 years old is virtually identical to the analogous correlation for individuals who terminated their schooling in recent years.[49] On balance, the available data suggest that the number of years of schooling attained by a child depends upon the social class standing of the parents as much in the recent period as it did fifty years ago.

Thus we have empirical reasons for doubting the egalitarian impact of schooling as the educational system expands to meet the continuing needs of economic growth. But what of those cases when education *has* been equalized? What has been the impact? We will investigate effects of three such cases: the historical decline in the inequality among individuals in years of schooling attained, the narrowing of the black/white gap in average years of schooling attained, and the explicitly compensatory educational programs of the war on poverty.

Though one's parents' social class has lost none of its influence on how far one gets up the educational ladder, the historical rise in the minimum legal school-leaving age has narrowed the distance between the top and bottom rungs. Measured by years of schooling, the dispersion of educational attainments has fallen steadily and substantially over the past three decades from 3.7 years in 1949 to 3.0 years in 1970. And had this led to a parallel equalization in the distribution of income? Jacob Mincer and Barry Chiswick of the National Bureau of Economic Research in a study of the determinants of inequality in the United States concluded that the 20 percent reduction in the standard deviation of years of schooling among white male adults would have had the effect—if operating in isolation—of reducing the standard deviation of the logarithm of income (a measure of income inequality) by a mere 2 percent.[50] And, of course, education was not operating in isolation. Aside from cyclical variations, there is no evidence that the U.S. income distribution has been equalized at all over this period. In fact, a 1972 Labor Department study indicates that as far as labor earnings (wages and salaries) are concerned, the trend has been unmistakably away from equality: and it is precisely inequalities in labor earnings which is the target of the proponents of egalitarian school reforms.[51]

[49] See Peter Blau and O. D. Duncan, *The American Occupational Structure* (New York: John Wiley, 1967).

[50] Barry Chiswick and Jacob Mincer, "Time-Series Changes in Personal Income Inequality in the U.S. from 1939, with Projections to 1985," *Journal of Political Economy*, Vol. 80, No. 3, Part II (May/June, 1972), pp. 34–66.

[51] See Peter Henle, "Exploring the Distribution of Earned Income," *Monthly Labor Review*, Vol. 95, No. 12 (December 1972). Inequalities in

The reduction in the black educational deficit—still measured in years of schooling—has been even more dramatic than the decline in the dispersion in educational attainments among the entire population. The difference between black and white males' median years of schooling fell dramatically between the late 1940s and the late 1960s.[52] And what has happened to the incomes of blacks relative to whites, or to their relative occupational disadvantage? Virtually nothing, again abstracting from cyclical variations.[53]

Last, consider that group of explicitly egalitarian educational programs brought together in the War on Poverty. In the most systematic economic survey of these programs, Thomas Ribich concludes that with very few exceptions the economic payoff to compensatory education is low.[54] The economic impact was so low, in fact, that in a majority of cases studied, direct transfers of income to the poor would have accomplished considerably more equalization than the educational programs in question.

But the liberal perspective on education cannot be rejected simply because it has not worked. Indeed, despite the above evidence that more equal schooling does not in fact equalize incomes, it is often argued that this theory still remains to be put to the test. The expanded reproduction, self-development, and equalization functions of the educational system may be quite compatible, yet the latter two may not have been strongly implemented. Schools may have significant reformist power within the framework of market capitalism, yet this power may lie dormant, or even may be turned against liberal aims.

Indeed, this argument is often used by those adhering to the liberal perspective. Thus Raymond E. Callahan traces the failure of Progressivism in education to the burgeoning of bureaucratization and efficiency orientation in educational practice at the same time progressive education was capturing hearts and minds

---

income (profit, rent, interest, and transfer payments plus labor earnings) may also have increased if the unmeasured income from capital gains and other tax dodges for the rich are taken into account.

[52] U.S. Department of Labor, Bureau of Labor Statistics, Report No. 375, *The Economic and Social Status of Negroes in the U.S., 1969* (Washington, D. C., 1969).

[53] Richard C. Edwards, Michael Reich, and Thomas Weisskopf, *The Capitalist System* (Englewood Cliffs, N.J.: Prentice Hall, 1972).

[54] Thomas Ribich, *Poverty and Education* (Washington, D.C.: Brookings Institute, 1968).

in educational theory. Callahan argues that "very much of what has happened in American education since 1900 can be explained on the basis of the extreme vulnerability of our schoolmen to public criticism and pressure and that this vulnerability is built into our pattern of local support and control . . . so long as schoolmen have a knife poised at their financial jugular vein each year, professional autonomy is impossible."[55] The direction the formal educational system took in this situation was dictated by the power of business interests and the triumphant ideology of "efficient management." Again Callahan: "What was unexpected [in my investigation] was the extent not only of the power of the business-industrial groups, but of the strength of the business ideology. . . . I had expected more professional autonomy and I was completely unprepared for the extent and degree of capitulation by administrators to whatever demands were made upon them."[56] This vulnerability had great implications for student, teacher, and administrator alike. "Business methods" in schools meant that administrators were to be recruited from the ranks of politicians and especially businessmen, rather than professional educators, and their orientation was toward cost-saving and control rather than quality of education. Business methods also meant that the teacher was to be reduced to the status of a simple worker, with little control over curriculum, activities, or discipline, and whose accountability to the administrator again ran toward her classroom authority rather than the quality of classroom experience. Last, the student was reduced to an "object" of administration, "busy-work" and standardized tests coming to prevail over play and self-development.

Cohen and Lazerson have aptly summed up this period of educational history:

> In our view this history has to be understood in the framework of the schools' adaptation to large scale corporate capitalism and the conflicts this engendered. Infusing the schools with corporate values and reorganizing them in ways seen as consistent with this new economic order has been the dominant motif. Education has been closely tied to production—schooling has been justified as a way of increasing wealth, of improving industrial output and making management more effective. . . .

[55] Raymond E. Callahan, *Education and the Cult of Efficiency* (Chicago: University of Chicago Press, 1962), preface.
[56] *Ibid.*

As a result, the schools' culture became closely identified with the ethos of the corporate work place. Schooling came to be seen as work or the preparation for work; schools were pictured as factories, educators as industrial managers and students as the raw materials to be inducted into the production process.[57]

In short, the history of twentieth-century education is the history not of Progressivism but of the imposition upon the schools of "business values" and a stratified structure of social relationships which mirrored the hierarchical division of labor in the burgeoning capitalist corporation. The evolution of U.S. education during this period was guided not so much by the sanguine statements of John Dewey and Jane Addams, who saw a reformed educational system eliminating the more brutal and alienating aspects in industrial labor, as by the "time-motion" orientation of Fredrick Taylor and "Scientific Management," with its attendant fragmentation of tasks and imposition of bureaucratic and hierarchical organizational forms.

Thus there is some ground for the opinion that the modern liberal view of the egalitarian and self-developmental capacities of schooling has not been refuted by recent experience in the United States; rather, it has never been tried. A historian of progressivism in U.S. education might well echo Gandhi's assessment of Western civilizaton: "It would be a good idea."

IV. PREFACE TO A CRITIQUE OF LIBERAL EDUCATION THEORY:
THE HIERARCHICAL DIVISION OF LABOR

Decades of false predictions cast strong doubt on modern liberal educational theory. But the anomalies which arise when theory and practice are juxtaposed cannot lay it finally to rest. As Thomas Kuhn has noted, even in the physical sciences only a recognizably superior alternative seals the fate of faulty but generally accepted dogma.[58]

All the more true is this observation in the social sciences. In the case of liberal educational theory, the anomalies we have presented are by no means decisive. Thus the necessary connection among reproduction, self-development, and egalitarian functions

---

[57] David K. Cohen, and Marvin Lazerson, "Education and the Corporate Order," *Socialist Revolution*, March, 1972, p. 13.
[58] Thomas Kuhn, *The Structure of Scientific Revolutions* (Chicago: University of Chicago Press, 1962), p. 53.

of education may appear only in the long run. Capitalism is indeed still young, and does seem to promote a rhetoric of tolerance and egalitarianism, as well as a supreme emphasis on individual freedom and human development. That this rhetoric is consistently thwarted in practice may simply represent a perverse institutional inertia. Similarly, the technocratic school may claim that while educational policy has failed in the past, maturity and increased expertise many render it vastly more potent in the future. No one ever claimed reform to be easy only ultimately possible with proper dedication. Finally, there may be ultimate limits—technologically determined—to the degree of social mobility, due to inherent differences in mental ability. The possibility has been asserted forcefully by such writers as Arthur Jensen and Richard Herrnstein.

In short, decent respect for liberal theory demands it be judged on theoretical grounds as well as in terms of the social outcomes it predicts, and preferably with an alternative in mind. This is the goal of the remaining sections of our paper. Our argument may be summarized simply enough: the failure of progressive educational reforms stems from the contradictory nature of the objectives of expanded reproduction, equality of opportunity, and self-development in a society whose economic life is governed by the institutions of corporate capitalism.

We first argue that a correct understanding of the relation between school and society begins with the social relations of production—the rules of authority governing the workplace and the laws of property governing the distribution of the product. In capitalist society these social relations appear in the form of the hierarchical division of labor and capitalist appropriation of a portion of the product in the form of profit, interest, or rent. It is these social relations of production into which youth enter upon assuming adulthood, and for which schooling is a preparation.

Second, we argue that in capitalist society the social relations of production lead to alienated work-activities—alienated in the sense that the criteria according to which work is determined do not take account of the needs of the worker. The worker is alienated from—divorced from control over—both the process of production and its product.[59]

---

[59] In part Dewey recognized this alienation as a significant problem for modern society (see for example *Democracy and Education*). However, even though he called for workers to have a "share in social control," he was quite

Third, we argue that an individual's ability to secure a certain position in the hierarchical division of labor depends upon five essential types of personal attributes: (1) adequate cognitive and psycho-motor skills; (2) productive affective personality traits (motivation, orientation to authority, diligence); (3) proper self-presentation for the associated status level (manners of speech and dress, acceptable class identifications and demeanor); (4) ascriptive traits, consonant with the power and status of the job, which govern social mores (race, sex, age); and (5) credentials (educational level, seniority) appropriate to the job. These personal attributes, which differ according to level in the hierarchy, not only enhance the efficiency of the organization, but, what is equally important, serve to legitimize the authority relations of the enterprise.

Fourth, we argue that the family and the educational system are the major forces in the generation, stabilization, and selection of these traits. Indeed, we propose a pair of "Correspondence Principles" whereby the social relations of family life and education—the social relation of reproduction—exhibit strong similarities of form and content with the social relation of production. The correspondence between the social relations of family life and production derives from the fact that experiences, authority relations, and interpersonal relations characteristic of a level in the hierarchy of production have an important bearing on the individual's attitudes, values, and behavior at home. The correspondence between the social relations of schooling and production derives from the fact that schools have evolved historically to produce a labor force consistent with the continuing accumulation of capital and the concomitant extension of the wage labor system. Changes in the structure of schools have corresponded to changes in the social relation of production.

This view of the educational system will guide our critique of liberal educational theory, both of the "democratic" and "technocratic" varieties. We shall argue that Dewey's error lies in characterizing the social system as democratic, whereas in fact the hierarchical division of labor is profoundly totalitarian. Moreover, his central thesis as to the "naturality" and intrinsic growth-

---

vague about the actual mechanism for achieving this. More important, however, is his belief that education, rather than being molded by this alienation, could actually correct it.

orientation of education is untrue under capitalism whether it be laissez-faire or that of the corporate liberal. Dewey's view requires that "work" be seen as a natural extension of "play," whereas alienated work in the corporate capitalist economy is the negation of all intrinsically motivated activity—including play. The major error in the "technocratic" school is its overemphasis on the first (cognitive and psycho-motor skills) among the requirements for job adequacy. We shall show that cognitive requirements are least crucial in all respects, and indeed, can account for little of the association of education and economic success. Had the "technocratic" school looked at the social rather than the technical relations of production, it might have been more circumspect in asserting the compatibility of expanded reproduction, individual development, and equality of opportunity functions of schooling.

We will go much further, and assert that the way in which the school system performs its expanded reproduction function—through its production of a labor force for the capitalist enterprise—is inconsistent with its performance of either the self-development or the equality of opportunity function. Under corporate capitalism, the correspondence between the social relation of production and the social relation of reproduction—the essential mechanism of the expanded reproduction function of schooling—precludes an egalitarian humane education under corporate capitalism.

The failures of the school system to serve individual needs for personal self-development and its poor showing as a promoter of equality of opportunity are thus not the result of errors in practice but rather flow directly from a fundamental theoretical error, namely the contradictory nature of the objectives of liberal educational reform.

Both the democratic and technocratic versions of liberal educational theory focus on the relations into which individuals enter upon adulthood. In the case of Dewey's democratic version, the social relations of political life are singled out as central, while for the technocratic version, the technical relations of production hold the honored position. Both have been blind to—or at least treated in quite unrealistic manner—the social relations of capitalist production.

In corporate capitalist society, the social relations of production conform by and large to the "hierarchical division of labor," characterized by power and control emanating from the top downward through a finely graduated bureaucratic order.[60] The social relations of the typically bureaucratic corporate enterprise require special attention because they are neither democratic nor technical.

For Dewey, democracy is, in essence, a "mode of conjoint communicative experience" which "repudiates the principle of external authority . . . in favor of voluntary disposition and interest."

In this sense, the dominant forms of work for which the educational system prepares youth are profoundly antidemocratic. Under capitalism, work is characterized not by "conjoint" but by hierarchical "communicative experience" and codified patterns of dominance and subordinacy, where personal interaction is dictated primarily by rules of procedure set by employers. By and large, the "voluntary disposition" of the worker extends only over the decision to sell his or her labor, upon which his or her work activities are indeed subject to "external authority."[61]

Dewey is aware, of course, of the undemocratic control of production in capitalist society; indeed he refers explicitly to "those in control of industry—those who supply its aims" (see quotation on p. 102). But he avoids the fatal consequence of this admission for his theory by suggesting that the brutal nature of work—in Dewey's time, exemplified by Taylorism and time-motion studies, and today by the "human relations" school of organizational theory—is attributed to their "one-sided stimulation of thought" rather than to structural features of capitalistic production. Thus he is led to believe that these severe problems are matters of personnel and conceptual error subject to correction by liberal educational exposure (see p. 103). Here Dewey exhibits in raw form the liberal proclivity to locate the source of systemic failures in the shortcomings of individuals and to propose

[60] For a more complete discussion see Richard C. Edwards, "Alienation and Inequality: Capitalist Relations of Production in a Bureaucratic Enterprise," Ph.D. thesis, Harvard University, July, 1972. Also, Andre Gorz, "Capitalist Relations of Production and the Socially Necessary Labor Force," in Arthur Lothstein, ed., *All We Are Saying* . . . (New York: G. P. Putnam's Sons, 1970).

[61] See Herbert Gintis, "Counter Culture and Political Activism," *Telos*, No. 12 (Summer 1972) for a more complete discussion of this point.

"expert" solutions which respect—even reinforce—the top-down control of social life under corporate capitalism.[62] Surely he could not have been unaware of the forces in a market-oriented economy pressing managerial decision continually toward profit-maximization to which end secure hierarchical authority and flexible control of the enterprise from the top are prime requisites.[63]

Similarly, the technocratic version of liberal educational theory suffers from an extremely partial characterization of the capitalist system. Seen from the present, the Industrial Revolution may appear as a simple up-gearing of the pace of technological change. From the point of view of those experiencing it, however, it constituted a thoroughgoing social upheaval which involved a radically different pattern of social interactions with demanding and pervasive requirements on the level of individual psychic functioning. Values, beliefs, modes of personal functioning, and patterns of social and economic loyalties were formed, transformed, and reproduced in the process of bringing the individual into line with the need of the capitalist class to accumulate capital and extend the wage labor system.

Thus the modern economy is a product of a social as well as a technical revolution. In the development of productive organization from precapitalist forms, through the relatively simple entrepreneur-worker dichotomy of the early factory system based on piece work, immediate supervision, and direct evaluation of job adequacy, to the modern complex, stratified and bureaucratically ordered corporation or governmental organ, the social and affective requirements of the job in addition to the purely technical demands of work have changed drastically.

V. REPRODUCTION AND SELF-DEVELOPMENT: THE EMPLOYABILITY CRITERIA

To understand the actual reproduction role of schooling, then, we must grasp the essential individual requisites for holding positions in the hierarchical division of labor, and exhibit how these are affected in the educational process. We shall now turn to the first of these tasks.

[62] See Karier, "Testing for Order and Control in the Corporate Liberal State." Also, Walter Feinberg, "Progressive Education and Social Planning," *Teachers' College Record*, Vol. 73, No. 2 (May, 1972).

[63] See Gintis, "Counter Culture and Political Activism."

The prima facie dimensions of job-relevant individual attributes are vast indeed. They include (at least) such features as ownership of physical implements (e.g., ownership by the medieval knight of his horse, armor, and retinue), membership (e.g., the feudal guild master), ascription (sex, race, social class, age, caste, religion), and personal attributes (skills, motivation, attitudes, personality, credentials). In capitalist society it is the last of these, along with a few important ascriptive traits—sex, race, and age—that come to the fore. Indeed even the relationship between social class background and economic success operates in large measure through differences in personal characteristics associated with differential family status. Employers never ask about social background.[64]

Thus our inquiry into the stratification process must focus on the supply, demand, and production of those personal attributes and ascriptive traits that are relevant to getting ahead in the world of work. We may begin with the demand for personal attributes by employers. While employers may have certain restrictions in their hiring practices (child labor and antidiscrimination laws, union regulations, social pressures), by and large their sole objective in hiring is to insure the ability of individuals to perform adequately in the work role in question. The requirements of job adequacy in any job, of course, depend on the entire structure of work roles, that is, on the social relations of production within the enterprise. Thus we must first inquire into the criteria by which work is organized. What determines the structure of work roles—in capitalist society characterized by hierarchy, job fragmentation, bureaucracy, and control from the top of the organization?

One objective of capitalists—both as a class and as individuals—is to perpetuate their class standing. Thus work roles must be organized so as to reproduce the position of capitalists and allied high-level management in the social relations of production. A closely related second objective is securing adequate long-term profits, without which the enterprise would cease to exist Thus profits are sought both as an instrument in maintaining the class

[64] Warner et al., in their extensive studies of stratification, place much emphasis on social class ascription. See Warner et al., *Who Shall Be Educated?* Compare Warner with Paul Lunt, *The Social Life of a Modern Community* (New Haven: Yale University Press, 1941). But this seems characteristic only of the "small town" economic community, rapidly becoming past history.

status of directors of the firm and as their major source of income.[65]

In the joint pursuit of profits and the perpetuation of their class standing, the directors of an enterprise seek to meet three immediate objectives—sometimes complementary, sometimes in conflict: technical efficiency, control, and legitimacy. Technical efficiency requires that the structure of work roles be organized so that for a given set of inputs—labor, raw materials, equipment, etc.—the maximum possible output will be produced. The second objective, control over the production process, requires both the retention of decision-making power at the top and the maintenance of labor costs in line with those prevailing in the economy as a whole. Both forms of control are highly problematic. First, as we have emphasized, the political organization of the enterprise is totalitarian, while the external political process is formally democratic. Where possible, workers demand control over decision making about working conditions toward improvement of their condition. Organizing production hierarchically and fragmenting tasks, by dividing workers on different levels against one another and reducing the independent range of control of each, both weaken the solidarity (and hence limit the group power) of workers and serve to convince them, through their day-to-day activities, of their personal incapacity to control—and even of its technical infeasibility. Thus hiring criteria and the structuring of work roles are based on the principle of "divide and conquer."[66] That the satisfaction of this control objective often conflicts with technical efficiency is illustrated by the many studies documenting significant increases in productivity and worker satisfaction associated with shifts toward worker participation in decision making, greater job breadth, and the use of work teams.[67] But efficiency and profitability are, of course, different things.

[65] Indeed under conditions of perfect competition the maximization of profits is a necessary condition for the reproduction of the capitalists' class position. We need not here enter into the complicated debate on whether firms do indeed seek to maximize profits. For a survey see Edwards, "Alienation and Inequality." We conclude that the relevant behavioral implication of the theories that posit other objectives (sales or employment maximization, for example) are, in the context of the by and large competitive milieu of the U.S. economy, virtually indistinguishable from those of profit maximization.

[66] Stephen Marglin, "What Do Bosses Do?," unpublished MS, Harvard University, 1973.

[67] For reviews of the evidence see Paul Blumberg, *Industrial Democracy* (New York: Schocken Books, 1969); Victor H. Vroom, "Industrial Social

A third objective is that work roles be organized so as to legitimize the authority relations in the firm. That is, relations among superiors, subordinates, and peers must not violate the norms of the larger society, and the right of the superior to direct as well as the duty of the subordinate to submit must draw on general cultural values. It is for this reason that a superior must always have a higher salary than a subordinate, whatever the conditions of relative supply of the two types of labor. It is also for this reason that in a racist and sexist society blacks and women will not in general be placed above whites or men in the line of hierarchical authority. Employers ordinarily structure work roles so that young people will not boss older people. In terms of personal attributes, modes of self-presentation are also important; however well they actually function technically, individuals must seem fit for their position and must actively protect their prerogatives and the structure of work roles (especially their own).[68] Educational credentials enter here as well: it is desirable to associate hierarchical authority with level of education, not only because higher levels of schooling may enable an employee to better do the work at hand or because the more educated seem more fit by their demeanor to hold authority, but also simply because educational achievement, as symbolized by one sort of sheepskin or another, legitimizes authority according to prevailing social values.

From this analysis of the capitalist objectives governing the organization of work roles in the enterprise, we may derive some insight into the employers' demand for particular worker attributes. Our analysis suggests five important sets of worker characteristics. First, we have noted the emphasis of the "technocratic perspective" on cognitive attributes—such as scholastic achievement—to which we may add concrete technical and operational skills (e.g., knowing how to do typing, accounting, chemical engineering, or carpentry). Second, there are, parallel to cognitive attributes, a set of personality traits (such as motivation, perseverance, docility, dominance, flexibility, or tact) that enable the

---

Psychology," in G. Lindsey and E. Aaronsen, eds., *The Handbook of Social Psychology* (Reading, Mass.: Addison-Wesley, 1969); Gintis, "Counter Culture and Political Activism"; and Gorz, "Capitalist Relations of Production."

[68] For more on this see Erving Goffman, *The Presentation of Self in Everyday Life* (New York: Doubleday and Co., 1959).

individual to operate effectively in a work role. Third, there are traits that we may call modes of self-presentation,[69] such as manner of speech and dress, patterns of peer identification, and perceived "social distance" from individuals and groups of different social position. These traits do not necessarily contribute to the worker's execution of tasks, but may be valuable to employers in their effort to stabilize, validate, and legitimize the particular structure of work roles in the organization as a whole. Similar in function are our fourth set of traits: ascriptive characteristics such as race, sex, and age. Finally we may add to our list of attributes credentials, such as level and prestige of education, which, like modes of self-presentation and the ascriptive traits, are a resource used by employers to add to the overall legitimacy of the organization.

The analytical problem, of course, is to determine the precise content of these five factors, and how each affects the stratification process. The problem is particularly difficult in that all five tend to occur together in a single individual. Thus an individual with more cognitive achievement and skills will also generally have the kind of personality that is acceptable for working at higher occupational levels. He or she will speak, dress, and exhibit a pattern of loyalties befitting the corresponding social class, and will have proper credentials to boot. But since there is still a great deal of variation among individuals in their relative possession of these various attributes, analysis is not impossible.

Concerning the importance of cognitive abilities in economic success, our empirical research reported in detail elsewhere supports two important propositions.[70] First, although higher cognitive abilities and economic success tend to go together, intellectual capacity is not an important cause of economic success. The statistical association between adult IQ and economic success, while substantial, derives largely from the common association of both of these variables with social class background and level of schooling.

Second, although higher levels of schooling and economic success also tend to go together, the intellectual abilities developed or certified in school make little causal contribution to getting ahead economically. Thus only a minor portion of the substantial statistical association between schooling and economic success can be accounted for by the schools' role in producing or screening

[69] See *ibid.* for a more thorough analysis.
[70] Bowles and Gintis, "IQ in the U.S. Class Structure."

cognitive skills. That is,very little of the differences in wages or occupational status among individuals having different levels of education can be accounted for in terms of measured differences in cognitive ability or attainment. White males with differing levels of schooling and similar levels of cognitive ability exhibit substantial differences in income. However, white males with similar education attainments and differing levels of cognitive abilities exhibit very similar levels of income. These results first developed by one of the authors, based on several data sources,[71] have been reconfirmed in several recent studies.[72]

We believe that all four of the remaining types of personal attributes—personality traits relevant to the work task, modes of self-presentation, ascriptive traits, and credentials—are integral to the stratification process. Indeed we shall argue that all four are systematically used by employers to affect the reproduction of the hierarchical division of labor, and, as such, their importance in the determination of economic success is not an expression of irrational and uninformed employment policies, subject to correction by "enlightened" employment practices and social legislation. Instead, we shall argue in our concluding section that the link between the social relations of production and the stratification process is so intimate that any qualitative change in the latter is contingent upon the transformation of the hierarchical division of labor as the archetype of productive activity.[73]

We do not yet understand precisely how these four noncognitive types of worker traits interact, or the extent to which each contributes to the stratification process. The strong association between education and economic success, plus the relative unimportance of cognitive achievement as a criterion of job placement,

[71] Herbert Gintis, "Alienation and Power: Towards a Radical Welfare Economics," Ph.D. dissertation, Harvard University, 1969.

[72] Bowles and Gintis, "IQ in the U.S. Class Structure," and Zvi Griliches and William M. Mason, "Education, Income and Ability," *Journal of Political Economy*, Vol. 80, No. 3, Part II (May/June 1972).

[73] We would like to show further that the hierarchival division of labor, far from flowing naturally from the exigencies of productive efficiency, has taken its present form in response to the continuous struggle of capitalists for hegemony in the control of economic activity. From this perspective the stratification system can be seen as the product of the class struggle between capitalists and workers. Given our present understanding of these issues, however, no brief survey of the evidence could do justice to the argument, to which we hope to return in a later paper. For extended historical and contemporary treatments that we find persuasive, see Marglin, "What Do Bosses Do?" and Edwards, "Alienation and Inequality."

nevertheless convinces us of their overall decisive impact. We shall present evidence for the importance of each in turn, beginning with the job-relevant personality traits.

The personality traits required of "efficient" workers must correspond by and large to the requirements of harmonious integration into the bureaucratic order of the enterprise. This order exhibits four essential characteristics. First, the duties, responsibilities, and privileges of individuals are determined neither by individual preference nor flexible cooperative decision by workers, but rather by a system of rules that precedes the individual's participation and sets limits on his or her actions. Second, the relations among individuals are characterized, according to the rules of the organization, by hierarchical authority and interdependence. An individual's actions are closely tied to the wills of his or her superiors, and the results of his or her actions have repercussions on large numbers of other workers. Third, while control from the top is manifested in rules, the principle of hierarchical authority implies that large numbers of workers have essential, though circumscribed, areas of decision and choice. Fourth, the formal nature of the organization and the fact that work roles are determined on the basis of profitability and compatibility with control from the apex of the pyramidal organization imply that workers cannot be adequately motivated by the intrinsic rewards of the work process.

These characteristics of the hierarchical division of labor determine the personality traits required of workers. Some of these are general traits valuable to the employer at all levels of hierarchy and status. All workers must be dependable (i.e., must follow rules) because of the strong emphasis on rules and the complex interrelations among tasks that define the enterprise. Similarly all workers must be properly subordinate to authority—diligent in carrying our orders as opposed to merely obeying rules. Further, all workers, insofar as they have areas of personal initiative and choice, must internalize the values of the organization—the crudest being threat of dismissal, and the more subtle including the possibility of promotion to higher status, authority, or pay. Thus the worker must work equally efficiently independent of personal feelings about the particular task at hand.

While these requirements hold for all workers, there are important qualitative differences among levels. These tend to follow directly from differences in the scope of independent decision making, which increases with hierarchical status. Thus the lowest level of worker must simply refrain from breaking rules. On the highest level it becomes crucial that the worker internalize the values of the organization, act out of personal initiative, and know when not to go by the book. In between, workers must be methodical, predictable, and persevering, and at a somewhat higher level, must respond flexibly to their superiors, whose directives acquire a complexity transcending the relatively few rules that apply directly to their tasks. Thus we would expect the crucial determinants of job adequacy to pass from rule-following to dependability-predictability to subordinateness to internalized values, all with an overlap of motivation according to external incentives and penalties (doubtless with penalties playing a larger role at the lower levels, and incentives at the higher).

Much of this description of functional personal attributes of job performance is based on the work of Richard Edwards, and has been supported by his empirical research.[74] Edwards argues that supervisor ratings of employees—as the basic determinant of hirings, firings, and promotions—are the best measure of job adequacy and are the implements of the organization's stratification mechanism. Thus Edwards compared supervisor ratings on these workers with a set of thirty-two personality ratings by the workers' peers. In a large sample of Boston-area workers, he finds that a cluster of three personality traits—which he summarizes as respect for rules, dependability, and internalization of the norms of the firm—strongly predicts[75] supervisor ratings of workers in the same work group, while such attributes as age, sex, social class background, education, and intelligence have little additional predictive value. In addition, Edwards noted that respect for rules was most important at the lower occupational levels, dependability appearing strongly for middle levels, and internalization of the norms of the firm predicting best at the higher levels.

When we pass to the literature documenting the importance of self-presentation as attributes relevant to the allocation of individuals to status positions, we are faced with a difficult problem

---

[74] See Edwards, "Alienation and Inequality."

[75] Edwards explained 38 percent of the variance of supervisor ratings using his three personality traits as explanatory variables (*ibid.*).

of assessment. Numerous studies have shown these personal attributes to be definite (albeit often covert) criteria for hiring and promotion.[76] Being descriptive and analytical rather than statistical, however, they defy comparison with other data on personal attributes as to importance in the stratification process. We must content ourselves with a simple presentation of the arguments.

"A status," says Goffman," . . . is not a material thing; it is a pattern of appropriate conduct, coherent, embellished, and well articulated."[77] That is, apart from the "reality" of task performance, role fulfillment requires the "contrivance" of legitimation—legitimation of the role itself as well as the individual's personal right to fill it. Thus the doctor not only must cure but also must exude the aura of infallibility and dedication fitting for one whose critical acts intervene between life and death. Similarly, the supervisor not only must supervise but also must exhibit his inevitable distance from and superiority to his inferiors, and his ideal suitability for his position. Thus role fulfillment requires a dramatic "theatrical" performance—an impulse toward idealization of role—on a routinized and internalized basis. Goffman documents the importance of self-presentation in a vast array of social positions: those of doctors, nurses, waitresses, dentists, military personnel, mental patients, funeral directors, eighteenth-century noblemen, Indian castes, Chinese mandarins, junk peddlers, unionized workers, teachers, and pharmacists, as well as in the relations between men and women and blacks and whites.[78]

Central to Goffman's analysis of self-presentation is his concept of the "front" of a performance, defined as "that part of the individual's performance which regularly functions in a general and fixed fashion to define the situation for those who view the

[76] We know of two major presentations, reviews, and over-all interpretations of these studies: Goffman, *The Presentation of Self*, and Claus Offe, *Leistungsprinzip und Industrielle Arbeit* (Frankfort: Europaische Verlaganstait, 1970).

[77] Goffman, *The Presentation of Self*, p. 75.

[78] Other studies may be cited. Gorz (fn. 60) provides a cogent analysis of the self-presentation of technical workers. Offe's analysis (fn. 76) includes evidence on the role of schools in docifying modes of self-presentation and reviews sociological studies of self-presentation and promotability. Finally, Bensman and Rosenberg analyze the importance of conscious manipulation of self-presentation among the upwardly mobile. See J. Bensman and B. Rosenberg, "The Meaning of Work in Bureaucratic Society," in M. Stein et al., eds., *Anxiety and Identity* (New York: The Free Press, 1960).

performance."[79] This front consists of personal behavior ("insignia of office or rank; clothing, sex, age, and racial characteristics; size and looks; posture; speech patterns; facial expressions; bodily gestures; and the like") as well as physical setting. Moreover, argues Goffman, these fronts are not merely personal and idiosyncratic, but are socially regularized and channeled, so there is "a tendency for a large number of different acts to be presented behind a small number of fronts."[80] Thus, on the one hand, "modes of self-presentation" take on a social class character, and, on the other, physical settings are allocated not to individuals but to hierarchical levels.

The role of self-presentation in social stratification arises from a similar social treatment of "personal fronts." Social class differences in family and childhood socialization, as well as the informal organization of peer groups along social class lines, are likely to reinforce social class lines from generation to generation by providing stable reproduction of modes of self-presentation. Similarly, social class differences in levels of schooling are likely to develop career identities, symbols and ideologies, organization loyalties, and aspirations apposite to particular levels in the hierarchy of production.

But does self-presentation play a role akin to IQ in the stratification process (i.e., is it by and large a by-product of allocation and socialization mechanisms based on other criteria), or does its importance compare with and perhaps even eclipse job-relevant personality traits? The answer awaits future research.

We may now consider the importance of our last two sets of employability traits: ascriptive characteristics (race, age, sex) and acquired credentials (e.g., educational degrees, seniority). We have argued that the legitimation of the hierarchical division of labor, as well as the smooth day-to-day control over the work process, requires that the authority structure of the enterprise —with its corresponding structure of pay and privilege—respect the wider society's ascriptive and symbolic distinctions. In particular, socially acceptable relations of domination and subordination must be respected: white over black; male over female; old (but not aged) over young; and schooled over unschooled.

We make no claim that these social prejudices originated as a capitalist contrivance, although a strong case could probably

---

[79] Goffman, *The Presentation of Self*, p. 22.
[80] *Ibid.*, p. 26.

be made that the form and strength of both sexism and racism here derive in large measure from the particular historical development of capitalist institutions in the United States and Europe. Save credentialist distinctions, all predate the modern capitalist era. "Rational business practice" has reinforced and extended them, while consigning less useful prejudices to the proverbial trash bin of history.[81] The credentialist mentality, as we have argued, was indeed contrived to perpetuate the concept of social rank in a society increasingly eschewing distinctions of birth.

The individual employer, acting singly, normally takes societal values and beliefs as data, and will violate them only where his long-term financial benefits are secure. The broader prejudices of society are thus used as a resource by bosses in their effort to control labor. In this way the pursuit of profits and security of class position reinforces the racist, sexist, and credentialist mentality. Thus black workers are paid less than whites with equivalent schooling and cognitive achievement;[82] it is similar for women relative to men.[83] Likewise those with more schooling are given preference for supervisory jobs, in the absence of compelling evidence of the superior performance of those less educated.[84] Last, pay and authority increase over most of a person's working life, out of all proportion to any conceivable on-the-job learning of increased skills.

We may now return to our critique of liberal educational theory. Our focus on the social relations of production bears directly on the compatibility of the reproduction and self-development functions of education. To reproduce an adequate labor force, the educational system must instill in its charges those attitudes, values, beliefs, personality traits, and patterns of motivation which induce adequate performance in the hierarchical division of labor. There

[81] At the same time, of course, the extension and development of capitalist wage labor tends to destroy class distinctions based on precapitalist social relations of production (such as nepotism, direct social class discrimination in hiring, slave status, caste, and nobility), as these are incompatible with the hierarchical division of labor. Similarly, capitalist development is destructive of the ideological underpinnings of all ascriptive norms—even those that are "respected" in the above sense in the day-to-day operation of the enterprise.

[82] Weiss, "Effect of Education on the Earnings of Blacks and Whites."

[83] See Marilyn Power Goldberg, "The Economic Exploitation of Women," in David M. Gordon, ed., *Problems in Political Economy* (Lexington, Mass.: D. C. Heath and Co., 1971).

[84] See Ivar Berg, *Education and Jobs: The Great Training Robbery* (New York: Praeger, 1970).

is no reason to believe these personal characteristics are conducive to healthy psychic development or personal liberation. In the capitalist enterprise, work activities are organized to conform to the abstract criteria of profitability and secure hierarchical control.[85] Thus work is "alienated" in the sense that the criteria governing its historical development do not conform to the intrinsic needs of the individual. Hence the personal characteristics necessary to adequate performance in work roles will also be alienated.

Given this situation, Dewey's reconciliation of the social reproduction and individual development function of education fails. If schools serve the intrinsic needs of individuals for growth, there is no reason to expect the mature individual to possess those personality characteristics opposite to "natural." Similarly, the envisioned "unity of work and play" will not result from conditions of alienated work, where labor is "constrained" precisely in Dewey's sense that "the consequences are outside of the activity as an end to which activity is merely a means." Since absence of control is the heart of alienated labor, an education which reproduces the labor force will not increase the individual's "ability to direct the course of subsequent experience."

Our analysis of the criteria of employability suggests a basic flaw in the technocratic version of liberal educational theory as well. Focusing on the technical relation of production, this theory asserts that the basic economic function of schooling is the transmission of cognitive and psycho-motor skills. Thus while preparation for adult work roles is not coextensive with healthy personal development, as in the "democratic" version of the theory, the two objectives are perfectly compatible; indeed, they are complementary. As we have shown, this proposition turns out to be empirically incorrect. The predominant economic function of schools involves not the production or identification of cognitive abilities but the accreditation of future workers as well as the selection and generation of noncognitive personality attributes rewarded by the economic system. And this process, we have argued, requires a pattern of personal development profoundly antithetical to the rhetoric of the liberal educational reformers.

---

[85] For support of this point see Herbert Gintis, "Power and Alienation," in James Weaver, ed., *Readings in Political Economy* (Rockleigh, N.J.: Allyn and Bacon, 1973).

VI. REPRODUCTION AND EQUALITY OF OPPORTUNITY: THE CORRESPONDENCE PRINCIPLES

Having surveyed the reasoning and evidence indicating the importance of our four sets of noncognitive worker traits—work-related personality characteristics, modes of self-presentation, ascriptive characteristics, and credentials—we turn now to our last question: how are these determinants of one's place in the hierarchy of production affected by education, in home, community, and school? This question is of utmost importance in grappling with the alleged compatibility of the reproduction and egalitarian functions of education. For clearly the school system can be egalitarian only insofar as it is potentially powerful in supplying these personal attributes equally to all members of society.

In neither the democratic nor the technocratic versions of liberal educational theory is this question particularly problematic. For Dewey, the "assimilative force of the American public school" is absolutely required in "a society to which stratification into separate classes would be fatal. . . ." But as we have seen, stratification by class, race, sex, age, and credentials not only is not fatal to American capitalism, it is positively required for the efficiency and perceived legitimacy of the hierarchy of production. Thus a smoothly functioning educational system under corporate capitalism is more likely to reinforce rather than undermine these stratification devices.

The technocratic school is in a similarly weak position. Were the prime economic function of schooling the transmission or identification of cognitive skills, then the school system could provide an adequate labor force in an egalitarian framework, given the fairly equal distribution of intellectual ability across social classes. But as we have shown, such is not the case: specifically, the production of cognitive skills is a nonproblematic by-product of schooling, not its major economic function. Moreover, the power of the educational system to generate those critical noncognitive attributes which distinguish successful from unsuccessful workers is tenuous. For while the school system is the prime source of cognitive skills, the development of noncognitive traits is first and foremost the province of other social institutions—family, peer groups, and community.

Our own approach to this question is summarized in our correspondence principles which may be stated succinctly as follows: the social relations of schooling and of family life correspond to the social relations of production. Unlike the technocratic perspective, the content of education is, we find, far less important than the form. And unlike Dewey, who asserts that schools are a "purified medium of action," we consider the educational system as a reflection of the actual economic order.

We have suggested above that the social relations of schooling are structured similarly to the social relations of production in several essential respects.[86] The school is a bureaucratic order with hierarchical authority, rule orientation, stratification by "ability" (tracking) as well as by age (grades), role differentiation by sex (physical education, home economics, shop), and a system of external incentives (marks, promise of promotion, and threat of failure) much like pay and status in the sphere of work. Thus schools are likely to develop in students traits corresponding to those required on the job. Gintis,[87] in a review of the educational literature, has shown that students are graded for personality traits associated with subordinacy, discipline, and rule following quite independently of the level of cognitive achievement. Several studies of vocational training by Gene Smith[88] exhibit the same pattern of reward, and our colleague Peter Meyer[89] has replicated Edwards's results, using the same personality measures, in predicting not "supervision ratings," but "grade point average" in a New York high school. Last, Edwards's analysis of data on high school records and data work supervision ratings collected by Brenner[90] indicates that variables measuring teacher's evaluation

[86] For a more extended discussion, see Herbert Gintis, "Education and the Characteristics of Worker Productivity," *American Economic Review*, Vol. 61 (May 1971), and "Power and Alienation"; and Samuel Bowles, "Unequal Education and the Reproduction of the Social Division of Labor," *Review of Radical Political Economics* 3 (Fall/Winter 1971).

[87] Gintis, "Education and the Characteristics of Worker Productivity."

[88] Gene M. Smith, "Usefulness of Peer Ratings of Personality in Educational Research," *Education and Psychological Measurement*, Vol. 27 (1967), and also his "Personality Correlates of Academic Performance in Three Dissimilar Populations," *Proceedings* of the 77th Annual Convention, American Psychological Association, Vol. 64 (1969).

[89] See Peter J. Meyer, "Schooling and the Reproduction of the Social Division of Labor," honors thesis, Harvard University, March, 1972. Also Edwards, "Alienation and Inequality."

[90] Marshall H. Brenner, "Use of High School Data to Predict Work Performance," *Journal of Applied Psychology*, Vol. 52, No. 1 (January 1968).

of student conduct are far more important than the student's grade point average in predicting the individual's work adequacy as perceived by the supervisor.[91] While more work in this area remains to be done, there are clear indications that the educational system does articulate with the economy in large part via these effective selection and generation mechanisms.

But recall that the work-related personality traits required of employees differ according to the work role in question. Those at the base of the hierarchy require a heavy emphasis on obedience and rules and those at the top, where the discretionary scope is considerable, require a greater ability to make decisions on the basis of well-internalized norms. This pattern is closely replicated in the social relations of schooling. Note the wide range of choice over curriculum, life style, and allocation of time afforded to college students, compared with the obedience and respect for authority expected in high school. Differentiation occurs also within each level of schooling. One needs only to compare the social relations of a junior college with those of an elite four-year college,[92] or those of a working-class high school with those of a wealthy suburban high school, for verification of this point.[93]

The differential socialization patterns in schools attended by students of different social classes, and even within the same school, do not arise by accident. Rather, they stem from the fact that the educational objectives and expectations of administrators, teachers, and parents, and the responsiveness of students to various patterns of teaching and control, differ for students of different social classes.[94] Further, class inequalities in school socialization patterns are reinforced by inequalities in financial

[91] This is particularly strong finding in view of the fact that the grades themselves are evidently determined in important measure by the teacher's evaluation of the student's conduct. For a discussion of these data, see Edwards, "Alienation and Inequality."

[92] See, for example, J. Binstock, *Survival in the American College Industry,* Ph.D. dissertation, Brandeis University, 1969.

[93] It is consistent with the pattern that the play-oriented, child-centered pedagogy of the progressive movement found little acceptance outside of private schools in wealthy communities. See Cohen and Lazerson, "Education and the Corporate Order," and Neil Friedman, "Inequality, Social Control, and the History of Educational Reform," unpublished MS, School of Social Welfare, State University of New York at Stony Brook, 1972.

[94] That working-class parents seem to favor more authoritarian educational methods is perhaps a reflection of their own work experiences that have demonstrated that submission to authority is an essential ingredient in one's ability to get and hold a steady, well-paying job.

resources. The paucity of financial support for the education of children from working-class families leaves more resources to be devoted to the children of those with commanding roles in the economy; it also forces upon the teachers and school administrators in the working-class schools a type of social relations that fairly closely mirrors that of the factory. Thus financial considerations in poorly supported working-class schools militate against small intimate classes and against a multiplicity of elective courses and specialized teachers (except disciplinary personnel), and preclude the amounts of free time for the teachers and free space required for a more open, flexible educational environment. The lack of financial support all but requires that students be treated as raw materials on a production line; it places a high premium on obedience and punctuality; there are few opportunities for independent, creative work or individualized attention by teachers. The well-financed schools attended by the children of the rich can offer much greater opportunities for the development of the capacity for sustained independent work and the other characteristics required for adequate job performance in the upper levels of the occupational hierarchy.

The correspondence between the social relations of production and the social relations of childhood socialization itself is not, however, confined to schooling. There is strong evidence for a similar correspondence in the structure of family life. The male-dominated family, with its structure of power and privilege, further articulated according to age, replicates many of the aspects of the hierarchy of production in the firm. Yet more relevant for our immediate concerns here is the evidence on social class, parental values, and child-rearing practices. Most clearly directed to our formulation is Melvin Kohn's massive ten-year study, under the sponsorship of the National Institute for Mental Health. Kohn's major results are that "middle class parents . . . are more likely to emphasize children's self-direction, and working class parents to emphasize their *conformity to external authority.* . . . The essential difference between the terms, as we use them, is that self-direction focuses on *internal* standards of direction for behavior; conformity focuses on *externally* imposed rules" (emphasis added).[95] Thus parents of lower-status children value obedience, neatness, and honesty in their children, while higher

[95] Melvin L. Kohn, *Class and Conformity: A Study in Values* (Homewood, Ill.: Dorsey, 1969), p. 34.

status parents emphasize curiosity, self-control, and happiness. Kohn concludes: "In this exceptionally diverse society—deeply marked by racial and religious division, highly varied in economy, geography, and even degree of urbanization—social class stands out as more important for men's values than does any other line of demarcation, unaffected by all the rest of them, and apparently more important than all of them together."[96]

To refine the relation between social class, values, and child-rearing, Kohn classifies his test subjects (fourteen hundred in number) according to the amount of "occupational self-direction" inherent in their jobs—using as indices whether the worker is closely supervised, whether the worker deals with things, data, or people, and whether the job is complex or repetitive. His analysis indicates that the "relationship of social class to parents' valuation of self-direction or conformity for children is largely attributable to class-correlated variation in men's exercise of self-direction in work."[97] And he concludes: "Whether consciously or not, parents tend to impart to their children lessons derived from the conditions of life of their own social class—and thus help prepare their children for a similar class position. . . . Class differences in parental values and child rearing practices influence the development of the capacities that children will someday need. . . . The family, then, functions as a mechanism for perpetuating inequality.[98]

Such differential patterns of child-rearing do affect more than the worker's personality and aspiration level. They also determine his or her style of self-presentation: patterns of class loyalties and modes of speech, dress, and interpersonal behavior. While such traits are by no means fixed into adulthood, their stability over the life cycle appears sufficient to account for the observed degree of intergenerational status transmission.

VII. TOWARD A PRODUCTIVE, HUMANE, AND EQUAL EDUCATION

Our argument is complete. The process of expanded reproduction serves—through the corresponding social relation of school, family, and workplace—to reproduce economic inequality and to distort personal development. We may go beyond our earlier

[96] *Ibid.*, p. 72.
[97] *Ibid.*, p. 163.
[98] *Ibid.*, p. 200.

assertion that under corporate capitalism the objectives of liberal educational reform are contradictory: it is precisely because of its role as producer of an alienated and stratified labor force that the educational system has developed its repressive and unequal structure. In the history of U.S. education, it is the expanded reproduction function which has dominated the purpose of schooling, to the detriment of the other liberal objectives. When education is viewed as an aspect of the process of capital accumulation, the history of school reforms in the United States appears less as an enlightened intervention in the process of capitalist growth and more as an integral part of that process. According to this view, the structure of U.S. education evolved in response to political and economic struggles associated with this process of capital accumulation and the extension of the wage labor system. The continued proletarianization of the U.S. labor force has not been a placid process of gradual accommodation to economic progress. Workers—at least since the 1840s—have fought to retain control over their labor and its products. Bowles[99] has argued elsewhere that the main periods of educational expansion and reform are coincident with the integration of major groups of workers into the wage labor system and were a response by the capitalist class to the political and economic conflicts arising from this continued expansion of capitalist production relations. Thus the two decades prior to the Civil War—which saw the rapid extension of public primary education and the consolidation of schools—were also a period of labor militancy associated with the rise of the factory system and the "degradation of the worker." The progressive education movement can be seen as a response to conflicts associated with the integration of peasant labor—both immigrant and native —into the burgeoning corporate capitalist relations of production. The recent period of educational change and ferment— covering the sixties to the present—is a response to the integration of two major groups into the wage labor system: uprooted southern blacks, and the once respectable "solid" members of the precorporate capitalist community—the small business people, the independent professionals, and other white-collar workers. The particular intensity of recent conflict and reform efforts in U.S. education may be explained by the simultaneous impact of these

[99] Bowles, "The Integration of Higher Education into the Wage Labor System," and Bowles and Nelson, "The Genetic Inheritance of IQ and the Intergenerational Reproduction of Economic Inequality."

two groups—the first mainly in elementary and secondary education and the latter chiefly in higher education.

Current educational reform movements are an expression of these contradictions in the larger society. The free-school movement and, more generally, youth culture are direct reactions to the proletarianization of white-collar labor and the expression of this process in repressive schooling.[100] The extent to which the educational establishment will embrace free schooling depends to some extent on the political power of the parents and children pressing these objectives. But the long-run survival of the free school as anything but a peripheral aspect of the U.S. educational system will depend on the extent to which the social relation of the free school can be brought into line with the changing social relation of production in the modern corporation. Here no firm answers can be offered, for the increasing complexity of work, the growing difficulty of supervising interrelated labor processes, and the rampant dissatisfaction of workers with their exclusion from discretion over their own labor may foretell a sustained effort by employers to redesign work roles consistent with limited worker participation in production decisions. Experiments with "job enlargement" and production team work are manifestations of what may become a trend in the "soft" human relations school of personnel management. A coopted free-school movement, shorn of its radical rhetoric, could play an important role in providing employers with young workers with a "built-in supervisor." This much at least is clear: the possibility of a free schooling which promotes truly self-initiated and self-conscious personal development will await a change in the workplace more fundamental than any proposed by even the softest of the soft human relation experts; for only when work processes are self-initiated and controlled by workers themselves will the free schooling be an integral part of the necessary process of growing up and getting a job.

The impact of the current movement for equalization of schooling—through resource transfers, open enrollment, and similar programs—likewise hinges on the future of the social relations of production. Education, and particularly educational credentials, play a major role in legitimizing the hierarchical division of labor. Equal access to these credentials is, of course, not in the cards. But were egalitarian educational reformers to win spectacular victories and gain their objectives, we can confidently predict that

[100] Gintis, "Counter Culture and Political Activism."

employers would quickly resort to other symbolic distinctions as a mechanism for the fortification of the structure of power and privilege within the enterprise.

So it turns out that Dewey was right. Where the society in all of its social relationships is democratic, a productive, humane, and equal educational system is possible. If the movements for free and equal schooling help to expose the contradictions both of liberal educational reform and of the larger corporate capitalist society, they will have made a substantial contribution toward that objective.

Technology and Community: Conflicting Bases of Educational Authority

Kenneth D. Benne

Western civilization in its modern phase has frequently been described as Faustian civilization. To recall the legend of Dr. Faustus is an appropriate beginning for this discussion. It was for the augmentation of his personal power, through knowledge and mastery of technology, that Faustus bargained with Mephistopheles. And the price that he paid for the mastery of technics was his soul. Without a soul to guide the powers with which his technology endowed him, he became a threat to his human community, and ceased to be a person. Unable to love or to trust others, he was equally unable to accept love and trust from them.

The salvation of Faustus, in Goethe's version of the legend, came through his restoration to humanity, to membership in the human community. It came also in the utilization of his unusual technical powers for humanly constructive purposes—the draining of the swamps. The angels chanted, as they carried the restored soul of Faustus to his eternal reward—"Whose restless striving never ceases, him we have power to save."

THE LURE OF TECHNOLOGY AND TECHNOLOGICAL SOLUTIONS

The legend of Dr. Faustus reveals a moral ambivalence toward the power to control nature that is deep within the traditions of western culture. Extraordinary mastery has been associated with malevolent, antihuman, black magic. But it has also been associated with white magic as well. Goethe revealed his own ambivalence toward the magic of technology—it could be black magic but it could be benevolent, humane, white magic, if its uses were controlled by a humanistic and humanitarian morality.

Until recently the traditional ambivalence toward technology has become increasingly absent from the modern Western world. An even more intricate and powerful technology, continually replenished and renewed by scientific research and maintained by powerful engineering professions, became the very measure of human and ethical progress.[1] The decline in moral ambivalence toward technique has been accompanied by a decline in the traditional humanistic checks on its undirected growth.

Nevertheless, the consequences of expanding technology were often far from benevolent. Technology often meant that community life was destroyed and then replaced by a functional and inorganic rationalization of personal life, a rationalization that served best the developing bureaucratic organization. These consequences were often explained away by the advocates of technology as part of the necessary price of human progress. To the advocates of the technological society, a technological solution is always available, even for the deeper concerns of human existence. The alienation of persons from themselves, from each other, from the social economy upon which they depend, will all be solved by the intensification of technique. Technology became the new faith, promising the believer an end to war, poverty, political disharmony. Only human beings stood in the way—a new problem for technology to solve.[2]

[1] Scholars like Thorstein Veblen, in *The Instinct of Workmanship* (New York: Macmillan Co., 1914) and C. E. Ayres, in *The History of Human Progress* (Chapel Hill: University of North Carolina Press, 1944) argued eloquently that technological advance furnished the only "real" measures of social progress. Both, but especially Veblen, believed that the morality inherent, but largely implicit, in the craft and mentality of "engineering" would not only order the uses of technology in society for good ends but would bring moral order to our predatory system of capitalist enterprises as well.

[2] An illustration of what I mean by a technological solution to a human problem may help to make my point clear. Let us accept without argument that some emotional difficulties of persons are induced by the technicalization and dehumanization of our society and economy. Chemotherapies, shock therapies, and cerebral lobotomies are examples of "technological solutions" to such difficulties. Their "technological" nature is revealed as they are contrasted with psychotherapeutic approaches to similar difficulties. In the latter, the person in distress is invited to enter and is supported in entering into a dialogic relationship with another person or with other persons, as in reeducative groups or therapeutic communities. The voluntary character of the relationship is sedulously maintained. It is assumed that he has regenerative strengths within

Voices have, of course, been raised over the years urging that education should be grounded in a moral authority that transcends and guides technological development. But most of these voices, whether religious or secular, have spoken in behalf of a traditional authority from a pre-industrial past. It was thus easy for a society committed to progress and to defining progress in terms of scientific and technological advance to dismiss these voices as echoes from a dead past.

DISENCHANTMENT AND DESPAIR

It was not argument and criticism but rather the evidence of cataclysmic historic events that cast initial doubt upon the beneficence of the technological god. After the day in August, 1945, when a U.S. bomber dropped a nuclear bomb upon Hiroshima, many sensed that mankind had moved, in Karl Jaspers's term, into a new Axial period of human history. Ingenuity and creativity had given us the power to pollute our planet and destroy all life.

The release of atomic energy was only the most dramatic event signaling to the modern world that we are living in a new period of human history in which moral responsibilities are vastly extended, in which continuation of the old moral irresponsibilities

---

himself, though the strengths are now concealed from or denied by himself. It is further assumed that such strengths are elicited by other persons committed to listen to him, to respond to him, to understand him, to care for him, even as he is invited to listen, respond to, understand and care for them. In the process, at least ideally, he finds himself, understands himself, comes to accept himself, assumes responsibility for managing his own choices and his relationship with others.

In the "technological solution," the person in distress becomes an object, an occupant of the patient role vis-à-vis the role of the expert therapist. The relationship is defined in nonmutual, nonreciprocal terms. The therapist withholds his feelings, values, and empathy, his subjectivity, from the process of treatment. He supplies only his know-how and expertise. The subjectivity of the patient is not seen or valued as a strength, a prime resource in the "communal" process of reeducation and renewal. The relationship is depersonalized, dehumanized in the interest of objectivity and predictability of results.

I have, of course, idealized the psychotherapeutic or reeducative approach for purposes of contrast with a "technological solution" of a "patient's problem" by an expert psychiatrist. In a technologically oriented society, the psychotherapist is continually tempted to externalize, objectify and standardize his "techniques," to treat his "patients," to withhold himself from participation in a process of dialogic regeneration. And no lobotomist probably can ever divest himself entirely of the human feelings evoked in transactions with his "patients," however hard he may try. The contrast is, nevertheless, valid.

in controlling the vast technological powers at our command is fatal. Yet the power of technology is such that even the likelihood of total human destruction is not sufficient to bring it under control, and in a vast number of ways we continue to destroy the "nature" upon which our life depends. We are mining and exploiting the resources of nature without replenishing them, meeting each new problem with an abstract technology sufficient to meet the present crisis only while generating new problems. For example, we create better highways to relieve problems of traffic glut. As a consequence, the hordes of cars moving into the city pollute the air to the point where health is threatened and if continued, life is destroyed. We are destroying, in a thousand insidious ways, the life support systems, the ecological balances, on which continuation of our existence depends.

One common reaction to awareness of the power of total destruction is despair. But despair does not by itself maintain life. The problem is for us to reeducate ourselves as we subordinate technique to moral ends. It is not difficult to locate the general area of human problems to which our new education must address itself. Disparate and contradictory moral visions guide the current uses of the plethora of powers with which our science and technology have endowed us. We live and choose within a maze of moral contradictions. A well-intentioned effort to rid farmers' crops of insect pests may unintendedly rob forests of birds and lakes and streams of fish. Our power to build and to destroy is evident in deserts made into fertile fields and in fertile fields transformed by bombs into eroded and defoliated deserts, with both sorts of projects financed by the same nation state. Our command of effective means in the biological sphere is evident in human lives restored, sustained and extended by people through applied biochemical and nuclear knowledges and in human lives indiscriminately snuffed out and horribly mutated by variant applications of the very same biochemical and nuclear knowledges. Our power to modify behavior finds expression in devoted and sensitive nurture and support of scientists and artists, of creative minds engaged in building new knowledge and new images of human potentiality, and in the brainwashing of masses of people into robot servitude to some fuehrer's or party's whim or will.

Such contradictions are not meant to suggest that the solution to the problems of the modern world is the total abandonment of technology. They suggest only that technology is not an unambiguous blessing. It is sometimes argued that since technology got us into the mess we are in, the way out is to return to some pre-technological state of nature—perhaps some time before the wheel. The intention is not willfully to condemn vast numbers of men and women now alive to starvation, disease, or lives of grinding toil unrelieved by comforts or leisure, but that would be the effect. Technology is not inherently evil or inherently good. What is bad is the uncritical adulation that people have recently granted it, along with the moral authority granted its expert practitioners to manage the lives and education of people. What is needed is not a rejection of the powers of technology but a moral community which can bring these powers under competent, humane control. In brief, we must make a commitment to seeking and creating "the Good" for our Axial period of human history and to bringing our recreated conceptions of the Good into play in human choosing, deciding, and planning at all levels of human organization.

People who have lost hope in something they have depended upon may try to return to some mythical, primitive state of nature or they may also try to rededicate themselves to a conception of the good found in traditional religious or nationalistic dogma and seek to impose it on life in a technological world. Northrop has warned us of the dangers of this approach to security:

> The East and the West are meeting and merging. . . . This is by no means an easy or a perfectly safe undertaking. . . . Neither war nor the peacetime problems of our world can be diagnosed as a simple issue between the good and the bad. . . . The very number and diversity of conceptions of what the good and the divine is give the lie to this diagnosis, and to the ever present proposal that a return to the traditional morality and religion is a cure for all our ills. All that such proposals accomplish is the return of each person, and religious denomination, each political group or nation to its own pet traditional doctrine. And since this doctrine (or the sentiments it has conditioned) varies from person to person, group to group, nation to nation, and east to west, this emphasis upon traditional morality generates conflicts and thus intensifies rather than solves our problems. This in fact is the basic paradox of our time: Our religion, our morality and our "sound" economic and political theory tend to destroy the state of affairs they aim to create.[3]

[3] F. S. C. Northrop, *The Meeting of East and West* (New York: Macmillan Co., 1946) pp. 4, 5, 6.

Our despair and our anguish are the result of the magnitude of our responsibility and of the inefficacy of our traditional ideas to build a moral community that can adequately control and direct our technology. During the time when they sought to find adequate authoritative bases for life and education in technological expertise and in technological solutions to human problems, people were buoyed up by a faith in inevitable progress. They did not despair but they also did not feel themselves to be responsible. They felt a confidence in a presiding providence which would automatically bring the conflicting plans and actions of individuals and groups into the service of a common good. Confidence in some preestablished ordering principle thought to guarantee that conflicting decisions will result in a coherent moral order has taken many forms in the history of human affairs, and has been given many names—the will of God, Fate, the Nature of Stoics and Taoists, the Unseen hand of Adam Smith and the free-market mechanism of the classical economists, the idea of progress in Western liberalism, the historical inevitability of socialism in Marxist thought. We can recognize the common function which all these versions have played in shaping men's view of their future without denying the differences which adherence to one version or another has made in the organization and deployment of human energies and resources. The effect of this confidence has been to narrow the range of human responsibility and to turn people's attention to the evaluation of means, to the neglect of an analysis of human ends. The recent decline of confidence has often resulted in despair, but it might also result in a widening of our responsibility for designing and inventing our own future. If we are to take responsibility for planning our own future, there must be an appeal to a principle that attends to the conservation and augmentation of human values. This principle cannot be imposed upon us from an external source such as the authority of the expert, but rather it must be constructed through the communal exercise of human intelligence and volition. Neither technology nor a forlorn return to some earlier set of traditions is sufficient for this task.

There are many paths toward the rehumanization of mankind which will need to be traveled, but one important path leads to a commitment *by those in charge of education* to building a human, moral community. Such a task requires the acknowledgment and criticism of normative assumptions which function authoritatively both in traditional culture and in technological society.

A FAUSTIAN EDUCATION SYSTEM

Despite the discontent with technology that has arisen in some circles, our formal educational system continues to be guided by those committed to the dominance of technological expertise which accompanies a "fatuous progress theory of history."[4] The "authority of technology" has permeated the orientations and practices of our educational institutions. Yet it is these very institutions which must be reconstructed if the task of moral reeducation is to be initiated, and this reconstruction requires a reassessment of the concept of authority. The authority of the technological expert has become a perverted expression of the more appropriate relation that can exist between an authority and a client. In order to clarify the effects of the technological expert it is useful to express the more ideal relationship that *can* exist between an authority and a client. The form of the expert-authority relation can be rather simply described: a person unable to meet some need or achieve some purpose through his own unaided powers puts himself under the guidance and direction of someone who claims to know how the need or purpose can be expeditiously met. This grant of authority is not an unlimited one, for the field of conduct in which the authority relation holds is delimited by the alleged competence of the bearer and the need or purpose of the subject. The triadic relationship between bearer, subject, and field is thus ideally collaborative in some degree, since it requires some mutual fitting of need to resource. The subject must legitimize the authority of the bearer in controlling and directing his conduct. After all, it is the subject's need and purpose that ideally are being served through the authority relation.

The collaboration, however, becomes minimal if the subject willingly grants to the expert the right to determine his need and purpose or if the expert assumes the right to tell the subject what his need really is as well as how to behave in meeting it. Because of the general adulation of the technological expert, many people in industrial society have been willing to grant him this extended power.

[4] This phrase is to be found in Charles W. Hendel's "An Exploration of the Nature of Authority" in *Nomos: Authority*, Vol. I, edited by Carl Friedrich (Cambridge: Harvard University Press, 1958). Hendel argues persuasively that Western man's distrust of authority is naturally linked to his faith in inevitable progress. After all, if progress is inevitable then authority simply becomes the cumbersome relic of a bygone age.

So far, I have spoken as though the subject of expert authority is an individual person. This, of course, is not always the case. Groups and organizations of various size depend on experts and expert information and advice in forming plans and policies and in finding their way out of or through recurrent crises. The staffs of industries, government agencies, universities, and school systems are made up largely of specialized experts. And even more specialized experts than the staffs provide are brought in for advice and recommendations in times of emergency and confusion.

The use of expert authority is, of course, no new thing in the history of human affairs. What is new is the kind of expertise which practical men consider useful and dependable, along with the increasing specialization and fragmentation which characterizes the composition of contemporary expertise, particularly in its scientific and technological forms.

Perhaps because the function of education presupposes informal relationships in a way that other functions do not, the commitment to the maintenance of intricate bureaucracies is more accentuated in the educational systems of America than in other institutions of similar size. This is particularly true of universities and colleges. Faculty members are chosen for their demonstrated expertise in one or another field of specialized knowledge. And the same credentials are considered meritorious for teaching as for research appointments. Since the basic credential is successful completion of a graduate school program and since graduate schools typically require a demonstration of research competence in some highly specialized field of knowledge as a condition of successful completion of advanced degree requirements, the university, even more than government or industry, has become, in Kelly's phrase, "a world steadily reduced to conceptual particles."[5]

The lack of cultivation of any common intellectual or moral basis to support communication between faculty members in a university led Robert Hutchins, when he was president of the University of Chicago a generation ago, to remark, exaggeratedly but truly, that the only thing that united the parts of the university was a central heating system. And Clark Kerr, when he was president of what he chose to describe as a multiversity rather than a university, noted that all that united faculty members in common debate were endless discussions of what to do about the

[5] George A. Kelly, "The Expert as Historical Actor," *Daedalus*, Vol. 92, No. 3 (Summer, 1963), pp. 529–48.

parking problems of the university. Technology may thus have a "communifying" function to perform, when all else fails.

George Kelly remarked that the novelty in the utilization of contemporary expertise is "that the form of official expertise seems finally to have caught up with the needs of a complicated bureaucracy and been assimilated to it". While Kelly had in mind the fit between the form of expertise and the needs of governmental and industrial bureaucracies, his observation is nowhere better validated than by the social organization of the contemporary university. Faculty members are organized by similarity of field of specialization, rather than by common concern with an issue or problem, into schools, departments, and sub-departments. Their teaching and research programs are, by and large, laid out along departmental lines. Transactions with members of other departments are not required by the norms of the social organization of the university. In fact, they are discouraged. Rewards are given to faculty members for staying within departmental boundaries. For example, publications in highly specialized journals are ordinarily considered more meritorious than publications in general journals with a concern for issues of broad human import.

The social organization is functionally rationalized and bureaucratic. It is designed to perpetuate a system of departmental segregation between people who are committed to accumulation of ever more specialized conceptual particles, or ever more specialized expertise. The social organization brings into play another kind of authority, the authority of the rules of the game which serves as a substitute for the real needs that the more legitimate authority is designed to meet.[6]

The bureaucratic social system is a mechanical system, in the sense that it operates by rules which try to eliminate surprise from the outcomes of its functioning and which try to guarantee a "high quality output" from its operations. It values predictability and quality control. Graduating students are on this view products of the system no more, no less, than specialized research papers. Each is expected to conform to institutional rules, whether or not a real human need is addressed.

---

[6] Kenneth D. Benne, *A Conception of Authority* (New York: Russell and Russell, 1971, originally published 1943). See especially Ch. IV, "The Authority of the Rules of the Game."

Kenneth Boulding has argued that human systems are somehow inherently and "naturally" organic and evolutionary, rather than mechanical, systems:

> One thing we can say about Man's future with a great deal of confidence is that it will be more or less surprising. This phenomenon of surprise is not something which arises merely out of man's ignorance, though ignorance can contribute to what might be called unnecessary surprises. There is, however something fundamental in the nature of our evolutionary system which makes exact foreknowledge about it impossible, and as social systems are in a large measure evolutionary in character, they participate in the property of containing ineradicable surprises.[7]

If Boulding is right about the nature of human systems, and I believe that he is, it is not difficult to understand why universities, having become so mechanical and bureaucratic, must depend on extrinsic motivations and rewards to maintain a minimum degree of morale and institutional identification among their various subgroups. Given the mechanical adherence to the rules of the game, it is not surprising that these systems have tended to be so uncreatively defensive and vulnerable in their responses to protests against their dehumanization, moral irresponsibility, and irrelevance.

Of course, the university system is not thoroughly mechanical in its organization or operation. Some of the most creative breakthroughs in knowledge understandably have come in the interstices between traditional university departments—biochemistry, nuclear studies (are they physics or chemistry?), social psychology, etc. And universities have experimented with alternative organizations that cut across departmental lines, such as centers, institutes, and area studies; often these alternative organizations select their personnel on the basis of the needs generated by the issues under examination. But traditionally, these organizations are breaks in the system which have been regarded as temporary, ad hoc, maverick suborganizations, and they have to struggle against continual pressures exerted upon them to become indis-

---

[7] Kenneth E. Boulding, "Expecting the Unexpected: The Uncertain Future of Knowledge and Technology," in Edgar Morphet and Charles O. Ryan, eds., *Prospective Changes in Society by 1980* (New York.: Citation Press, 1967), pp. 199–213.

tinguishable from departments. These pressures arise from the influence of the norms of the larger system operating in crucial day to day areas such as promotion, budgeting, and accounting procedures.

Of course, the content—the conceptual particles—offered to students through the intricate system of bureaucratized relationships is highly various. The content is by no means all technological, in the narrow sense of information translated, readied, and developed for particular application and use. In fact, most professors in arts and sciences pride themselves on selecting and presenting nonutilitarian content in their courses. Nevertheless, professors are selected for their technical competence. They are professors of "know how," albeit a "know how" for finding and testing conceptual particles in their own specialized field. Most operate under the "scientific" norm of "not taking sides" on issues of large human concern, on the assumption that "universal" knowledge is morally neutral, applicable to both good ends and bad. Generally overlooked, however, are the choices they have made in selecting and organizing the content, and the emphasis that these choices generally give to one cultural tradition at the expense of another. Often neglected too are the moral implications of the information selected, and the likely use that will be made of it given the power and direction of private industry and government.

An even more powerful norm operating in selecting and presenting content is a kind of territorial imperative. This might be stated as "Thou shalt not in thy teaching get into another faculty member's field of specialization." Of course, the moral implications of conceptual particles ordinarily do not become evident until it is understood how they fit together, but it is precisely this understanding that is taboo. The atmosphere of the learning situation is ordinarily competitive and individualistic. Rewards, in terms of credentials such as grades, honors, and recommendations, are determined by a comparative ranking of individual students, according to individual achievement. Students' cooperation and helping of each other with their work is considered a violation of the norm and is called cheating. Relations between teachers and students are impersonalized, often to the point of depersonalization.

When the various aspects are taken together, however, potentially liberalizing the content involved, the result is a technicalization of education. Its basis is noncommunal. Its human "products" issue from its programmed processes as specialists, motivated to get ahead in their own fields, with little awareness of the relationships of their specialties to the moral and political issues which divide the "human community." "Generalists" and "moralists" do not function happily or entirely safely in such an environment.

There have been strong resistances in the university to the extension of its facilities and resources into programs of continuing education and reeducation for persons, groups, organizations, and communities outside the university. Part of this resistance is no doubt due to economic considerations—the university never has enough funds to support all the campus programs which its ingenious faculty members imagine as desirable to do. But, even where continuing education programs might add to its inadequate funding, the resistance persists. The resistance is least in "vocational" fields like agriculture, engineering, business, health, and welfare. It is greatest where general moral, political, and civic enlightenment and empowering of outside persons and groups is the aim of the continuing education project or program. Probably, the main resistance rests on grounds similar to those which led Abraham Flexner, arch exponent of the technicalized university I have been describing, to urge a stance of social irresponsibility upon the university so far as the melioration of social life and the resolution of society's moral and political dilemmas are concerned. Flexner feared that university people who assumed responsibility for social improvement would be corrupted into soothsayers, alchemists, magicians, astrologers, prescientific recommenders to society on the basis of faith, lore, and superstition, rather than on the basis of valid knowledge. The corruption he feared was corruption of the role he passionately recommended to and for university-based men and women, that of the pursuit and propagation of disinterested, scientific and, for him, *valid* knowledge. That his recommendation was based on a positivist faith in the objectivity of knowledge should be apparent. But such a faith is still widely shared in university circles. It is a faith that consigns the university to a priestly rather than a prophetic role in its relations with the established society that environs it.

The technicalization of schools below the college and university level has proceeded concomitantly with the technicalization there. This is due partly to the fact that the credentialing of teachers and administrators in public schools more and more involves successful completion of college and university programs of instruction. It is also due to the increased influence of university professors in shaping of school curricula and in establishing efficient pathways of preparation for students to become successful recruits for higher education.

The attempt to substitute educational technology for human teaching has probably made greater inroads in the schools than in colleges and universities themselves. University experts have played increasingly larger roles in developing curriculum materials on the lower grade levels. Much of this material is still printed, but more and more of it is issued with accompanying tapes and films. Whatever the media, however, the big selling point is often the extent to which these instructional devices are teacher proof. They are advertised as enabling the student to proceed with his own learning at his own individual pace and they are designed to relegate teachers to the role of technicians implementing a *prescribed* learning program.

The "best" materials are thought by many to be self-instructional, providing immediate feedback to students as to whether a certain response is right or wrong. Students can proceed to learn through interaction with their materials without any necessity of messy, subjective, and unpredictable dialogue with either their teachers or their fellow students. Such materials are urged as a technological solution to problems of large numbers of students and a paucity of well prepared teachers. They are urged also as an efficient way of individualizing instruction, usually without awareness of the irony involved—that "individualization" in this usage seems to be equivalent to further "depersonalization" of the instructional process.

Thus the search for technological solutions to the human problems of teaching and learning goes on among educators who have not heard the news that we are living in an axial period, a tragic period, of human history. And the exploitation of multiple media of "communication"—visual, auditory, electronic—is part of the search. A limerick which went the rounds recently shows, in exaggerated fashion to be sure, the absurdity that has been reached in the reliance upon educational technology as a substitute for the freely chosen action and suffering of human experience.

The news is now out, clear and clean,
That by aid of a teaching machine,
King Oedipus Rex
Has learned all about sex
Without ever touching the queen.

COMMUNITY AS THE BASIS OF EDUCATIONAL AUTHORITY

The ultimate bearer of educational authority is a community in which people are seeking fuller and more valid membership. Actual bearers and subjects of this authority must together build a proximate set of mutually helpful relationships in which the aim is the development of value orientations, perceptions, skills, and knowledges which will enable the subjects to function more fully, adequately, and autonomously as participants in a still wider community life.

Authority relations are educationally valid insofar as they operate to cultivate mutual processes of association and dialogue which, by design, reach beyond these relationships into the life of the wider community. All such education, whether occurring in schools or elsewhere, is at once a mothering and a weaning, a rooting into ongoing authority relations and a pulling up of roots.

The educator develops his authority in relation to a community process in which he works as a co-participant in that process. The authority of a teacher is exercised as he seeks to give form, focus, and direction to the participative medium. Yet the justification of his efforts to shape processes of learningful participation cannot be found primarily in the intrinsic satisfactions of the school. He is granted his authority only by virtue of his efforts to mediate between the present community involvements of those being educated and their expanding and deepening affiliations in the common life of a wider community. His authority derives both from the mandate of the wider community and from the fundamental interest of those associated with him in growing up into free and responsible men and women.[8]

---

[8] See Benne, *A Conception of Authority,* especially Ch. V, "Community as the Basis of Pedagogical Authority," for an explication and defense of this position. See also Kenneth D. Benne, "Authority in Education," *Harvard Educational Review,* Vol. 40 (August, 1970), pp. 385–410 for a contemporary application of this view of authority. I have leaned heavily on this article in the later pages of this essay.

It is the traditional bases of community that the advance of our technological civilization has destroyed. And the rebuilding of open, future- rather than past-oriented communities of inquiry to sustain the continued growth of people has not been a high priority. In education, the focus has been on the development of special skills and knowledges, because people with highly special-ist mentalities have been placed in charge of curricular planning. Even when the need for *general* education has been recognized it has been handled by requirements that students study with *spe-cialists* outside their major field of specialization for some per-centage of their course work. Or it has been conceived as a need for a smattering of *general knowledge* of man, nature, and society drawn in diluted form from various specialties. Rarely has the need been interpreted as a need for people to live and be in a community of developing persons, of various ages, backgrounds, cultures, life styles, and moral and religious outlooks as each together inquires into the meaning of being a human person, a man or woman, today and tomorrow, in our increasingly inter-dependent but increasingly segregated and alienated world, learn-ing primarily from the experience of building a community and from trying to understand what happens to self and to other selves in the process, using specialist knowledges and skills, of course, but using them to face and meet the choices and dilemmas of com-munity living. Such education, if widely practiced, might very well undermine the Faustian educational system and the unexamined authority of expertise and of bureaucratic rules of the game, as well as the larger social and political system from which the edu-cational system draws its models and support. And that is why the bureaucrats and the experts will not tolerate it.

Community, in a normative sense of that term, as an associa-tion of people, mutually and reciprocally involved with each other, caring for each other, aware of the human effects of their actions upon those within and outside the association, committed to being responsible for these effects, is dangerously missing both in our institutions of formal education and in the society which environs those institutions. The resistance of the bureaucrat and the expert notwithstanding, a validly authoritative education must become committed to building and utilizing community both in places set apart for learning the arts of living, loving, knowing, choosing, working, and playing and in other parts of society not focally responsible for the "education" of people as well. The range of reeducative community must, in idea at least, extend to the inclusion of all mankind in its scope.

THE SOCIAL VALUE OF THE SELF

Since John Locke, much of Western thought has popularized the idea of man as an atomistic and passive creature molded by and reacting to his environment, but it took the unhampered development of technology to institutionalize this idea in the bureaucratic organizations of human beings. This idea, so institutionalized, is a major retarding force in the development of human educational communities.

Schooling has remained a process in which the "correct" environmental influences, predetermined by adults, are brought to bear upon passive learners to produce the educational "products" needed by "society." Where resistances to these influences are encountered, they are seen by educators as defects arising out of extraschool socialization rather than as the efforts of inherently creative persons to choose and create the goals. Thus the resistance is looked on as something to be overcome either through punishment or through the postive reinforcers that modern day behaviorists tell us will motivate learners to learn gladly what they are expected to learn. In the history of American schooling we have turned to technical experts in various fields of specialized knowledge to set the curriculum and away from parsons and possessors of folkwisdom like the "Hoosier Schoolmaster." Yet the social valuation of the oversocialized self has not changed.

Throughout the history of American and European education there have been periodic outbreaks of reform against this passive, environmentally determined view of man's nature and nurture. These have been generated by various "Romantic" emphases upon an inherently active self, creating, becoming, through its own choosing, action, and contemplation. In the modern age, however, visions such as those generated by Froebel, Dewey, and others have been coopted by the triumphant environmentalism of established schooling and managerial techniques.

The idea of man as inherently passive has affected almost every aspect of social science and thereby has had a wide influence on both the form and content of schooling. This view of the self links together various theories in economics, sociology, political science, and psychology. The assumption of passive man has become the new moralism of the university and, through it, of other educational institutions as well. In this view, thinking is separated radically from the living contexts of the human organism. Intellect is separated from spirit, emotion, and will. The "idolatry of intellectualism," as Ortega once named it, separates intelligence both from the social and natural contexts of life and from the other functions of the feeling, willing, aspiring, valuing human being. The enunciation and publication of pure and correct doctrine is elevated as the main criterion by which the excellence and worth of a person is to be judged.

Intellectualism (the name that is given to various social "scientific" theories which are built upon the assumption of the passive self) becomes a mask behind which many of the dehumanizing and depersonalizing tendencies of American society are concealed. It makes a virtue of moral and political irresponsibility on the part of the person of knowledge by demeaning or denying the part which evaluation and decision-making play in any robust intellectual process and product. It actually supports the growth of irrationalism in the practical affairs of society because of its distorted, limited, and purist conceptions or reason and rationality. Erich Fromm has pointed to a tragic aspect of man in modern society in the determined separation of thinking and feeling, a separation which intellectualism in education condones and reinforces. "In fact, this separation between intellect and feeling has led modern man to a near schizoid state of mind in which he has become almost incapable of experiencing anything except in thought."[9]

But men are not passive, nor are they so easily divorced from their culture as the relation between the active environment and passive man suggests. Invention, creation, and renewal must, in the last analysis, come from inventive, creative, and self-renewing persons, if they are to come at all. Social and cultural institutions live from generation to generation, from day to day, only as living persons recreate them in their imaginations, their habits, and their moral commitments, and only as living persons continue to endow them with value. The widespread dropping out of persons, actually or psychologically, from the institutions of our culture

[9] Erich Fromm in his Introduction to A. S. Neill's *Summerhill* (New York: Hart, 1960), p. xii.

is a signal that many are withholding investment of their imaginations and moral commitments from *any* and *all* institutional life. The very survival of social life and culture requires reconstruction of our traditional value-orientation toward ourselves. We must accept ourselves as creators, not as passive products, of society and culture.

IS IT POSSIBLE TO BUILD VALID AUTHORITY RELATIONS IN TODAY'S
SCHOOLS AND COLLEGES?

The fact that we possess the power to destroy our lives and the lives of all other human beings on earth constitutes the essential moral plight of contemporary mankind. The responsibility for bringing this power into the service of common human purposes and values is a human responsibility. Tradition alone can not direct people toward the good of human survival. The idea of progress, conceived of as the development of an ever more refined and powerful technology, continually replenished by scientific research, has betrayed us. If there is to be a viable future for mankind, those now alive must invent and create it.

The task of reeducation for modern mankind involves major reconstruction of traditional normative orientations and the creation of new value orientations more apt to the purposes of human survival. There can be no technological solution to this task. Only the sustained deliberations of human communities, cutting across various extant lines of human segregation and cleavage, and addressed to the resolution of conflicting views of what human beings should do and be, can accomplish rehumanization and moral regeneration.

Our present system of schooling and education is inadequate for this task of reeducation because it operates under the authority of technical expertise reinforced by the authority of a functionally rationalized organization of work and learning. It has largely forsaken the arduous tasks of general education and reeducation. Its priorities and its social organization must be radically altered if it is to accept the authority of community as its basis of operation. I do not know whether our institutions of formal education will successfully achieve this reorientation, but we should make the effort.

The outlines of the authority relations now required in education become clearer through a probing of three major difficulties confronted by educators as they try to locate and build a community adequate to our contemporary moral plight.

Uncertainty about the Future. We do not know the shape of the future society into which we as educators, along with those we are helping to educate, are moving. We can be sure that it will be different from the society and culture that shaped our own development, and from the society and culture in which we, along with our colleagues and students, are now enmeshed. The traditions of the past and the "realities" of the present offer us suggestions. They cannot provide any certain grounding for our authority as educators.

The unpredictability and ambiguity which color all attempts to anticipate the future are frightening and anxiety-producing. We should acknowledge and accept our fear and anxiety. Such acknowledgement and acceptance are a first step toward the wise exercise of educational authority, whether as bearers or as subjects.

But uncertainty and ambiguity are conditions of hope as well as of fear and anxiety. An open future is one in which our aspirations for a better society can make a difference in shaping a culture that is still to be formed, partly through our own decisions and efforts. Human beings must now invent their future, and it is in the context of this project that educational authorities can help others to acquire the disciplines needed to create a more desirable way of life, one which can take into account both the validity of different cultures and life styles as well as the overarching needs of human survival.

Certainly the expert has a case; our knowledge of some matters is more trustworthy than our knowledge of others. It is wrong, however, to build our contemporary curriculum around what we know best. For we can have no prior assurance that what we now know best is what we most need to know in order to meet the responsibilities of our new historical situation. We must make value judgments about what it is most important for us to learn. And our best knowledge alone cannot automatically determine these judgments for us. Whatever the eventual judgments may be, however, they will affect all of us and hence the process by which they are made is as important as the nature of the judgments themselves. The process must be communal, involving cooperative thought and dialogue about issues for which there are no experts. Thus the judgments and the issues must be determined by those engaged in the inquiry, teachers along with students, and the selection of the knowledge most needed must wait upon this determination. It is a determination that must be revised continually by those engaged in learning and teaching, not alone in the light of new knowledge and new technology, but more fundamentally, in the light of new human aspirations, new actions, and new evaluations of actions taken. The basis of educational authority will change as the outlines of the community into which men and women, boys and girls are learning their way are altered in the minds of educators and of those with whom they work. We must honestly acknowledge the fallibility of our authority even as we work to decrease its fallibility.

Conflicts over What Is Desirable. The second difficulty in defining the basis of educational authority arises from the existence of deep and pervasive conflicts among nations and between groups within nations as to what is the desirable shape of future society and culture. This issue is closely linked to the various images of the kinds of personalities that will be required to build and maintain a self-renewing society and culture. Determinations of educational purposes, curricula, organization, and management are bound to be affected by these moral and political conflicts even though technological society attempts to deemphasize such issues.

The current conflicts between clashing utopias and ideologies in and around educational programs and institutions in America —indeed throughout the world—are a sign that denial and suppression of conflict is no longer a viable or desirable strategy for educators. The function of a nontechnical authority is to focus processes of cooperative deliberation and inquiry upon the very issues involved in the conflicts. For within these conflicts may be found the alternatives which will allow people to create a desirable future for themselves. However, the method of learning from conflict presupposes that the status and prestige of parties to the conflict are equalized and it presupposes too that some people are available to encourage communication between the partisans. It also presupposes that conflicting feelings and partisan attitudes be respected and that such differences be recognized as part of the materials to be utilized and reconstructed within the processes of conjoint learning, and that part of the outcome of the dialogue is a commonly accepted commitment by all parties to deal with each other in mutually respectful ways, as members of a human community. Wielders of educational authority must learn to support others as they learn to build community out of conflict. In other words, educators must seek to use the conflicts of value and interest that arise openly and responsibly and in a way that is educative both for themselves and for others.

Once the context of a communal educational authority is established, then the role of the expert can be reevaluated in terms of its subservience to the purpose to which the communal commitment is directed. When such a reevaluation takes place, it will not be the rules of the game or the pressures generated by a self-serving bureaucracy that will determine the requisite skills and knowledge, but rather the needs generated by the communal process itself.

If communal authority relations are to be built and rebuilt in our disoriented and tension-ridden institutions of education, teachers and administrators must learn to accept conflict as part of the reality of contemporary life. Once such acceptance occurs then the conflict itself can be used to provide a focus and a motivation to the learning process. This requires an orientation to education as dialogically regenerative and reconstructive, not monologically transmissive. Teachers and administrators can learn much of this orientation from each other if they invest themselves in projects of mutual self-reeducation addressed to the meaning of education in our historical period. But part of their reeducation will require them to learn from their students as well.

Whether such learning communities can be designed into the life of the educational institution as a legitimate and accepted part of its mission, and not just as grudging and ad hoc accommodation to "trouble-making" students, blacks, women, and utopian professors is, of course, an open question. The future offers no promises that are independent of the will and efforts of human beings.

Relationships of Old and Young. The processes will require a reeducation of men and women of all ages and it will require too that in at least some educational programs, younger people will validly take the lead. As Margaret Mead has noted, the upsurge of youthful rebellion and protest against established ways of life and education is worldwide in scope.[10] Its occurrence in capitalist, socialist, and communist countries, and in both technologically developed and developing societies, discourages ex-

[10] Margaret Mead, *Culture and Commitment* (New York: Natural History Press, 1970).

planations in terms of the injustices and inequities of particular forms of economic and political organization alone. The increase in tension between generations suggests to her that a turning around of human culture and of human enculturation is now underway on a worldwide scale. She believes we are on the threshold of a world culture still largely to be built—a world culture in which traditional forms of human enculturation have become outmoded.

As Mead observes, we are all living today as immigrants in a new and strange culture. We have considerable knowledge of how immigrants handled their problems of enculturation in the strange lands to which they came. Much of this knowledge is available from American experience. Adult immigrants to America could not coach and guide younger members of their families in ways of coping with a culture that was strange to them. They were forced to depend on their children, who learned the ways of the strange culture from their peer group experiences, inside and outside of schools. In turn, the younger members became the educational authorities for their parents in inducting them into the new culture which the younger members had come to know better than the older members.

We have already moved, in fact if not in idea and ideal, from a post-figurational culture, in which people sought and found ways of handling their present and future by lessons learned in and from the past to a pre-figurational one. Of necessity, immigrant families developed a mixture of cofigurational processes of enculturation (the process of peer-learning just described) and tradition-directed patterns. Today, we are all—young and old—living as immigrants in a pre-figurational world culture. At the least, we need to develop a pattern of education in which old and young learn to collaborate in inventing and reinventing a future which none of us can predict in any detail. The pattern of authority must become a collaboration of equals. A rigid hierarchy of old over young or of young over old will not work. We elders must accept the fact that, at times, those younger than we are closer to the authentic pulse beat of the future as it reveals itself in the present than we are. And this applies to the most prestigious and doughty wielder of technical expertise. At such times, we must learn to put ourselves under the educational authority of the young without losing our self-esteem.

The problem of maintaining a livable continuity with the past (for the past is within us however much we may try neurotically to deny it) will remain a genuine problem in a pre-figurational culture. Contrary to Mead's emphasis, when such problems are uppermost in learning communities, the lead will shift from younger to older, as it will in expert authority relationships as well. The building and rebuilding of viable authority relations for a pre-figurational world culture will become a never-ending task, in which older and younger people must learn to collaborate. Established authority relations will always be open to challenge. The cooperative determination of the *right* locus of authority from situation to situation will place that locus now here and now there, insofar as age and the proper weighting of past and present experiences are concerned. Credentialing must take on a new meaning.

A fundamental reorientation of authority relations is now required in families, schools, colleges, work situations, churches, and social and political planning and action projects—wherever the tasks of education go on. More, not less authority, is required; more mutual and reciprocal giving and receiving of help will be needed in the schools, colleges, and universities of tomorrow if they are to survive. But such authority relations must work in the interest of optimizing personal freedom within the context of interdependence.

The temptation of teachers and administrators may be to reject the very conception of authority as I have tried to develop it. Many will continue to seek adequate bases of authority in modernized and refined or perhaps in refurbished traditional rules and codes, or in the invention and use of ever more powerful and specialized expertise. There is nothing wrong with refined rules or specialized expertise. We need and will continue to need both. But unless both can be placed in the service of the claims of a more fundamental moral, communal authority, still largely to be created, education will fall victim to a process increasingly alienated from the central dilemmas of human beings in a strange world.

Whether or not such tasks will actually be accomplished is impossible to say, but if progress is possible it will arise not as a blessing of history, but out of the will and effort of human beings.

Our civilization is a Faustian one. The salvation of Faustus, his restoration to membership in the human community came through the utilization of his unusual technical power for humanely constructive purposes—the draining of the swamps. The angels chanted, as they carried the restored soul of Faustus to his eternal reward—"Whose restless striving never ceases, him we have power to save." And so too, perhaps, may be the projects and the salvation of mankind in contemporary times.

Art and Technology: Conflicting Models of Education? The Uses of a Cultural Myth

Marx Wartofsky

There is a current and popular distinction made between art and technology as conflicting modes of human activity. Art, as we all know, is creative, liberating, free activity. Technology, as we all know, is mechanical, constraining, subject to rote and rule. Where art calls for originality, invention, the fullest play of the imagination, technology is no more than acquired skill, transmitted by training, requiring at most imitation, or an ability to follow instructions. Such a popular characterization takes on mythic proportions: the alternative modes easily become "models," emulated and mapped onto various domains. We recognize the distinction, or its analogy, in talk of alternative or conflicting "life styles": the liberated and the repressed. We see its reflection in the contrast between play and work. In social contexts, the counterposition becomes one between a privileged elite, able to exercise its leisure creatively, and a mass, condemned to the workaday repetition of dead tasks merely instrumental, or, as "alienated labor," required by the system. Inevitably, the distinction comes to be mapped onto education, where art and technology may serve as conflicting models of the educational life and process as well.

This crude and current myth has little to recommend it; yet it is pervasive, accords with a common understanding and a prevalent mood, and perhaps worst of all, permits us to build theories of education which appear to be on the side of God, the angels and poor little Johnny. Who, after all, will *not* want children to have the opportunity to be "creative," "liberated," "free" from the automatism of the factory system (whether in industry or in education), from the tyranny of rule and rote, from the dead hand of mere artisanal skill? The technological model of education, so the myth suggests, is dedicated to the production of cogs for the machine. The "cogs" are well-fitted and well-trained products needed to keep the system going. The schools are therefore nothing but the factories and assembly lines for such social production, and their ends are dictated not by the needs of children, for growth and development as human beings, but by the needs of the system, for craftsmen and functionaries. Much follows, on this model, concerning the details of education: the role and function of the teacher; the requirement and rationale for discipline; the shape and aims of the curriculum. The force of a model as metaphorically rich as the technological one, is that it suggests so clearly how all these details fit into a coherent pattern. And it permits—even encourages—us to think that we can understand and explain the phenomena at issue—the crisis in education, the anomie of the student, the frustrations of the humanist-teacher, the vagaries of funding.

As with any myth, there is enough of the truth in its stark formulation of alternatives to evoke in us an assent which draws its force from what we add from our own and varied experience to flesh out the details of the dramatic sketch. Surely art is a liberating and exhilarating experience, in which the highest powers of human imagination and creativity find expression. Certainly art is an exaltation of the human spirit, an intensification of everyday experience, a fit activity for free men and women, and therefore a fit model for the education of children. Just as surely, the image of the educational system in the bleak and utilitarian colors of a training ground for the industrial and technological army has a notable veracity. The school as factory, as ideological preparation for service to the industrial-capitalist system, as inculcator of the proper habits and attitudes required by "the system" has been the object of a long and devastating critique, as well as of more and less successful efforts at humanistic and liberal reform. That mass public education as a legal requirement grew out of the needs of the industrial revolution is a patent fact. It is nowhere more vividly described than in Karl Marx's chapter on the Factory Acts in England, and on the institution of compulsory education for working children as part of the Child-Labor laws.

What is wrong with the myth, however, is not that it somehow embodies an enlightened attitude toward the aesthetic and a critical one toward technology, but rather that it falsifies both art and technology, misunderstands the very activities which it takes as its abstract models, and ends with a shallow and comfortable humanism where what is needed is a deep-going and hard-headed radicalism.

Therefore, I want to make a case against this model of an antithesis between art and technology, and specifically, against its interpretations in educational theory and practice. I will suggest further that there is much that is culturally and educationally vicious in this confrontation of the two modes. Moreover, I will argue that it is politically vicious as well, and that this counterposition of art and technology hides, beneath its rosy humanist appearances, a bourgeois-liberal myth, whose effect, like that of Plato's Royal Lie, in the *Republic*, is to keep the working masses in their place. My argument is somewhat perverse, for it will *appear*, in the context of the myth at least, that I am arguing for repression, against liberation of the free spirit of the imagination, and for rote and rule. In fact, I am arguing against the myth, against that view of art and the concomitant view of technology, which yields this counterposition in the first place. And I want to show that the conceptions of "art" and "technology," in this mythic form, are sham conceptions, and that their perpetuation is part of a self-serving "liberal" ideology; that this ideology (which often pretends to the title "radical") simply seeks to cast education in the image of allegedly enlightened middle-class values, to the denigration of working-class values; and that its effect, were it successful, would be to plaster over the worst failures of our mass-education of the young with a fig leaf to hide our shame. Now it is clearly *not* my intention to denigrate either art in the schools, or the richness of an aesthetic model of education. It *is* my intention to rescue the technological from the elitist disdain in which it has been held by often well-meaning liberal and humanist social and educational theorists. The confusion is clear: "technology" has been identified with the abuses of a technological-scientific society, with the misuse of rationality in the service of exploitation and war. This is the superficial Luddite critique of technology: smash the machines, get back to the soil and the sunshine, and all will be well. The deeper critique of technology argues more sophisticatedly that the very conditions of social organization and work made necessary by a rationalized technology are inherently brutalizing, anomic, alienating; that the essential requirements of technological advance inevitably pollution, ecological disaster in the rape of resources to feed the machine, and a mechanized and dehumanized form of human labor. Both versions, however, offer no solution short of deindustrialization, or the more vicious alternative of "zero-growth." More to the point, in the popular forms in which antitechnology is disseminated, technology is seen as no more than the soulless, amoral, and value-free means to an end, whereas ends themselves come, somehow, from beyond the "merely technological," i.e., from a "value-system" or from the "culture." The fact-value dichotomy is neatly packaged so that human judgment concerning ends is abstracted from the concrete contexts in which choices become practical and actual: within the constraints of actual needs and of actual means to satisfy them. Once the separation is effected, the ease with which a rosy humanism can generate ends at its pleasure and leisure becomes boundless. Utopianism is the name of the game. Pie in the sky is the name of the payoff. The masses of the poor and the underprivileged suffer because utopias can be realized only in colonies, in "experiments," in "model-programs," which filter down only into the reports of committees, or into the glossy paperbacks which serve dreamy educators in much the same way that "True Romances" or "Muscle Power" served the dreamy youth of an earlier generation. The teacher, surrounded with broken desks, deprived and disturbed children, inadequate supplies, an impossibly tough and retrograde school committee, and a proliferation of blindly bureaucratic paperwork, dreams of the "child-centered school," of the "authentic educational encounter," even of Room 222 with its inane mix of happy children with happy problems, cutesie teachers, and a Jewish Mother principal. My point is that the ends separated from the means (political, technological, practical, humdrum, organizational) become shallow and effete; and that the antitechnological model of technology serves in practice to effect this separation.

I'm exaggerating for effect, and being deliberately cruel in this characterization. For, in effect, the specter of technology which haunts the bourgeois-liberal theory of education needs desperately to be laid to rest. A specter, we know, is a construction of the imagination; thus, we are able to invest it with our fears, anxieties, and hatreds. Specters *are* embodied fears, after all. But the specter of "technology" has been invested with the evils of education, much as has the goat which bears our sins for us.

The dulling and deadening characteristics of mass-education, the packaged lesson plan, the programmed sequence which determines which of our cortical centers shall fire when, the "transmission" of "knowledge," as a stuffing operation, by the book and by the clock, the bureaucratization of the school systems, the standardization of "progress" in learning, the lockstep grade-system, the uses of the IQ, all have the earmarks of "technology": the school as assembly line; the teacher as a one-operation mechanic, coming in at the appropriate year, or semester, or hour, and then leaving; the student as product—all of these very real problems conduce to the characterization of the technological in these terms, as the source and "model" of our educational ills.

Enter art. Here, not the constraints of necessity, but the air of freedom reigns. The feelings expressed, the mind open to inspiration, invention, discovery; the unique and the individual in each of us fully encouraged. Gone, the serried ranks, gone the knee-jerk responses of obedient little minds, gone the barracks atmosphere. Air, light, and sun. O art! O freedom!

This vision of art as a liberation from the constraints of a mechanical necessity, as a corrective to the very real problems of a bureaucratized and inhumane educational practice, fails not merely on the grounds of its utopianism, but fails as a vision of art. Art as an escape from drudgery and necessity is escapist art. It changes nothing. It accommodates the present situation and its oppressive tendencies. But beyond this, it falsifies the very nature of that disciplined creativity which art requires, that necessity of craft and skill, that training without which "art" becomes a sham.

The artist—the real, live working artist—is no less, and often more a "technologist" than any assembly-line mechanic or production lathe operator. He has to be, for the expression of his art requires the discipline of his craft. But perhaps the term "technologist" grates here. We think of technologists as engineers, perhaps, or as computer technicians. They occupy a middle range between "scientists"—i.e., theoreticians, creative types who "use their minds"—and mere "laborers" who use only their muscles, with whatever minimal skill which is required. The "technologist" somehow effects what the scientist thinks out, but he has to use his mind little, and under supervision and direction. He is, at least, a high-school graduate, but not an academic. The internal class and status differentiation, while interesting, is beside the point here.

On the model of "technology," as opposed to "art," it becomes the work of the world, the practical, and therefore constrained activity in pursuit of some tangible goal, in answer to some articulated need, and thus tied to earth, and more particularly, to the means for carrying out a prescribed end. In this sense, science too is easily misunderstood either as a theoretical tinkering or invention, or as purely theoretical "art," as an activity whose only constraints are aesthetic, or formal, which is therefore divorced from practice, or the conditions of application. But I want to use the term "technologist" more broadly here, for the sake of the argument against the model which counterposes art to technology. The artist as "technologist" in this sense is simply the artist aware of the limits of his medium, and therefore of its possibilities as well; aware therefore also of the requirements for practical skill and technical understanding in the service of his vision. To the extent that work has been degraded so that vision and imagination play no part in it, skill itself has sometimes been raised to the level of creative application. The counterpart in art is virtuosity, as a quality abstracted from vision and understanding. The worker, deprived of any role in the planning and shaping of the product or the production process, will elaborate his skill and take pride in it. When even this possibility is removed, and work becomes rote performance of an unthinking and easily learned procedure, then even the dignity of craftsmanship is robbed from work. By analogy, when the imaginative refinement of skill and craftsmanship is denied to the child, in educational contexts, he is likewise brutalized; just as he is demeaned when skill itself is not informed with a vision whose ends it subserves. But the model I am criticizing consigns skill and craftsmanship to the domain of a denigrated technology, and conceives of art, by contrast, in the image of an inane and empty "freedom" and "creativity," in which wish becomes reality without the mediation of work. The falseness of the separation works the other way as well: it denies the aesthetic component of skilled performance itself. The child, caught in the intricate web of an electrical circuit design, or in the weighty determinations of fitting a tongue and groove, or of constructing the proof of a geometrical theorem, has (or should have) as much aesthetic experience in the situation as he has wielding a brush or dancing. The fact that this is not the case in much actual school practice reveals the extent to which technology itself has been subverted in the interests of sheer rote learning for manpower needs. But the subversion of the humane content of technological activity is not overcome by the subversion of the technical requirements of aesthetic activity. The humane content of technological activity is precisely that it is the activity by which human beings produce the means of their existence. It is that conscious praxis in which human teleology, the deliberate and conscious organization of human skills toward a human end, is first developed historically, and is renewed again as each generation transmits its productive genius and achievements to the next. The dehumanization of technology comes with the separation of the process from its ends, and with the embodiment of this separation in exploitative class societies, in which one person works for another's weal, and becomes no more than an instrument for ends not his or her own. But the dehumanization of technology calls not for its continued, and even sharpened separation from "free," i.e. end-controlling, teleological activity, but for its *re*humanization. Here, the myth abdicates the struggle utterly. In its place we have a poultice misnamed "art" or "creativity," in which the very idea of artistic creation has degenerated into some notion of the "production" of instant art, of "objects" requiring neither skill nor the delicious deliberation required for the difficult work of coordinating hand, eye, and heart.

So, not yet to the issue at hand, concerning "alternative models of education," but rather to the characerization (or mischaracterization) of art and technology themselves: Whence the distortion?

Santayana, in his discussion of work and play (in *The Sense of Beauty*), reconstructs the puritan myth for us. He writes:

> We may call everything play which is useless activity, exercise that springs from the physiological impulse to discharge the energy which the exigencies of life have not called out. Work will then be all action that is necessary or useful for life. Evidently if work and play are thus objectively distinguished as useful and useless action, work is a eulogistic term and play a disparaging one. It would be better for us that all our energy should be turned to account, that none of it should be wasted in aimless motion. Play, in this sense, is a sign of imperfect adaptation. It is proper to childhood, when the body and mind are not yet fit to cope with the environment, but it is unseemly in manhood and pitiable in old age, because it marks an atrophy of human nature, and a failure to take hold of the opportunities of life. Play is thus essentially frivolous. . . . At the same time there is an undeniable propriety in calling all the liberal and imaginative activities of

man play, because they are spontaneous, and not carried on under pressure of external necessity or danger. . . . It is spontaneous play of his faculties that man finds himself and his happiness. . . . Work and play here take on a different meaning, and become equivalent to servitude and freedom. The change consists in the subjective point of view from which the distinction is now made. We no longer mean by work all that is done usefully, but only what is done unwillingly and by the spur of necessity. By play we are designating, no longer what is done fruitlessly, but whatever is done spontaneously and for its own sake, whether it have or not an ulterior utility."[1]

Work, therefore, is what is imposed on us. Play is our "free activity," our "holiday life." Art then becomes either (*a*) an adornment, an idle pursuit, a frivolous matter at best (or in the deathless words of the New York City Board of Education of some three decades back, a "useless frill"); or (*b*) the activity of the ideally free person, not hung up in the toils of daily necessity and survival; in either case, not essentially part of our lives, as they are in fact lived. It is easy to meld the metaphors "work" and "technology" (for assuredly, both are highly metaphorical terms in the context of this discussion). "Technology", according to the myth connotes "technique" and *techne*, or skill. It separates the artisan from the artist, the worker from the creator, the mass from the elite. Technology is what trade schools or vocational schools teach. And we all know who they are for. Indeed, the liberally educated man and the child who is to become that man need to "know about" such things. So we go slumming, educationally, and include such peripheral and "special" subjects as "shop," "home economics," and "personal typing"—(not "business typing," for that already connotes a vocational track)—in our schools. The liberally educated person has to be democratic and "well-rounded"—but not a mechanic!

Carry this mythology one step further: for there it separates "fine art" from "craft" or "skill" even further, in a peculiar perversion of "art": drafting or mechanical drawing is a technical subject. Drawing from the figure, or painting still lifes still has an air of 'rule' about it: there are judgments of better and worse, correct and incorrect to be made; and the last thing we want our spontaneous and free young "artist" to be subjected to is the backward

---

[1] George Santayana, *The Sense of Beauty: Being the Outline of Aesthetic Theory* (New York.: Dover, 1955), pp. 17–19.

and reactionary notion that what he has drawn or painted is
"incorrect." As long as it is an "authentic" and "imaginative" expression (of what? his "feelings"? his plastic intuitions"? his
"color sense"?), it makes its own rule. The child is genius in germ,
giving the rule to art. The only "art" which suits this image of the
spontaneous creator is a spontaneous "art," a use of the imagination unhampered by the strictures of craft, of rule, of tradition, of
"better" and "worse." ("That's *fine*, Cecily—isn't that *beautiful!*
Did you make it up *all by yourself?*")

To be sure, this fairy tale about permissiveness in child art
has its grim complement in the rigidities and aesthetic idiocies
of the "color-inside-the-line" school, or the "color-the-grass-green-
and-the-sky-blue" school, or the "trace-carefully" school. It is
socially revealing that the permissive anti-art practices abound in
upper-middle-class schools, and that the repressive anti-art practices abound in working-class and ghetto schools. But they are
complementary practices, for both reinforce, and are reinforced
by the myth, with its false separation of "necessity" and "spontaneity." To be sure, there are exceptions, and there is a body of
intelligent art-education theory, and a noble corps of intelligent
and sensitive teachers of art who struggle daily with the physical
impossibilities of schools which lack facilities and supplies, and
with the curricular and intellectual impossibilities which demand
either that art be taught in an entirely "vocational" way, or that
it be consigned to the limbo of its disutility or that it satisfy
doting parents who just love all that creativity as a release from
the burdensome constraints of the "real" subjects. (It ranks with
gym and "free-play" periods, since, as we all know, art is a release
of tension.)

Granting the dominance of the more repressive modes of art-
activity, one needs to separate them from the legitimate demand,
in art, for discipline and for skilled craftsmanship. For the myth-
engendered version of freedom and spontaneity in art is equally
perverse in at least two respects.

One perversion is that what is being demanded of the child
is something he or she cannot deliver; and yet, the assumption
is that it is *always* being delivered, on every occasion. Spontaneity,
one of the greatest of human *achievements*, has been cheapened
into randomness; and thereby, freedom into license. The child
has been cheated, because achievement is so cheap.

A second perversion socially more degenerate is that the child's attitude toward (and aptitude for) disciplined work, as an avenue of delight and satisfaction in achievement, has been sold short, cut short, impugned. The requirements of craft, of skill, the acquisition of the historical and cultural achievements of the species, have been denigrated as tired requirements imposed by a dead traditionalism. However, the social effect of "liberation" from this tradition is *not* the production of a humanistic or aesthetic elite, but rather of a generation of humanistic and aesthetic illiterates; young people robbed of their potentiality for creativity, in whatever field, by the myth that creation is easy: all you have to do is do it!

The social context of this view of art and of art education is not the art world itself. Here, struggle with ideas, with the limits of skill and style, with the medium *and* with the message, is daily and fierce. No joy without pain there. Rather, the social context of what I would call the "arty" view of art (its dilettantism aside) is the separation of hand and head, of feeling and intellect, of work and leisure, of production and creation. And thus, because work and the workday unfortunately *do* have the connotations Santayana ascribes to them, in our society—they constitute, most often, activity under constraint, done because it must be, for the sake of survival—the infelicity of work, its dullness, its lack of spiritual life, its sheer and weighty necessity are all burdens. And in this image of work, the workaday—and therefore also, the "technological"—is framed.

Art then becomes escapist. It becomes Sunday art, holiday art, museum art, divorced from life and from the social and personal demands of life. And by "life," here, I mean no grim prison of daily needs, but *whatever* it is that is the ongoing, self-preserving activity of a man, or a society. To the extent that the mass of men are required to become mere production machines, in order to "preserve their being," to that extent a society has become de-humanized, as the cost of its self-preservation; and for this, there are social and political remedies, one hopes. Yet to surrender human labor, work, production of the very means of one's existence to the level of dull routine, or to work as a necessary evil, seems to admit that life itself can be preserved only at the expense of the spirit; or worse yet, that one person's spiritual freedom from toil can be purchased only at the expense of another person's labor; that human exploitation is the condition for the freedom of art.

This social and ideological consequence, it seems to me, is at one with the separation of art and technology, as "free" and "slavish" activities. Technology is assigned to the precincts of toil—it is for "them," for those who have no recourse; whereas art is for "us," by virtue of our enlightenment—and more, by virtue of our leisure. And if we ourselves are caught in the daily grind ("technology") then our saving grace, our escape, our "other world" is art. Art becomes the dream-world, the heaven of the imprisoned spirit; and therefore, the separation of art from real life becomes absolute: not merely acknowledged, but accepted and reinforced. The model of art as freedom, in a world and a life caught in the constraints of necessity, is therefore, at best, an escapist model; far from being a vision of a world-to-be-achieved, it is assigned the status of a vision of what real life can never be like, and of what we may enjoy only on the margins and in the rare moments of felicity in our ordinary lives. It is pie in the sky. The myth thus puts art beyond reach—an interlude, in the "free periods" of our learning, sandwiched between serious subjects like mathematics and social studies, and good for letting off steam, or as therapy for disturbed children, or for providing the "regular" teachers with a coffee break (at the expense of "messing up the room"—for despite its exalted status as the realm of free creation, art is seldom accorded the literal room which "necessary" subjects deserve). The separation of "art" and "technology" therefore acts to preserve and enhance quietism and passivity: an acceptance of the "unaesthetic" conditions of a workaday life, as inevitable, since that's what "technology" inevitably is like.

Worse yet: having fostered an illusion concerning art, we lose the reality of technology as well. For one thing, we lose (and lose for our children) the breathtaking realization of the capacity of people to produce their own existence, to support and maintain life by their labor, their inventiveness, their capacity for social cooperation, their plain hard work. We give up the conceptual and ideological importance of the dignity of labor, in the face of its perversion by an often repressive industrial-technological social organization. We forget that human beings make things for human use, even in the context where the only aim of production seems to be either sheer survival, or sheer profit from the work of others. And so, we forget that people become human, by means of their work, just as they may become dehumanized by it. Human skill,

artisanship, craft, technology,—the human ability to shape means
to ends, by deliberate intelligence and imagination—is not something we can afford to surrender. Yet on the mythic view of
technology as repressive, regimented activity, it is surrendered.
In a world desperately in need of human productivity and skill,
we can hear complaints about the "work-ethic," and mewlings
about "greening" and "self-liberation." Where it is plain that
we cannot survive without technology, it becomes a mark of almost insane self-privilege to insist that we dump it. Such attitudes
are, in effect, the marks of privilege of an elitism which holds
itself beyond the social needs of a struggling mankind. At best
they are the marks of petit bourgeois despair over the possibilities
of effective social change. The other side of this despair is cynicism
and escapism—the same escapism which leads to a perversion of
the concept of art.

This is not to deny the importance of a critique of an alienated
technology—one which has lost its basis in the humanism of labor
as the productive activity by which human needs are satisfied.
There are social roots for this abstraction of technology from its human contexts, certainly. Technology has become an instrument for
repression. It has been used for conquest, for inhumane ends, for
the profit and power of the few. It has produced mega-death,
to order. Political and military abuses of technology aside, the
division of labor has gone so far in complex industrial societies
like our own that we each, simply, produce practically nothing that
we need, but contribute only to that collective social production
which generates anonymous products for use. Indeed, one of the
appeals of art is that its products are often autographic, uniquely
identified with personality and individuality, in the face of technological anonymity. Yet, the solution which the myth proposes
is to kill the goose because the golden egg has been stolen from
us. Instead of an effort to regain technology for human ends, it
is condemned in toto, and abstractly. Those who have benefited
most from it—in terms of relative affluence, or freedom from dire
need—are often most anxious to persuade others to surrender it.
But this seems to me more a cry of impotence, in the face of
failure to control and use technology for human welfare, than a
rational and militant program for regaining control over it.

What eventuates is a disdain for technology, and with it, a
disdain for labor and craft (except in the hothouse or drawing-
room versions of a quaint or primitive artsy-crafty activity, or in

the escapist versions of commune greeneries, where "doing your own thing" is reminiscent of nothing so much as Marie Antoinette's "milkmaids" in the pastoral dairy, set up in the midst of a suffering, prerevolutionary France). This disdain for technology, for labor, for craft expresses itself most precisely in the misconstrual of technology, and in the "slumming" attitude toward vocational education.

The translation of this cultural myth into alternative and conflicting models of education is not so blatant as to be obviously self-condemning. In fact, dressed up in the language of "freedom" versus "repression," this confrontation of art and technology cannot help but win our liberal sympathies. The rhetoric of the myth, in educational contexts, is persuasive enough, if we swallow the primary error in the characterizations of art and technology themselves. Very simply, and schematically, the cultural myth would translate educationally thus: deemphasize all rote learning, all the inherited disciplinary forms, all the quasi-military features of the school. Deemphasize or eliminate the merely "vocational." Let the child flower in the exercise of a free imagination, unconstrained by backward notions of grading, of the "correct" and the "incorrect." Let spontaneity rule, for the child must be free to discover what he or she can or will. Let the child be an "artist" in all of his educational enterprises, playing with the materials and resources, rather than being trained in their use. At best, simply have these resources available so that the child can choose them in the course of his free and creative exploration. Eliminate the punch-in-punch-out tyranny of the clock, the seating plan, the lesson-plan. Let the teacher be another such available resource, not directing, or guiding, but rather enhancing the child's own motivations. Eliminate the conceptions of disciplined work, of a schedule of achievements, of a linear scale of required "progress"; eliminate the training of "skills"—let them rather be acquired "naturally" where needed (as in learning to walk). School is not "work"—it is play. We are not producing trained automatons, but creative agents. Not every child has to learn the same thing— rather, let the child learn at will what he or she wills. You can lead a horse to water etc., etc.

What, by contrast, does the cultural myth see as a technological model of education? Again, very schematically: find out what the needs of society are. Fit the educational program to the most efficient satisfaction of these needs. Screen children for their vocations, either by merit or by social class (no matter, the quotas will be fulfilled). Thereafter, train, condition, direct, mold so that the proper products will be produced for the needs at hand. The curriculum requires literacy specific to the tasks to be performed by the "products" in their eventual vocations. Teach the discipline needed for "real life" later on: obedience, perseverance, responsiveness to reward and punishment. Teacher says what's what. Authority reigns.

The technological model is, in many essentials, Plato's, in the *Republic*. I present it in its horror-show version here just to be fair to the spirit in which it is rejected.

To say that these are the models of education which the myth proposes is not to say that such models exist only in the mythic imagination. They exist in fact. The myth has its embodiments. Certainly the permissive and the repressive exist side by side, in real life; they are perfectly compatible. They are two sides of the same coin, and no conflict or struggle ensues as long as each remembers which side of the coin it is on. And it is this separation, in real life, this abstraction and one-sided existence of the permissive and the repressive which is reflected in the myth. That the separation is "false" is a normative claim for the unity and complementarity of the aesthetic and the practical, of freedom and necessity. But the "false" separation does exist, and can be abided by a society which needs its art to be escapist and its technology to be exploitative. The myth doesn't invent the division; it dignifies it, and in this case, under the guise of a liberal humanism. What is at issue here is not simply the rosy model of a "free" educational environment, nor the grim model of the school-factory, as instrument of society and authority. Rather, it is the misidentification of the first as somehow based on the model of "art," and of the second, on the model of "technology." What is at issue is whether some normatively adequate conception of art and technology could entail such educational interpretations. The answer is "no"; and therefore, the conceptions of art and technology which do entail such interpretations are normatively inadequate. That is to say, they are wrong. Were one to argue that "normative adequacy" begs the question, and that the question is not what art and technology ought to be, but what they in fact are in this time and place, I would argue that "art" and "technology" are normative terms to begin with, and that it depends upon whose norms one is willing to adopt.

Since the issue lies in the dissection of the cultural myth, let me proceed to an alternative account of art and technology, not as conflicting models of education, but as complementary ones.

First, what positive features are there to art as a model for education? Art, among other things, is an exploration; an exploration into the properties and potentialities of a medium, first; for color, shape, movement, sound, language itself, are malleable, manipulable, and resistant, and the exploration of their possibilities is a piece of juvenile education without which fingers, eyes, ears, and limbs will remain underdeveloped. Moreover, the medium offers scope to the imagination. For art is, second, an exploration of the possibilities of the imagination. It is a search for precise expression, for adequacy in the presentation and representation of a feeling, an idea, an image, Moreover, since images do not come pre-formed in the mind, only *then* to be objectified, art concerns the process of forming or creating ideas or images, as plastic or visual or aural constructions. And so it is, at the same time, an exploration of modes and capacities one has both for creating and communicating such feelings, ideas, images.

The model for education is clear enough, at two levels at least: *First, that the practice of art, the exploration which art affords, is a necessary part of the education of any human being.* Without it, the capacities of people for technical skill and empathetic understanding of the materials of their world will remain cramped and debased. For the materials of their world are all the materials of their human praxis. These include words, sounds, and colors, as well as wood, steel, plastic; the medium of expressive gesture, as well as the medium of the visual image, or the vivid phrase. So, at one level at least, art is the model for education in the simple sense that a proper education includes aesthetic exploration, not as a frill or adornment, not as an escape, or a therapy, but as a necessity for the education of the child's sensibility to the world. In this sense, education should simply include what is necessary for human life—for a good life, in which abilities and sensibilities are most fully realized; and so, art proper, beyond the school, is simply the highly perfected expression of such a human need. What art includes in its perfected expression, is therefore a model for what education should include, as an introduction into a fully human life—or at least, into the expectation for such a life, and the appreciation of it which will help make it worth struggling for.

Second, art is a model for education in a more analogical, less direct way, *insofar as it involves delight, or enjoyment, or plea-sure in its achievements.* But this is not simply an argument for the values of pleasure; rather, it involves the social education of the child, to the community of shared feeling, shared delight. The appreciation of art is a profound mode of social feeling, of the appreciation of other people. This is a subtle matter. For it is not simply that in viewing a great work of art, or hearing great music, we are awed by a Michelangelo or a Beethoven. We are rather awed by the art work itself;   we delight in it, exercise and expand our sensibilities in the experience of it, enlarge our intellectual scope by the demands it makes on our understanding. All this is response to the art work itself, and not to its label, or its reputa-tion. Yet, in the aesthetic experience of the work of art, we are in concourse with others; more than that, we are shaped, in our sensi-bilities, and in the modes of our response, to the cultural inheri-tance of the species, across time and space and in a communion as profoundly human as the sexual or the religious. In a word, we are humanized by great art; and can become dehumanized by base art. The lure of our enjoyment takes us beyond ourselves, just as love and faith do, and helps to make us species-beings, not mere atoms in a crowd. Thus, at two levels, as an activity which involves us with the materials of human *praxis*, and as a mode of humanizing and socializing our responsiveness to the human community, art provides a very general model for education.

Now in what ways does technology provide an alternative or even conflicting model for education? I confess I do not know. For what I refuse to accept is the dichotomy, in the first place. Suppose we construct a minimal model of the "technological," as having to do with means, applications, the "how" of things. We take technology to be related to science, ordinarily, and not to art (except as "industrial art or "craft"). In relation to science, technology presumably has to do with the embodiment, or the carrying out in practice, of principles or truths established "theo-retically" in the sciences. Landing on the moon is therefore, simply, the application of Newtonian physics—the distances and speeds being too small to require any Einsteinian considerations of a relativistic sort; and too big to involve quantum-theoretical considerations. The technology, at least insofar as trajectories, masses, and forces are concerned, is simply a matter of engineer-ing an embodiment of a theoretical idea already established. The landing is regarded as a feat of applied theory, an engineering achievement, not a theoretical one. (We discount the auxiliary technology and theory of fuels, of television transmission, of optical and radio guidance systems, etc. in this account). But surely, this view of the relation of technology and science is simpleminded! Granted that there is established theory, and that the engineering applications are not devised either as tests of the theory, nor as explorations of alternative theories; it is still clear that new theory, in a number of scientific fields, grows out of just such contexts of application. Further, apart from serendipity, scientific discovery is so closely linked to the development of instrumentation, to the technological possibilities opened up by new hardware and engineering techniques, and to the host of new problems which crowd in upon the solution of old ones, that the sharp division of scientific theory proper from technology may be retained only as a formal distinction, and not a distinction in practice. One may grant with impunity the valuable distinction between "mission-oriented" scientific research and "basic" research, and even insist that a good deal of scientific theorizing goes on in a way detached from contexts of solution to given practical problems (though not detached from the context of solution to given theoretical problems). The relations between theory and practice in science *and* in technology are complex and subtle. For all this, in the living practice of science, the neat formal divisions between the theoretical and the practical become fuzzy, the membrane becomes highly permeable, and especially so in periods of active scientific-technological development.

To press the point: if one were to separate the technological so discretely from the theoretical, in science, and then to insist on its further separation from the free and imaginative intellect on the one hand, and from the creative aesthetic sensibility on the other, the caricature left of technology would be thin indeed. Yet, one may argue, it is the case, right or wrong; that in actual practice, in actual social and production contexts, this division is enforced. Some are creators, some mere imitators, or mechanics. The division of labor *has* reduced many human activities to *mere* technology, to uncreative, rote repetition of a procedure, devoid of any but the meanest skill, and certainly devoid of any intellect or sensibility. And, it will be argued, this is what we mean by "technology"—the brute function of effecting what someone else has prescribed, no matter what skill is required.

But there is a not-so-subtle shift here, from the idea of carrying theory into practice, to the idea of sheer, mechanical, untheoretical practice, which violates the very sense of technology proper. That technology can become alienated is no more astounding than that theoretical science and art itself can become alienated. There is no special virtue of art or of science that can prevent them from becoming dehumanized; and no special vice of technology, that leads to its dehumanization. It is quite clear (both historically, and at present) that fine art and theoretical science can be dehumanized very effectively; and equally clear that technology can become humanized. What this means is that the sense of the human—the need for wholeness, for socially just and humane ends, for joy in work—is not prescribed or proscribed by the limits either of art, or science, or technology. What we require is that theory and practice, discovery of new truths and the deployment of old ones, imagination and skill, be closely linked to each other, so that their interaction ensures their mutual integrity.

What has this to say of a technological model for education? Simply that if we separate the requirements of craft, skill, and application from the requirements of free, imaginative exploration, we have doomed the imagination to impotence, and skill to brute and blind activity. The effect of this is to leave the "creative" either as an effete and ineffectual fantasy life; or worse, to create an elitist and hierarchial ideology, in which the "creative" person is forever provided with the assurance that others, less fortunate, will carry out his ideas in practice, will do the "dirty work." In educational contexts, this connotes a disdain for practice, for sustained work, for the sense of a collaboration among equals. Does this mean that there is *no* division of labor, no special talent, no leadership, expertise, genius? I think not. Rather, it means that an alienating division of labor should not be imposed on our children in their education; for the "creative" child can become just as alienated in his alleged "creativity," suffering from a lack of means to make his free imagination count for something, as can the "backward" child, assigned to his "vocational" tasks.

The disdain for technology has another effect, related to these: the workaday, the technical, the applied is itself a domain of creativity and freedom. The child knows this clearly, before he becomes corrupted by an elitist ideology. He can transform a task into a game, a skill into an exploration; his fantasy and imagination see possibilities in the ordinary, and he is magical with it. Work and wonder are not yet at odds in the child. The child's insight is profound here, though not self-conscious. We are responsible to recapture it in a self-conscious way, to nourish it and recognize it, and to discover (or rediscover) for ourselves this unity of play and work, of free vitality and disciplined form. Technology, on this model, is not the alternative, or conflicting model to that of art, but is part of what a viable model of art contains; conversely, the aesthetic, the explorative, the creative is what a viable model of technology contains. Far from conflicting, these are complementary models of a unified mode of human activity.

What, then, is politically and educationally vicious about the counterposition of these two models? Not simply their counterposition, nor even the distinctions one may draw between their relative emphases. Rather it is the uses and interpretations to which such counterposition gives rise. It is the false, exclusive and mythical models of art and technology which are vicious. They are vicious because they accept and harden the separation of two requisite and complementary modes of human activity; in doing so, the two modes are abstracted and seen as exclusive of each other. We invest, in these abstracted models, the very abstraction and alienation of those activities which plague our social and economic life. That is to say, we embody in these models a falseness which is *objective* in our own social life—the human falseness of a division between creation and work, between free human agency and slavish toil. Instead of liberating work, labor, technique, from its sheer instrumentalism, we denigrate it as slavish, and pretend that we can transcend its slavishness by eliminating it altogether. In favor of what? Why, art of course. But such an art would be devoid of its social role, its seriousness, its demands upon skill, craft, and discipline. It would be a pretense at art, not the living practice of it.

Far from being a liberating conception, this contrast of the two modes accepts the status quo and accommodates it. In doing so, this contrast encourages social attitudes in our children which tend to denigrate not only the technological, or the technically productive activity, abstractly, but the people who are engaged in it. In short, what is encouraged is a disdain for working people; and in the case of working-class students, a self-disdain, and disdain for their parents. Similarly, the contrast of the two modes encourages admiration for those freed from the necessities of toil, for the creative spirits who have risen above the dull necessities of life. Unfortunately, these few are dream figures: they have escaped the system, or have dominated and used it. Such mythic models (of the "artist," presumably) are our contemporary versions of the "star," of the folk hero who beats the system and "makes it" on his own. And our contemporary version of this myth has the same social function as did the Hollywood version of a generation ago: the goal is not to change or improve the system, but to beat it. The solution remains individual and not social. And the social and political effect is to displace real social change with a fantasy of self-achievement.

People need art; and people need technology. The world needs to be made aesthetic, humanized for mankind. But the conquest of war, of disease, of hunger demands the education of a generation technologically capable of effecting such changes, and morally and aesthetically committed to them. The cultural myth which disarms us in the face of such needs must be put to rest.

A Phenomenology of
Man-Machine Relations

Don Ihde

INTRODUCTION

There is often a gap between what is explicitly dealt with in academic circles concerning technology and technological culture and the concrete experience of and with machines as used by human beings. Moreover, the academicians do not even agree on the proper status and functions of machines; indeed two divergent interpretations are at war with one another. On the one hand there is a series of ideologies which at bottom are "utopian" in their understanding of machines. Machines, as the embodiment of a rational-technological culture, are the hopes of mankind. They are potentially the mechanical "slaves" which can eventually free us from our enslavement to labor and create a New Greece or Utopia. Further examination of this school of thought usually reveals that the holder tacitly assumes that here is a *mere use* of machines and thus all that is needed is an ethical perspective on their proper use. On the other side stand another series of ideologies basically "romantic" at bottom, which hold that machines are ultimately the tempters which have caused man to fall from a pristine organic relation with Nature. Unlike the utopians, romantics see machines as nonneutral; but in a pessimistic way: machines are essentially dehumanizing, they are the sources of an alienation between man and Nature.

The following approach to technological culture, focusing on man-machine relations, is conceived of as an *alternative* approach by way of a phenomenology of man-machine relations. Through such a descriptive psychology, a phenomenology reveals that machines *amplify* certain basic human ambiguities. But also at a higher level, the use of machines opens the way to a second level ambiguity which ultimately implicates the entire range of our understanding of ourselves and our world. Thus against "utopian" ideologies, this interpretation would hold that there is no mere use of machines, but the very use of machines implicates a wider set of existential relations. And equally against the view that the machine is inherently a source of alienation, the phenomenology of man-machine relations reveals that *as a relation* there is no *necessary* alienation in the use of machines. To the contrary, it would seem to be the case that there is often a type of symbiosis between man and machine. The approach here aims at a basic uncovering of the experiential relations man has with and of machines.

I. A PHENOMENOLOGICAL FRAMEWORK

The machine[1] is an essential, concrete embodiment of technological culture. Man's relations with machines are complex, varied and pervasive. They include the range of relations from invention and development to the use of machines and their products. In order to show that these relations require a fresh perspective on the nature of work, technology, and education it is not necessary to explore them all, and consequently I shall concentrate only upon our "use" of machines herein. Even more narrowly, I shall select as my examples ordinary and familiar man-machine relations such as may be found in home and school.

There are several reasons for this selection: first, these ordinary man-machine relations are clearly widespread in technological culture and thus may serve as a broad point of reference for certain states and implications of technological culture as a whole. Second, these ordinary man-machine relations are also those which are typical of the formative educational years and thus bear a more direct relation to education and the role it plays within technological culture. And third, I believe this selection ultimately is symptomatic of the dilemmas and ambiguities of technological culture and of an emerging change of experience in which our perceptions of the world and of ourselves are implicated.

The fact that the man-machine relations I have chosen to analyze are familiar makes the task not at all easier. To the contrary, the

---

[1] I shall use "machine" in the broadest sense possible to cover the range from simple tool to complex computer.

familiar is precisely that which is closest to us and thereby it often hides those implicit and taken for granted presuppositions which we accept, usually without our even realizing that the acceptance was made. The task of the analysis is threefold: first, to lay a descriptive basis for man's experience of machines in man-machine relations; second, to note some implications of this experience for the wider situation within technological culture; and third, to take account of a certain discontinuity between the experience of machines and education.

The analysis will focus upon a descriptive psychology of man-machine relations. I wish to describe some essential features of man's *experience* in his relations with machines, and assume as my operational model a form of the phenomenologist's *being-in-the-world* scheme. This model may be simplified as follows:

$$\text{Man} \longrightarrow \text{World.}$$
$$(a) \qquad\qquad (b) \qquad\qquad (c)$$

By this diagram I mean to suggest that (*a*) Man as experienc*er* is (*b*) experientially always involved with, directed toward (the arrow) a (*c*) World or experienc*ed* environment. Furthermore, although one may focus relatively upon either the "subject-pole" (the experiencing) or upon the "object-pole" (the experienced), neither is to be considered separable. Each "pole" is implicated in the other, in the experiential *relation*.

This model is as yet incomplete in two ways. First, although it may stand as the generalized symbol for man's experiential involvement in his lifeworld (experienced environment), it does not yet place the machine in the relation. This may be done first as follows:

$$\text{Man} \longrightarrow \text{machine} \longrightarrow \text{World.}$$

The justification for placing the machine *on* the relational line will become apparent in the descriptions to follow. At this point it need only be noted that the machine *as* relation may be thought of as a "means" of relating to World.

And finally, the model is incomplete here because it indicates only the "first" movement of man's relations with his lifeworld, the "outgoing" involvements of everyday concerns with the tasks at hand. To complete the model a second relational line is needed:

$$\text{Man} \longrightarrow \text{World.}$$
$$\longleftarrow \; — \; — \; — \; — \; — \; —$$

By the dashed line I mean to suggest that *reflected from* the World, man also enjoys a form of self-experience; such a reflective experience, however, is *not direct*.

It is by way of the world that one arrives at a "self-image." Phenomenologically, there is no self-enclosed and abstracted experience apart from the experience *in* the world. The World as Other is thus essential for one's self experience. Thus the way that World is perceived and understood affects the way we conceive of ourselves.

II. MAN-MACHINE RELATIONS

Once a reflection upon man's relation with machines is begun perhaps the first impression is one of being astounded by the sheer pervasiveness and multiplicity of these relations. Were a catalogue of even the familiar and ordinary machines of home and school to be made the list would soon be quite long:

Home		School
automobile	furnace	projector
lawnmower	washer	tape recorder
power tools	drier	public address system
telephone	dishwasher	microscope
television set	vacuum	telescope
radio	fan	teaching machines
etc.		typewriters
		etc.

And were the sheer number of explicit man-machine relations counted during a given day the number would undoubtedly be surprisingly large (day begins with alarm clock, progresses to electric shaver, toaster and stove, coffeepot, on to the car to the office, the dictaphone, and on to the evening with TV or maybe an electric martini stirrer). This is without even beginning to think of the quiet background presence of machines (furnace, electric lights, air conditioners, etc.). Man-machine relations in our lifeworld are the familiar *omnipresence* of technological culture.

Machines and their presence thus "surround" us. Their reassuring hum is the Holy Spirit of the twentieth century. They provide us with a technological "bubble" which some take with them wherever they go. For example, the walker on the country road today is just as likely as not to have his transistor radio blaring. The camper now views nature as a spectacle from his "camping machine" complete with TV, flush toilet, and picture window. Our lifeworld in its most familiar form may be spoken of as the *technosphere*.

But this first impression of the sheer pervasiveness of machine presence is too undifferentiated to lay the groundwork for a subsequent understanding of how man-machine relations transform the quality of experience. It does, however, suggest that both the pervasiveness of the machine and the taken-for-granted familiarity we have with it is a dominant characteristic of daily life.

From this general impression the reflection upon man-machine relations turns to specific instances of these relationships in order to discern more fully what is involved with man's experience of and with machines. What are the essential features of this experience?

Begin with certain "primitive" man-machine relations which may be actually experienced or recalled: you pick up an electric drill in the basement of your home and begin to drill a hole in a piece of metal—if you take careful stock of this experience you may discover that you actually *feel* the resistance of the metal *at the end* of your drill, that is, the experiential focus is not so much the hand/drill juncture as it is the drill/metal juncture. An even simpler example of this same phenomenon may be experienced by tracing a pencil over a rough surface where again you *feel* the surface *at the end* of the pencil.

What is this quality of experience? Two things may be simultaneously noted: first, the machine "extends" the experience *through* itself and "stretches" that experience to the environment. Conversely, the machine is taken "into" our self-experience. I feel *through* the machine *into* the World and the machine becomes part of "me," of my experiencing subject-pole. I shall speak of this experiential phenomenon as the *transparency function* of this type of man-machine relation. The machine becomes "transparent" in the sense that it is not the object of experience but is embodied within the experiencing subject. I shall call such man-machine relations *embodiment relations*.

If we now relate this first observation about the experience of man-machine relations to the simplified Man-World diagram the following symbolizes this phenomenon:

(Man-machine) ——————————→ World.

The parentheses indicate that the machine is not the object of experience, but is taken into the subject's experiencing. The object of experience is in the World, the experience *of* the hardness of the metal, *of* the rough surface of the desk. Thus the machine is a "means" of experience, or better, in this man-machine relation one relates to the World *through* the machine.

Upon examination of a vast number of examples this turns out to be an essential feature of a large number of specific man-machine relations and includes the "use" of a wide variety of machines. Its range includes the simple tool (pencil) but also extends to very large and complex machines. One ordinary example is the automobile. In driving, one's intention traverses the car and is directed outside at the driving environment: the roadway, other cars, traffic signs, getting there. In extreme situations, such as the "use" of the car as a racing machine, the skilled driver *feels* the juncture car/road surface through his body. His hands are gloved to maximize the feeling of the road rather than the wheel;[2] the sensitive steering and rough springing allows the road to be felt at each crucial turn. One race driver reports, "In a corner it's right on tiptoes, finely balanced on the very edge of adhesion . . . you glide through it though at a rhythm which has by now become natural. Only after you've cleared the corner can you take pleasure in knowing that it has gone well." Here is a prime example of the "first" concentration toward World, the feeling or experiencing of World *through* the transparent machine, and—later—the reflective enjoyment of this man-machine phenomenon. Far simpler and more ordinary is the felt extension of the subject-body experienced by the driver who knows quite well how to parallel-park without extensive visual cues. The driver feels through the whole car and is able to move the unseen bumper only inches from the other car without touching it just as easily as one who is able to slip one's body by another's chair without seeing one's own backside. The sense of body is "extended through" the machine.

Such examples of *embodiment relations* may be extrapolated indefinitely from the ordinary examples of cars, boats, and tools to specialized examples such as wrecking cranes, airplanes, and bulldozers. In each case we may speak of the machine as becoming transparent, taken into the sense of one's body, and of the ex-

---

[2] Gloves muffle even further the hand/wheel feeling and at the same time allow the car/road feeling to be heightened.

perience traversing the machine to find its fulfillment in the World.

Note that these descriptions remain strictly within the limits of experiential man-machine relations. The embodiment relation characterizes the "normal" relation of man to certain machines in use, but there remain the possibilities of other relations as well. For example, the relation *through* the automobile may be radically changed to a relation *with* the automobile as an object of experience. Should it suddenly malfunction while I am driving it (there is the flap-flap of a flat, or the missing of the engine), the car then suddenly looms up between me and the world as an intrusive object and usually my first actions are to try to get it back into its transparency role.

There is a second factor which requires comment here. The embodiment which the relation through the machine allows may be a form of enjoyment *reflectively*. Once the most intense involvement with making the curve is over the race driver "enjoys" the man-machine act as well done. Indeed, this enjoyment is very much the same as that which the athlete feels in relation to his own body when he has performed his feat well. The parallelism is instructive, for the machine in the embodiment relation is "taken into" one's body-experience: just as in any physical activity the body is not the focus of attention, so in the "use" of the machine the machine is not the focus. Body and machine are within the experiencing subject-pole as a functional symbiosis.

The transparency function of embodiment relations is an essential one, but it is not the only aspect of the experience worthy of note. Return to the examples of embodiment relations. In this case think about the "use" of a typewriter. Whether one is composing or copying with a typewriter, the relation is one which follows the embodiment pattern. The typewriter is transparent and the intention traverses through the typewriter to the project at hand. If one switches one's attention deliberately to the typewriter ("what key do I use now to get the *t*?") that same typewriter becomes not the means of experience, but an object of experience intruding into the relationship between man and his project in the world, or, in other words, the machine loses its transparency and becomes an object to be related *to* rather than *through*.

The phenomenon I am after now, however, is a more subtle one. The "use" of the typewriter also *transforms* the experience of the "user." Take composing by typewriter as the example. The accomplished composer-by-typewriter types rapidly; the thoughts flow smoothly and take shape on the paper in written form. Now substitute a quill pen for the typewriter. The difference for the philosopher of experience is immediate and vast. The pen still embodies the project, but in an altogether different way. The "user" finds first that his speed of composition is greatly reduced, no matter how familiar and facile he is with the use of the pen. But he also finds something else going on—his thoughts, now racing far ahead of his writing, may go through many variations before actually being concretized on the written page. His style begins to change and he may begin to appreciate the style of belles lettres of old.

The rather illusive phenomenon I am trying to isolate here is the transformational function of machine use which occurs through the use of a machine. Not only does the machine "extend" one into the world, it also transforms that extension according to a selection or focus. The "use" amplifies certain possibilities while reducing others. I shall characterize this as the *extension-reduction function* of man-machine relations.

This phenomenon is perhaps more difficult to isolate in full embodiment relations precisely because the degree to which the "user" of a machine learns the full potential of the machine the less he can be aware of the subtle changes occurring along with transparency. In other words, the more intuitive and taken for granted the "use" of the machine, the less dramatic and covered over may be the transformational function which is equipresent with the relation.

But a second set of relations does begin to make the transformational function clearer because there is still a partial basis by which to make a comparison. These examples I shall call *sensory-extension-reduction* relations (SER). They are again familiar as "uses" of machines which "extend" the senses. Such are the uses of telephones, television sets, tape recorders, movies, and the like. These machines may be single-sensed (telephone=hearing; telescope=seeing, etc.) or multi-sensed (television=hearing and seeing, etc.). I am unaware of any which are full-sensed in ordinary uses.

In this set of examples the transparency function remains partially operative, but in a changed way. When I listen to you on the phone it is *you* I hear, not the instrument; when I watch television I see the actors through the television set, etc.—but the

transparency is located within perception. Thus although in strict-
est phenomenological terms one perceives with one's body, the
focus upon one or two senses and the lack of a fully felt extension
allows the subject's sense of his body to recede into the background. The machine then, becomes not so much transparent as
translucent, and the embodiment relation is reduced to a perceptual relation. This translucence may be symbolized as:

Man ⟶ (machine) ⟶ World.

The parentheses indicate that the perceptual relation, often a
distancing relation, is where the translucence occurs.

But the essential feature I wish to underline here is the *transformational* function of man-machine relations. With perception
there is a comparative basis in reference to perception through
machines and perception without machines—the transformation
function is partly apparent.[3] Take as a first case "using" a telephone, a single sensed machine. I listen to you, but as a "reduced
presence," *you* as or through *your voice*. The machine "extends"
my hearing, but "reduces" your presence. Your presence is a
quasi-presence rather than a fully embodied presence. There is
a "distance" between us.

This "distance," however, is somewhat strange because in the
use of the telephone the experience of space-presence is transformed. It makes little difference whether you are "actually"
speaking from the next block, California, or Europe (if the
technology is good); your quasi-presence is equally "vivid" in
any case. Objective distance is eliminated and you are present
in a "here and now" immediacy of "near distance."

The same transformation into a "near distance" of machine-
induced immediacy occurs with time in the use of stored SER
machine products. The movie, the TV tape, and the tape recorder
"reduce" time to a quasi-present. One may go see a double feature
of *Klute* and *Barbarella* and watch Jane Fonda "age" within the
same evening. One may see Perry Mason's DA, now dead, still
cautioning against cigarettes in the "near distance" of the quasi-
present. The "use" of the machine extends and reduces our previous experience *of* the World. The implication is one which
points toward the conclusion that there is no *mere* use of ma-

[3] With effort a similar comparison could be made with embodiment relations
between experience without a machine and experience through a machine.

chines. Rather, when we use machines, we in turn are "used" or affected within our experience.

In embodiment relations and SER relations the machine is experienced transparently or translucently. There is, however, another set of machine relations which may be spoken of as experience *of* machines. This feature was anticipated in those cases where the machine intrudes as *object of* experience where transparency is lost due to malfunction. But the machine as object of experience is not always a negative form of experience. The mechanic who listens to, treats, and repairs the malfunctioning engine relates *to* the machine as focal entity. (One should also note that there are some persons who have only what I call *opacity* relations with machines—the driver unable to feel himself through the car has his partner get out and guide him into the space.) These abrupt changes of man-machine relations still do not elicit the full positivity of man-machine relations in which the machine is "normally" Other.

There is such a set of relations among ordinary examples in the home. When using the gas stove, the washing machine, or the dishwasher, the relation is briefly with the machine (setting the dial) and then the machine is left to do its work.[4] It is true that one may still speak of an intention directed toward the world through the machine in the sense that the *result* of the machine's work is the fulfillment of the mode of involvement. But the machine is *not experienced* as transparent, nor is the fulfillment directly experienced through the machine. The person using the stove or dishwasher does not *feel* the object being cooked or the dishes being washed. Thus we may note that the transparency function is quite radically altered. At this point we may diagram the situation thus:

$$\text{Man} \longrightarrow (\text{machine-World}).$$

The machine is still part of the man-world relation in that it facilitates a world project, but the machine is now opaque and "other" between man and the project.

---

[4] It is interesting to note that many machines used in the home are automatic or semi-automatic. If work is not shared between husband and wife the woman often has more experience with such opacity relations than the man. Furthermore, the dishwasher (opacity relation) is clearly preferred to the vacuum cleaner (embodiment relation). The implications for both a theory of labor and for so-called alienation are interesting.

In some cases relations may actually be *with* machines. The typewriter-computer teaching machines with a program in mathematics or logic which our children "use" are closer to experiences *with* machines. There is a "conversation" between the machine and the "user" and the machine emerges as a quasi-Other. Such machines in use parallel not the body-experience, but the experience of others. One attends to what the machine "says" in its typing. One may even be amused or angered at the response.

The relations in which machine and world become paired in an *opacity function* may be taken one step further even within the range of familiar machines. In those machines which are "normally" fully automatic, the machine becomes environment or part of the World itself. In home and school such machines are those which form a part of the ordinary background of our environment: heating furnaces whose fringe presence is at best the whir of the motor; electric lights; the water system supplied by unseen and unheard distant pumps. Here the machine is neither taken into the body-experience nor is it a transparency through which perception occurs. It rather produces the experienc*ed* opaqueness of World itself.[5] The machine as Other becomes intertwined with the whole sense of the World, it becomes a quality of the surrounding environment. It is here that the familiar presence which is taken for granted fills in the plenum of World as *technosphere*.

The relations I have oversimply and briefly traced may now be seen to form a continuum ranging from the machine as part of the subject's self-experience in its transparency function to the machine as Other in both focal and field objects of experience in an opacity function. The machine has some kind of presence throughout the whole range of man's experiences. And throughout this continuum runs the subtle and hard to isolate transformational functions of the use of machines in man-machine relations.

III. MAN-MACHINE RELATIONS AND SELF-UNDERSTANDING

If this sparse descriptive phenomenology rings true to our experience of, through, and with machines, the implications for a second level speculative reflection now become important. How

[5] The machine as a world-part may be experienced either focally, as in a direct relation with a machine, or as a part of the background or field. Many automatic machines "normally" function as background.

do our relations with machines affect our situation within our world and ultimately our understanding of ourselves?

Perhaps the opening to this stage of thought is best made by looking again at the transformational functions revealed in man-machine relations. Three general and preliminary features may be noted: (1) First, the "use" of machines is nonneutral in the sense that any use of machines transforms the quality of experience whether or not this is explicitly noticed by the naive machine user. (2) There is also something like an inverse ratio within the transformational factor between what is first starkly apparent and what later becomes intuitive and taken for granted in the successful use of the machine. That is, the more adept the machine user becomes in learning the machine's use, the less likely he may be aware of the transformation which has occurred. Here the process of learning is involved crucially. And (3) the nonneutrality of machine use may be spoken of as a transformation by *inclination* rather than *determination*. The use of the machine allows a learning, sometimes quite gradually, of a path of least resistance rather than a necessary path. The machine "calls for" a selective response if it is to be well used. Just as in the early days of large machine design the machine could not "dictate" that the use of pseudo-gothic frillery be abandoned, yet as the machine began to emerge in its uses more fully such frillery was gradually seen as superfluous. Again, in the use of a typewriter the machine cannot "dictate" the abandonment of a belles lettres style, but it can, through its speed, "incline" the user away from the style by making that style more difficult to produce.

Nor is it necessary that the user ever fully learn the best way of machine use. I have never yet seen a child who on being given a bow and arrow did not first "pinch" the arrow between thumb and forefinger—a method of shooting which distinctly limits the pounds of pull one is able to shoot and a method still used by some aboriginal tribesman. The archer who has learned to pull the string with his fingers, resting the arrow lightly between them, not only may use a more powerful bow, but soon develops an accuracy unmatched by users of the more primitive position. The bow's potential does not dictate but it does open a pathway. This "soft determinism" of the machine in no way weakens its non-neutrality; to the contrary, it plays a role in the subtlety with which the transformation of man's entire experience occurs.

The transformational role vis-a-vis experience spans the entire continuum of man-machine relations. Beginning with the "primitive" man-machine embodiment relation, the transformation of the sense of body in relation to the World may be noted. "Man," may well have been technological in that first instant of picking up a club to "extend" his striking power *and his experience through the club* when he emerged millennia ago. The "use" of the club is already a transformation of the sense of "I can." In this primitive use of a machine a certain isomorphism of the existential ambiguity of man's "I can" occurs between the primitive and the modern. The sense of power *through* the embodiment relation, enjoyed by clubber as well as by the adolescent expressing his sense of power through the automobile, is constant even if the means by which the embodiment occurs are more complex now. The potential *hubris*, as well as the potential *symbiosis* of man-machine relations, may be seen in this existential "use" of machines.

This man-machine relation is "primitive" in another sense as well. For although even primitive man already surrounded himself with a rather vast array of "machines" (clubs, boats, tools of various sorts, rope ladders, levers, etc.) the use of these machines relied little on the surrounding presence of complete technospheric transformations. At the opposite end of the continuum the surrounding presence of the machine as the context or field of experience at the "object-pole" transforms the entire sense of World. For example, in that contemporary "primitive" embodiment through the automobile, although the enjoyment of the automobile is *through* the embodiment relation, the world-field in which the automobile functions is also a machine-world. The system of roads, signs, and other cars, let alone the background systems of repair, refueling, and other machine-oriented systems, is what makes possible this enjoyed embodiment. The automobile driver lives and moves and has his or her being *in* a technosphere. The comparative status of "raw nature" in ancient and modern times is illustrative: the man with the club needed only a wild animal to provide him with a project for embodiment through his "machine." His world-field was a pretechnological context just as his "technology" was concentrated within the subject-pole of embodiment relations. Today "raw nature" is either a fringe feature or, better, a feature which has increasingly become a museum piece *within* the technosphere. Conservationists who ask for city

green belts and the preservation of wild lands are actually request-
ing that those pieces of "raw nature" be set aside for aesthetic
appreciation *inside* the wider world-field of the machine-transformed otherness of the world. As the machine presence becomes
more pervasive, not only as a means of human expression, but
as a background quality of the world as a technosphere, a certain
inescapability from this dominant quality of our world experience
appears. The organicist who wishes to live "simply" but also to
retain his record player and electric guitar carries with him not a
simple instrument, but a whole world. Nor do we often want to
totally escape that technological quality of the world. The kidney
machine, the artificial lung, the temporary and perhaps permanent
artificial heart of medical technology literally allow our life to
continue. The plenum of machine presence spanning the continuum from self-experience (embodiment relation) to the machine as Other (opacity relation) is full.

But again, the most dramatic occurrence of the profound transformation of man's experience of himself and his world may be
seen in SER relations. Here the gradual, subtle, but sure transformation of very perceptions occurs. We have already noted
the degree to which SER relations transform both the sense of
presence of the Other through the machine and the sense of "near
distance" into a "here and now" space-time situation. The Other,
space, and time are immediate, but immediate as quasi-present.

This quasi-presence creates its own ambiguity. On the one hand
the "extension" through SER relations allows all sensory "distance" to come within reach; on the other hand the presence remains short of full embodiment. It is always partial or disembodied.
The result is what I would like to think of speculatively as a spectator effect—the World through SER relations becomes a Spectacle.
Thus although the seven o'clock news, the cartoon, the TV movie,
and the documentary are "different" they all bear the same machine-transformed presence.

Nor does the transformation effect remain limited to the dura-
tion of watching. The transformation effect exceeds its immediate
context. For example, I have often noted an experience frequently confirmed by students which I call a cinematographic effect.

I look out my office window at the chemistry building, situated
in a bulldozed field from which issues a series of steam plumes
from the heating tunnels. The one-way windows opaquely reflect
the outline of the Life Sciences building and I have the strange

sense that I have seen this Antonioni movie somewhere before in a strange inversion of ordinary experience with that of the cinema. The SER relation trains us to see differently now just as painting once did. And this transformation enters daily life.

At first this sort of experience might be thought of as "strange" were it not familiar at least with so many of the young. However, upon deeper reflection this inversion of ordinary and machine-transformed "reality" is not new at all, but one further extension of the technosphere. An earlier and hence more familiar and taken for granted inversion is already part of our whole understanding of the world. The transformations of perception and the sense of "reality" through SER relations are as old as machine-induced scientific observation, at least as old as Galileo and his telescope. The stars we see today with the naked eye are far outnumbered by those available through the SER relation of the telescope—and it is the latter machine-present stars which have become the measure of the "real."[6]

The implication I am pointing to is that the sensory extensions and reductions which arose out of the scientific community's use of observational machinery are now in a wider and more profound sense paralleled by a transformation of a more total sensibility through the public use of SER relations. The suggestion is that just as the view of the cosmos was earlier transformed through an instrumental context, so the view of the human world through a media context may likewise be occurring. But in this latter case the "spectator attitude" which is induced spans a more complete set of human experiences than the carefully limited set of scientific observations. The televised landings on the moon illustrate the crossings of these transformations. The moon becomes a "near distant" quasi-presence as never before. But its presence is not a strictly controlled "scientific presence," but a public presence. The moon has become "scientific object" and "spectacle" at one and the same time. We are very far from knowing what the effect of such a possible transformation of sensibility might entail, precisely because of the inherent ambiguity of machine-induced "near distance" and its "spectator" or quasi-aesthetic attitude inclination for the human user of SER man-machine relations.

Thus within the technosphere, it is the whole of our experience which undergoes transformation. Our experience of self, includ-

---

[6] See Patrick Heelan, "Horizon, Objectivity and Reality in the Physical Sciences," *International Quarterly*, Vol. 7 (1970).

ing the sense of body and one's "I can," the very perception of the world and others, and the machine-pervaded presence of the world itself undergoes transformation.

IV. EPILOGUE: MAN-MACHINE RELATIONS AND EDUCATION

What does the phenomenology of man-machine relations with its possible resultant implications for man's self-understanding have to do with education and schooling? At first, in terms of *direct* and *explicit* connections it would seem there is little connection. Within the school there is a little interrogation of the taken for granted experiences with machines as elsewhere, both in terms of the learning process vis-à-vis machines and in terms of direct connections between man-machine relations and the usual conceptual-ideological treatments of technology.

Yet while this may be the case, the schools are prime users of technology. The schools' use of machines covers the full range of relations previously described. Embodiment relations in driver's education, in various forms of "shop" and in technical education are employed. At the other end of the continuum an increasing use of teaching machines, computers, calculators, and the like employ opacity relations. Also, the all-pervasive machine presence as surrounding background is evident in the public address system which can instantly bring the principal's voice to all, in the productions of the mimeograph machines, in the enclosed and controlled "environments" for living which the buildings themselves are, etc. But above all, the machines which are "tools for learning" are of the type which focally relate to the transformation of perception and understanding, those which use SER relations: the audio-visual aids such as movies, television, tapes, records; scientific instruments such as telescope, microscope, magnifying glass, all use the nonneutral man-machine relations which ultimately affect our whole range of self-understanding.

On a second look the lack of *direct* and *explicit* connection is not so startling precisely because much of the actual learning of machine use is *implicit* and *tacit*. In learning embodiment relations, for example, at best one may be "coached." The actual learning comes in the doing itself which occurs sometimes gradually, but equally sometimes occurs at a stroke. Conceptual and theoretical knowledge plays a very distant and indirect role here —one may know much physics and remain incapable of riding a motorcycle—or equally know none at all and be an excellent rider.[7] Here the learning process is one which occurs as the machine *becomes* embodied. It comes into its "normal use" relation when it ceases to be an object or obstacle and becomes increasingly transparent within the subject's sense of the man-machine conjunction.

Furthermore, this tacit learning is in no way limited or even focused in the school as such. The child comes to the school already taught in the use of television, the movies, the record, and perhaps also the telescope and microscope. The tacitness, implicitness, and familiarity are already learning imparted within the technological culture. This is to say that the school is as immersed in the implicit and taken for granted involvements of technological society as any other unreflective element of the culture. Yet at the same time, the universal pervasiveness, the tacit qualities, and the implicit aspects of basic experience indicate that here lies an essential element of technological man's experience itself.

There is a learning *from* machines, a learning which needs its own type of investigation. In comparing human and machine "intentionalities" one often discovers that the machine "intentionality" is quite different from the human one and from it there is a learning out of which new perspectives upon the world may be gained. For example, the human listener in a noisy auditorium can and "normally" does hear the speaker. But an ordinary microphone "hears" everything in terms of its "physical" qualities. Thus coughs, the squeaking of chairs, fans, may well blur out the words of the speaker. This machine "intentionality" is much closer to that of the empiricist's sense-data entities than any human—and the machine context is closer to the scientific constitution of "reality" than some forms of ordinary experience. It is in the *difference* that we learn what we did not previously know both about ourselves and about the world.

In short, the result, of these analyses which seek to reexamine the *experiences* within man-machine relations is that there is a need to reformulate the question of man's relations to machines. At the deepest level what emerges here is an understanding that man's relations with machines are *not* themselves *mechanical*—

---

[7] I do not deny that a theoretical knowledge enriches rather than impoverishes experience. The motorcyclist who is also an informed mechanic both feels and knows the workings of his or her machine.

they are rather *existential*. They are a way of being-in-the-world, a technologically oriented way of being-in-the-world. And until that way is explored, understood, and criticized in terms of the experiential bases of man-machine relations we will not have gained a grasp on many of the fundamental dilemmas and ambiguities of the twentieth century. If I have just now located a beginning it is because the beginning often lies the farthest from our considerations. And if this phenomenology constitutes a good beginning of an alternate view of man and machine, then our debates may be reconstituted and a way found of returning to human beings' primal experiences of the world in which they now live.

Toward a Humanistic
Conception of Education

Noam Chomsky

I had the very great personal honor to deliver some memorial lectures for Bertrand Russell at Trinity College, Cambridge,[1] and in the course of thinking about and preparing for them I had the pleasure of reading and rereading a fair amount of his work written over many years. Russell had quite a number of things to say on educational topics that are no less important today than when he first discussed them. He regularly took up—not only discussed but also tried to carry out—very interesting and provocative ideas in the field of educational theory and practice. He claimed throughout his years of interest in this area that the primary goal of education is to elicit and fortify whatever creative impulse man may possess. And this conclusion, which he formulated in many different ways over a period of years, derives from a particular concept of human nature that he also expressed in many different forms. It grows from what he called a "humanistic conception," which regards a child as a gardener regards a young tree, that is, as something with a certain intrinsic nature, which will develop into an admirable form, given proper soil and air and light."

Elsewhere he pointed out that "the soil and the freedom required for a man's growth are immeasurably more difficult to discover and to obtain. . . . And the full growth which may be hoped

This paper is a slightly revised version of a talk given at the University of Illinois at Urbana-Champaign on April 1, 1971, under the sponsorship of the College of Education and the G. E. Miller lecture committee.

[1] Published as *Problems of Knowledge and Freedom* (Pantheon: New York, 1971). Unless otherwise noted, all specific references to Russell's writings are given in that volume.

for cannot be defined or demonstrated; it is subtle and complex, it can only be felt by a delicate intuition and dimly apprehended by imagination and respect." Therefore he argued that education should be guided by "the spirit of reverence" for "something sacred, indefinable, unlimited, something individual and strangely precious, the growing principle of life, an embodied fragment of the dumb striving of the world." This is one view of the nature of education, based on a certain conception of human nature that Russell called the humanistic conception. According to this conception the child has an intrinsic nature, and central to it is a creative impulse. Pursuing that line of thinking, the goal of education should be to provide the soil and the freedom required for the growth of this creative impulse; to provide, in other words, a complex and challenging environment that the child can imaginatively explore and, in this way, quicken his intrinsic creative impulse and so enrich his life in ways that may be quite varied and unique. This approach is governed, as Russell said, by a spirit of reverence and humility: reverence for the precious, varied, individual, indeterminate growing principle of life; and humility with regard to aims and with regard to the degree of insight and understanding of the practitioners. Because he was well acquainted with modern science Russell was also well aware of how little we really know about the aims and purposes of human life. Therefore the purpose of education, from this point of view, cannot be to control the child's growth to a specific predetermined end, because any such end must be established by arbitrary authoritarian means; rather the purpose of education must be to permit the growing principle of life to take its own individual course, and to facilitate this process by sympathy, encouragement, and challenge, and by developing a rich and differentiated context and environment.

This humanistic conception of education clearly involves some factual assumptions about the intrinsic nature of man, and, in particular, about the centrality to that intrinsic nature of a creative impulse. If these assumptions, when spelled out properly, prove to be incorrect, then these particular conclusions with regard to educational theory and practice will not have been demonstrated. On the other hand, if these assumptions are indeed correct much of contemporary American educational practice is rationally as well as morally questionable.

The humanistic conception of man leads to what might be

called libertarian educational theories. It also leads in a natural and direct way to libertarian concepts of social organization that incorporate closely related ideas concerning, for example, the central and essential concept of the nature of work. In this context Russell quoted a remark by Kropotkin that ". . . overwork is repulsive to human nature—not work. Overwork for supplying the few with luxury—not for the well-being of all. Work, labor is a physiological necessity, a necessity of expanding accumulated bodily energy, a necessity which is health and life itself."[2] Elaborating on this theme, Russell pointed out that ". . . if man had to be tempted to work instead of driven to it, the obvious interest of the community would be to make work pleasant," and social institutions would be organized to this end. They would provide the conditions, in other words, under which productive, creative work would be freely undertaken as a part of normal, healthy life. To place these particular remarks in an appropriate historical context, one who conceives of the "species character" of man as "free, conscious activity" and "productive life," in the words of the early Marx,[3] will also seek to create the higher form of society that Marx envisioned in which labor has become not only a means of life, but also the highest want in life.

There is a contrasting and more prevalent view of the nature of work, namely, that labor is a commodity to be sold on the market for maximal return, that it has no intrinsic value in itself; its only value and immediate purpose is to afford the possibility to consume, for on this account humans are primarily concerned with maximizing consumption, not with producing creatively under conditions of freedom. They are unique and individual not by virtue of what they make, what they do for others, or how they transform nature; rather individuality is determined by material possessions and by consumption: I am what I am because of what I own and use up. Thus on this view the primary aim of life must be to maximize the accumulation of commodities, and work is undertaken almost solely for this aim. The underlying assumption, of course, is that work is repulsive to human nature—contrary to Kropotkin, Russell, Marx, and many others—and that leisure

---

[2] "Anarchist Communism." Quoted by Russell in *Proposed Roads to Freedom: Anarchy, Socialism and Syndicalism* (Henry Holt and Co.: New York, 1919), p. 100.

[3] Specifically taken up in the *Economic and Philosophical Manuscripts*.

and possession, rather than creative labor, must be the goal of humankind.

Again, the issue involves factual assumptions. On this conception of human nature the goal of education should be to train children and provide them with the skills and habits that will fit them in an optimal way for the productive mechanism, which is meaningless in itself from a human point of view, but necessary to provide them with the opportunity to exercise their freedom as consumers, a freedom that can be enjoyed in the hours when they are free from the onerous burden of labor. Such an idea is, of course, repugnant to one who accepts Russell's humanistic conception of human nature, but it bears repeating that between these contrasting views of work and education there is a factual judgment involved with regard to intrinsic human nature.

This question, in short, is whether creative work can be the highest want of life or whether labor is a burden, and idleness and consumption of commodities the highest want and goal of life.

It may be that the humanistic conception expressed by Russell, Kropotkin, Marx, and many others is wrong. I believe it is correct, but in either case there are direct consequences with regard to social organization as well as education. This possibility has been recognized by social critics who tried to elaborate the humanistic conception and draw appropriate conclusions from it. For example, Russell quoted a pamphlet of the National Guilds League, a British working-class radical socialist organization of the early part of the century, which tried to develop a point of view rather like the humanistic one outlined above. In the course of speaking about what Russell called the humanistic conception of man, it admits that "there is a cant of the Middle Ages and a cant of 'joy in labor.' " But it goes on to declare that "it were better, perhaps, to risk that cant" than to accept a philosophy that makes "work a purely commercial activity, a soulless and joyless thing." Again, my personal bias is toward Russell and the "medieval cant," but I am not directly concerned to defend this position here so much as I want to suggest a connection between the concomitant view of human nature—specifically with regard to creativity and productive work—and certain questions concerning educational practice: namely, whether it should be oriented toward freedom and challenge or toward guidance, direction, and control.

This debate between the positions did not originate in the present century. To mention one case of considerable historical importance, Wilhelm von Humboldt, an extremely important and too-neglected thinker whose works have only been made readily available in the last few years, wrote about educational practice and its foundation in a certain concept of human nature, along the lines of the humanistic conception we have been considering. He said that ". . . to inquire and to create—these are the centers around which all human pursuits more or less directly revolve." "All moral culture," he wrote, "springs solely and immediately from the inner life of the soul and can only be stimulated in human nature, and never produced by external and artificial contrivance. . . . Whatever does not spring from a man's free choice, or is only the result of instruction and guidance, does not enter into his very being, but remains alien to his true nature; he does not perform it with truly human energies, but merely with mechanical exactness." If a man acts in this way, he says, we may "admire what he does, but despise what he is."[4]

This view has implications for educational practice similar to Russell's, and, of course, related implications for social theory. Again, one who regards human nature in this light will proceed to search for social forms that will encourage the truly human action that grows from inner impulse. In this case, Humboldt writes, ". . . all peasants and craftsmen might be elevated into artists; that is, men who love their labor for its own sake, improve it by their own plastic genius and inventive skill, and thereby cultivate their intellect, ennoble their character, and exalt and refine their pleasures. And so, humanity would be ennobled by the very things which now, though beautiful in themselves, so often tend to degrade it."[5]

Humbolt was an important educational theorist as well as a practitioner. He was one of the founders of the modern university system and at the same time he was a great libertarian social thinker who directly inspired and in many ways anticipated John Stuart Mill. His rationalistic conception of human nature, emphasizing free creative action as the essence of that nature, was developed further in the libertarian social thought of the industrial period, specifically in nineteenth century libertarian socialist and

---

[4] Wilhelm von Humboldt, *The Limits of State Action*, ed. J. W. Burrow (Cambridge: Cambridge University Press, 1969), pp. 76, 63, 28.

[5] *Ibid.*, p. 27.

anarchist social theory and their accompanying doctrines concerning educational practice.

Let me reiterate the point that these views involve questions of fact concerning human nature, and that there are certain conclusions that one may draw from these factual judgments with respect to educational theory and practice, social theory, and the activism which naturally flows from a conscientious commitment to the conclusions of that theory. Judgments about these matters are, in fact, very often determined not so much by evidence as by ideological commitment. This is not particularly surprising, though it is not too happy a state. It is not surprising because there is very little evidence that bears on these issues, yet we cannot avoid making judgments on them. We may, and commonly do, tacitly accept most of the judgments which prevail in a given society. In other words, we make these judgments rather mindlessly in conformity to prevailing ideology. It requires effort to make them thoughtfully, recognizing the inadequacy of the evidence. But there are no other alternatives.

In this kind of situation the null hypothesis would be the point of view that Bertrand Russell expressed. That is, in the absence of conflicting evidence, the proper course should be to approach these problems with the reverence and humility that Russell suggested in discussing his "humanistic conception." In the absence of compelling reasons to the contrary, one should be quite cautious about trying to control someone else's life and character and mode of thought. The acceptance or rejection of the null hypothesis has political and social as well as pedagogic consequences for the educator and teacher. There are, in other words, significant consequences to one's thinking or lack of thinking about these issues and a corresponding personal and professional responsibility.

To become somewhat more concrete, consider the matter of control of behavior. In a certain sense this will be abhorrent to the person who accepts the humanistic conception of education. There is no doubt that control of behavior can be carried out to some degree. Effective techniques of conditioning and control exist that have been investigated experimentally in great detail. But it would surely be a mistake to consider that these investigations have significantly advanced our understanding of learning processes. For example, there are numerous results on the effects of various schedulings of reinforcement on the frequency of simple responses. Have we learned that learning takes place through conditioning, by the application of such methods in a natural or contrived environment? Of course we have not learned anything of the sort. Learning involves the interplay of an innate endowment, innately determined maturational processes, and a process of interaction with the environment. The pattern of this interaction and the nature of the various factors is largely unknown, as any honest investigator will concede. In some domains—language is an example—such evidence as is available seems to indicate that the innate component is extremely significant and that, in considerable detail, the form and character of what is learned is determined by an innate schematism of mind. In fact, precisely those characteristics of language that make it an effective instrument for free thought and expression seem to have their origins in this innately determined structure. It is fairly clear that language cannot be seriously regarded as a system of habits and skills acquired through training. Rather it must be understood as an elaborate mental structure largely determined by innate properties of mind. This point of view may be right or wrong when it is spelled out in detail, but there is no inherent mystery about it. One could make it quite precise and quite explicit; it is in no sense mysterious. What is mysterious, perhaps, is the biological or neurophysiological basis for these (and other) mechanisms of mind, but that is another question entirely.

There is a point of confusion that might be mentioned here, a confusion that one finds among many linguists who have identified the free creative use of language with the system of rules that permit that free creative use, that is, with the recursive property of grammars that permits arbitrarily many utterances to be constructed. These two notions, although related, are not to be confused. To do so would be a category mistake, a confusion of performance and competence. There are rules that permit an indefinite range of possible expression. Such rules are an indispensable component in the creative use of language. But a computer that produced sentences randomly would not be acting creatively. There is an interplay, a complex relationship between constraints and rules and creative behavior. If there is no system of rules, no system of constraints, no set of forms, then creative behavior is quite unthinkable. Someone who is throwing paints at a wall in an arbitrary fashion is not acting creatively as an artist. Similarly some system of constraints and forms and principles and rules is presupposed as a basis for any kind of creative action. But creative action has to be understood in different terms, with this being only one fundamental component.[6]

Returning to the question of what has been learned from the study of conditioning, it could not be true that these investigations have demonstrated that learning results from conditioning for the very simple reason that the fundamental problem of learning theory has barely been posed, let alone answered, within the theory of learning as it has developed over the years. There is an important conceptual gap in the theory of learning which makes it very difficult to pose this fundamental question and therefore casts a good deal of doubt on the significance of any results that are achieved, however interesting they may be in their own terms. The conceptual gap is basically this: the theory of learning is concerned with situation and action; that is, it is concerned with stimulus and response. But there really is no concept of "what is learned." The fundamental problem of learning theory, properly understood, is to determine how what is learned is related to the experience on the basis of which it is learned. We can study, if we like, the relation between stimulus and response, but it is very unlikely that such a study will contribute to solving the problem because that relationship is surely mediated by the system of knowledge and belief that has been acquired, by what has been learned.

Take again the case of language, which is perhaps the clearest example we can consider. Stimuli impinge upon the organism, which carries out certain "verbal behavior." It is prefectly obvious that the person's behavior as a speaker of a language is affected by what he knows as a speaker of this language, by the system of rules that is mentally represented in some fashion, which provides the framework within which the largely free, creative behavior takes place. If we want to study learning of language, we are going to have to study the relationship between experience and what is learned, between experience and knowledge, experience and this internally represented system of rules. We can then go ahead to study behavior, that is, interaction among many factors, including immediate stimuli, mediated through the already known

[6] These linguistic themes are taken up in more detail in *Problems of Knowledge and Freedom*, pp. 3–51.

system of rules. We can study the relationship between these factors and behavior. But to try to study the relationship between stimuli and responses directly is a sure road to triviality.

We could not expect to find a direct connection between experience and action, omitting any reference to what is learned. Nor could we even pose the questions of learning theory with that concept—what is learned, what is known—with that concept missing. To pose the problem of learning theory in the first place, one must face the task of systematizing what it is a person knows or believes, or has acquired or learned at a certain stage in his or her development. (The same is true of animal learning, for that matter.) Later we can ask how that system of knowledge or belief arose from the various factors that enter into it—experience, maturational processes, and so on. But to avoid any concern for the nature of what is known and what is learned is simply to condemn the enterprise to barrenness in the first place.

When we pose the question of what is learned, the few tentative answers that seem plausible are remote from the tacit and generally unargued assumptions of many learning theorists. The belief that conditioning is an important feature of learning may conceivably be true, but at the moment it stands as a kind of dogma. And if, in fact, the humanistic conception of human nature, work, and education mentioned earlier is correct, then the theory of conditioning may be a dangerous and possibly pernicious dogma. Recall again Humboldt's remark that "whatever does not spring from a man's free choice, or is only the result of instruction and guidance, does not enter into his very being but remains alien to his true nature; he does not perform it with truly human energies, but merely with mechanical exactness."[7] The fact that this observation was made by a profound social critic does not make it correct, of course, but there is not any scientific evidence to suggest that it is false. Indeed, I think that our own experience and the insights that arise from it—which are not to be discounted in areas where scientific evidence is so sparse—lend a certain credibility to this view. At an experimental level there is some evidence that voluntary, self-willed action plays a very significant role in learning and acquiring knowledge. This work supports the observations and guesses concerning the intrinsic, self-willed character of anything of real human significance that is acquired

---

[7] Humboldt, *The Limits of State Action*, p. 28.

by a child in the course of learning—or an adult as well, for that matter.

What about the concomitant idea that knowledge is acquired in small incremental steps? Consider a teaching program for geometry. Again there are inherent dangers in any such approach. Perhaps the dangers are even greater if the approach begins to work. To educate a mathematician, you do not train him to face problems which are just on the border of what he has already learned to do. Rather, he must learn to deal with new situations, to take imaginative leaps, to act in a creative fashion. If he is going to be a good mathematician, he must have a good imagination and use it frequently. We really do not understand what is involved in taking such imaginative, creative leaps in mathematics, or in any other domain. But it is plausible to suppose that the ability to undertake these essentially creative efforts is acquired through the experience of coming to grips with interesting, complex problems that are challenging and which attract one's attention but are not at all closely related in any incremental fashion to the skills that one has achieved and acquired. Programs that work quite successfully in teaching some fixed domain through small incremental steps may precisely deprive persons of the opportunity to develop these poorly understood abilities that enable them to act in a normal human fashion, occasionally with genius; and perhaps much the same is true of normal human behavior.

The schools have taken quite a beating in recent years and I do not want to join in the pummeling. Personally, I do not really agree with the more radical critics like Paul Goodman or Ivan Illich who imply that the solution to the problem of the schools is virtually to eliminate them. (On the humanistic conception of education, it is important to provide the richest and most challenging of environments for children so that the creative impulse will have maximum utilization, and a well-planned school should be able to provide just that environment.) But I think one cannot discount a good deal of what Goodman and Illich say. A close friend of mine came from Europe at age 15 and went to an American high school in New York. He was struck immediately by the fact that if he came to school three minutes late he had to go to the principal's office to be properly chastised, but if he did not do his work in a particularly intelligent fashion or if he was not creative or original, then people might not be too happy about it but at least he did not have to go to the principal's office. And quite generally, punctuality and obedience were very highly valued and were the values that definitely had to be instilled. As to originality or achievement, well that was nice too, but it obviously was not of paramount importance.

An approach to education which emphasizes such values as punctuality and obedience is very well suited for training factory workers as tools of production. It is not suited at all to the humanistic conception of creative and independent individuals, which brings us back again to those assumptions concerning human nature and the social forces and educational practices that give due regard to intrinsic human capacities.

The consideration of assumptions of this kind is particularly important in a rich and a powerful country with immense potential for good and for evil. The early experiences of citizens of this country are a matter of enormous human significance. It is a cliché to say that the responsibility of the teacher to the student, like that of the parent to the child, is beyond calculation, but it is further amplified to the extent that this child can affect history. Here in the United States we are clearly dealing with that situation. One of the worst forms of control, developed to very dangerous extremes in totalitarian states, is indoctrination of children. We very rightly deplore it elsewhere. We rarely recognize it at home. I do not pretend to be well-versed in this matter but I do have several children in school and I look over their shoulders occasionally. Some of the kinds of indoctrination that face them are, to state it frankly, frightening. I went through an issue of the *Weekly Reader*,[8] a children's newspaper, which discussed the problem of American prisoners in North Vietnam. It said, "A war is going on in Vietnam. The war has been going for many years. North Vietnam and South Vietnam are fighting each other. Americans are fighting on the side of South Vietnam. Many Americans have been taken prisoner by North Vietnam." Then it talked about some American children. "The children sent their letters to the president of North Vietnam. The children asked him to set American prisoners of war free and to let the men come home to the United States." There is also a teachers' edition which goes along with the paper, which explains how the teacher is supposed to elicit the appropriate answers.

Look at what the *Weekly Reader* was telling these impression-

[8] *Weekly Reader*, January, 1971; fourth grade edition.

able young children: first that there was a war between North Vietnam and South Vietnam. That is of course totally false. Anybody in the government knows that that was false. They know perfectly well that it began as a war between the United States and the peasant societies of Indochina, in particular South Vietnam. It never was a war between the North and the South. If you ask when the first regular units of the North Vietnamese Army were discovered in South Vietnam, you get the curious answer that it was in late April, 1965—one battalion of 400 men, approximately two and a half months after the regular bombardment of North Vietnam and South Vietnam, approximately eight months after the first bombing of strategic targets—at a time when there were 35,000 American troops deployed. In fact U.S. military forces had been engaged in direct military actions for four or five years. So it is hardly a war between North Vietnam and South Vietnam.

Second, the impression that the *Weekly Reader* tries to convey is that the pilots were captured while defending South Vietnam from North Vietnam. There is not a word about what the pilots were doing when they were captured. What they were doing, of course, was destroying everything in North Vietnam outside of the central population centers, a fact which is still not admitted in the United States. There is also not a word about prisoners captured by the United States and South Vietnam; for example, those who were dropped to their death from helicopters or those who were tortured or those who found their way to the tiger cages in Con Son island. And there is no particular explanation in the *Weekly Reader* as to why prisoners should be released while the United States continued to drop 70,000 tons of bombs on Indochina as it did during the month in which this article appeared, January 1971.[9]

But worst of all there is not a word about what the United States soldiers have been doing in South Vietnam and in Laos. These countries, of course, have borne the main brunt of the American aggression in Indochina, not North Vietnam. Now this kind of distortion, which we see in the *Weekly Reader*, continues to pound on children through most of their adult lives as well. The corruption of the media in this respect is extreme.

Children have to be spared indoctrination but they also have

[9] For a fuller, non–Weekly Reader account, see Noam Chomsky, *At War with Asia* (Pantheon: New York, 1969).

to be trained to resist it in later life. This is a very serious problem in our society and every other society. Let me give another example. I have a daughter in junior high school, and in looking at her history book on the topic of the countries of the communist bloc, I came across the following: "In no case did a revolution merely happen. The shift to Communism was skillfully brought about by groups of dedicated, Moscow-trained revolutionaries." In China and Cuba, for example? This is certainly nonsense, but it is pernicious nonsense, and when it is drilled into people constantly, day after day, week after week, throughout their lives, the effects are overwhelming.

This section of the book goes on to discuss peaceful coexistence. It says, "We all believe first in the existence of different systems of government and society, and second in the right of every people to settle independently all the political and social problems of their country. We have always had respect for the sovereignty of other nations and have adhered to the principle of non-interference in internal affairs. And we strongly believe in and practice the policy of trying to settle all international questions by negotiations." Then the book turns to the leaders of the Soviet Union. It says that "they claim they want to end the cold war," and so on. Before this can happen, the book continues, "we have to learn to trust each other"; but "Such actions as those the Soviet Union has taken in North Korea, in North Vietnam and in Cuba, in which Soviet-trained communists have taken over the reins of government have given the United States ample cause to doubt the sincerity of Mr. Krushchev's pronouncements about peaceful co-existence." [10]

There was often good reason to doubt the sincerity of Mr. Krushchev's pronouncements, but on the basis of Soviet actions in North Vietnam, such doubt would be difficult to defend, particularly since this book was written in 1963 when there were no Soviet actions in Indochina. There were, however, plenty of American actions: in that year a substantial part of the population of South Vietnam was forcibly removed by the U.S.-imposed regime to what we would call "concentration camps" if any other country had built them.

Let me give a third example, also from the text book of one of

[10] C. Kohn and D. Drummond, *The World Today* (McGraw, Hill and Co.: New York, 1963).

my own daughters—this one in the fourth grade. It is a social science reader called *Exploring New England*. The book has a protagonist, a young boy named Robert who is told about the marvels of colonial times. In the course of the narrative the extermination of the Pequot tribe by Captain John Mason is described as follows: "His little army attacked in the morning before it was light and took the Pequots by surprise. The soldiers broke down the stockade with their axes, rushed inside, and set fire to the wigwams. They killed nearly all the braves, squaws, and children, and burned their corn and other food. There were no Pequots left to make more trouble. When the other Indian tribes saw what good fighters the white men were, they kept the peace for many years. 'I wish I were a man and had been there,' thought Robert." That is the last that Robert hears or speaks about this matter. Nowhere does he express or hear any second thoughts.[11]

I think it is very important to consider such passages and to take them seriously—I do not know how prevalent they are—especially in the light of My Lai or the many incidents like it.

Even more important, perhaps, than direct and gross indoctrination is the general pattern of authoritarianism that one finds in the schools, and the associated pattern of the technocratic, problem-solving mode of thought combined with a great awe of expertise—quite natural in an advanced industrial society. In some areas of our lives this latter pattern has reached dimensions that can really only be described as pathological. To take only one dangerous example, the domain of counterinsurgency theory has been developed into an effective technique of mystification during the last decade. The idea is to formulate the problems of repression of popular movements in purely technical terms. Thus, two experts in counterinsurgency writing in *Foreign Affairs* ex-

[11] Harold B. Clifford, *Exploring New England* (Follett and Co.: Chicago, 1961). The example and precedent set by Mason was not forgotten by later soldiers. It was, for example, cited by General Leonard Wood while justifying the Army's killing of 600 Moro men, women and children in the Philippines in 1906: "The renegades had from 3 to 6 months supply on the mountain, with an abundance of water. There was nothing to do but take the place. . . . I believe that some of our hard-praying ancestors dealt with the Pequot Indians in a somewhat similar manner, and on a great deal less provocation." Quoted in R. O'Connor, *Pacific Destiny* (Boston: Little, Brown and Co., 1969), p. 295. The analogy is actually fairly accurate; like the Pequots, the native Moros were armed with bows, spears, and rocks (against Wood's machine guns, bombs, and howitzers).

plain to us that all the dilemmas of counterinsurgency are "practical and as neutral in an ethical sense as the laws of physics."[12] In short, the situation is a very simple one. We have the goal of establishing the rule of certain social groups in the society that is selected for the experiment in counterinsurgency. A number of methods are available, ranging from rural development and commodity import programs to B52s and crop destruction. And the policy maker faces the task of combining these methods in such a manner as to maximize the probability of success. Quite obviously, only a hysteric or a self-flagellating moralist could see an ethical problem in this situation; it is just like an experiment in physics.

Academic terminology can be put to very mischievous use in this connection, and it often is. For example, driving people into government-controlled cities by fire power and chemical destruction is called "urbanization," which is then taken as a key index of the modernization of the society. We carry out what are called "experiments with population control measures." We should learn, one RAND Corporation theorist tells us, to disregard such mystical notions as attitudes; rather we should control behavior by appropriate arrangements for positive and negative reinforcements such as "confiscation of chickens, razing of houses, or destruction of villages." Or consider, for example, "the offer of food in exchange for certain services. . . . If this has in the past been a strong stimulus, it can probably be weakened by increasing local agricultural production. If it has been a weak or neutral stimulus, it can probably be strengthened by burning crops." This is from a publication of the *American Institute for Research*, 1967.[13] Whatever such experts may be, they are not scientists, and the concept of "science" suggested by such pronouncements is not one that Russell—or any other honest commentator—could endorse.

Christopher Lasch once pointed out that one of the dominant values of the modern intellectual is his acute sense of himself as a professional with a vested interest in technical solutions to political problems. The schools to a large extent are training professionals, and they are training the general population to accept the values and the ideological structures that are developed by professionals. All of this is particularly important in a "post-indus-

---

[12] George Tanham and Dennis Duncanson, "Some Dilemmas of Counterinsurgency," Vol. 48, No. 1 (October 1969), pp. 113–22.

[13] See also Noam Chomsky, *American Power and the New Mandarins* (Pantheon: New York, 1969).

trial" or advanced industrial society where the intelligentsia are increasingly associated with the exercise of power. This is, of course, not a criticism of professionalism or of technology or science, but rather of the subversion of intellectual values as part of a new coercive ideology that seeks to remove decision-making even further from popular control by exploiting the aura of science and technology, by pretending that social planning is much too complex for the common man and must therefore be the domain of experts who claim to be value-free technicians, but who in fact quite generally accept with-out question the most vulgar forms of official ideology as a basis for their planning.

If you have read serious social science journals or foreign policy journals over the last few years, you have seen that it is very common to counterpose the "emotional approach" of certain people with the "rational response" of others. For example, the people who worry about the slaughter of peasant populations—these people are overcome by emotion. On the other hand, those who talk about arranging inputs to realize a certain outcome are "reasonable" commentators. This is an interesting development, the counterposing of emotion to reason, because it departs significantly from the Western intellectual tradition. For example, David Hume wrote that "Reason is and ought to be the slave of the passions." And Russell, commenting on the observation, noted that every reasonable man subscribes to this dictum. He surely would be an "unreasonable" commentator by the standards of today. Reason is concerned with the choice of the right means to an end that you wish to achieve, taking emotional and moral factors into consideration. Unfortunately too many modern technocrats, who often pose as scientists and scholars, are really divorcing themselves from traditional science and scholarship and excluding themselves from the company of reasonable persons in the name of a kind of reason that is perverted beyond recognition.

All of these are matters that require the most careful attention of teachers. We have to learn to adopt the questioning and iconoclastic approach that is highly valued and carefully nurtured in the physical sciences, where an imaginative worker will very often hold up his basic assumptions to searching analysis. We have to adopt this approach as teachers, and also as citizens who must be social critics, recognizing that in the domain of social criticism the normal attitudes of a scientist are feared and deplored as a form of subversion or as dangerous radicalism.

I have been discussing the negative potential of American power. There is also a positive side, one that should make the work of teachers particularly demanding but highly exciting. The United States has a real potential for revolutionary social change to a libertarian democratic society of the form that probably cannot be achieved anywhere else in the world. As compared with other societies, libertarian instincts are reasonably strong in the United States. There is also very little class prejudice as compared with most other societies. But most of all, in an advanced industrial society the rational and humane use of resources and technology provides the possibility to free people from the role of tools of production in the industrial process. It provides the possibility, perhaps for the first time in modern history, to free human beings from the activities that, as Adam Smith pointed out, turn them into imbeciles through the burden of specialized labor. This, then is the real challenge of the twentieth century in the United States: to create social forms that will realize the humanistic conception of man. And it is the responsibility of teachers, of citizens, and of ourselves, to liberate the creative impulse and to free our minds and the minds of those with whom we deal from the constraints of authoritarian ideologies so that this challenge can be faced in a serious and an open-minded way.

The Contributors

JAMES D. ANDERSON is an Assistant Professor of History of Education at the University of Illinois, and a graduate of Stillman College and the University of Illinois. His contribution to this volume was taken from his doctoral dissertation, which he is currently revising for publication as a book.

KENNETH D. BENNE is Professor Emeritus of Human Relations and Philosophy at Boston University. He was one of the founders of the Human Relations Program at Bethel, Maine, and he has written numerous articles and books on education. His latest book is *Education for Tragedy*.

SAMUEL BOWLES is Professor of Economics at the University of Massachusetts—Amherst. He has taught at Harvard University and has published articles in educational, economic, and popular journals. His monograph *Planning Educational Systems for Economic Growth* appeared in the Harvard Economic Series (No. 133) in 1969.

NOAM CHOMSKY is the author of *Syntactic Structures, Aspects of the Theory of Syntax,* and *Cartesian Linguistics*—among other works—which are responsible for the preeminent position he occupies today in the discipline of linguistics. He is equally well known for his critiques of American foreign and domestic policies, contained in *American Power and the New Mandarins, At War with Asia,* and most recently, *For Reasons of State.* He is Ferrari P. Ward Professor of Linguistics at the Massachusetts Institute of Technology.

WALTER FEINBERG is Associate Professor of Educational Policy Studies at the University of Illinois, and Associate Editor of *Educational Theory*. He has published articles in many educational journals, and is the author of *Reason and Rhetoric: The Intellectual Foundations of 20th Century Liberal Educational Policy*.

HERBERT GINTIS is Associate Professor of Economics at the University of Massachusetts—Amherst. In addition to his collaborative efforts with Samuel Bowles, he has contributed to the *Quarterly Journal of Economics, the Harvard Educational Review, Social Policy, American Economic Review*, and other professional, political, and popular journals. He is coauthor, with Christopher Jencks, of *Inequality*.

DON IHDE has taught at Boston University, Southern Illinois University, and the State University of New York at Stony Brook, where he is now Professor of Philosophy. In addition to published articles in educational and philosophical journals, he has written *Hermeneutic Phenomenology: The Philosophy of Paul Ricoeur*, and *Sense and Significance*.

HENRY ROSEMONT, JR., is Associate Professor in the New School of Liberal Arts, Brooklyn College of the City University of New York. The author of articles in philosophical, educational, and Asian journals, he is also Review Editor for *Philosophy East and West*, and is currently completing a book, *The Principles of Confucianism*.

JOEL H. SPRING has been affiliated with Ivan Illich at the Center for Intellectual Documentation (CIDOC) in Cuernavaca, Mexico, and is presently Associate Professor of Education at Case Western Reserve University. He was written *Education and the Rise of the Corporate State*, and coauthored *Roots of Crisis* and *The Superschool and the Super State*. His most recent work, *Anarchism, Marxism, and Neo-Freudianism: A Study of Radical Forms of Education*, will be published this year.

MARX WARTOFSKY is Professor of Philosophy at Boston University. He is a member of the editorial boards of *Synthese*, the *Journal of Value Inquiry*, and *Teaching of Philosophy*, and is editor of *The Philosophical Forum*. In addition to many articles in philosophical journals he has published *Conceptual Foundations of Scientific Thought* and is coeditor of *Boston Studies in the Philosophy of Science*.